THE OMNI-AMERICANS

ALBERT MURRAY the
omni-
americans

Some Alternatives
to the Folklore
of White Supremacy

with a foreword by
HENRY LOUIS GATES, JR.

LIBRARY OF AMERICA

CONTENTS

Part III | GETTING IT TOGETHER

FOREWORD

BY HENRY LOUIS GATES, JR.

Perhaps only someone who hasn't taken the time to study the history of slavery and the rollback to Reconstruction, or hasn't read Ta-Nehisi Coates's painstakingly detailed brief for reparations, could fail to see that black people have suffered devastating economic consequences from a quarter of a millennium of slavery followed by seven decades of *de jure* Jim Crow segregation. But reasonable people might wonder about the timing of making an endorsement of reparations, at the commencement of a presidential political campaign whose ultimate goal is the defeat of Donald J. Trump, one of the litmus tests for support of a Democratic candidate by the black or liberal electorate. And some might take the decidedly politically incorrect position that doing so at this time could be a costly mistake, given the fact that polls consistently show that relatively few white Americans support the idea of reparations. As I watched the hearings at the House of Representatives on H.R. 40 and listened to the compelling testimony of Mr. Coates, Danny Glover, Senator Cory Booker, and several other equally eloquent speakers, I wondered if the evening news would feature any black speaker raising this matter of timing. I wondered if anyone would have the courage or inclination to state a counterargument, to go, as it were, against the grain, if only as an exercise in the healthy exchange of ideas, without fear of being ostracized. It occurred to me that this was precisely the moment in which Albert Murray seemed to delight, the moment when he most eloquently found his voice: standing within the circle, yet critiquing it with the clear insight of someone outside of it. Going against the grain, registering counterpoint, insisting on polyphony was, for Albert Murray, not just an enjoyable intellectual exercise; it was an ethical principle, as well as an aesthetic one.

Albert Murray was one of the greats, and it was my honor to be in his orbit. When I was a junior faculty member at Yale, I used to take the New Haven line down to New York to spend Saturday afternoons with him at Books & Company on Madison Avenue. Both have long since crossed over to the mythical side of New York City life. "The King of Cats" I called him, easily one of the twentieth century's most important aesthetic theorists of American culture.

Commanding on the page, Murray was equally impressive in the flesh: a lithe and dapper man with astonishing verbal fluency. He was a teacher by temperament and as he explained a point he'd often say that he wanted to be sure to "work it into your consciousness." The twentieth century had worked a great deal into Murray's consciousness. He was fifteen when the Scottsboro trial began, twenty-two when Marian Anderson sang at the Lincoln Memorial. He joined the Air Force when it was segregated and rejoined shortly after it had been desegregated. He was in his late thirties when *Brown v. Board of Education* was decided. He was in his forties when John F. Kennedy was killed and the Civil Rights Act was passed. He was in his fifties when King was shot and Black Power was proclaimed. He was ninety-two when Barack Obama was elected president, and ninety-six when Obama shocked the world by doing it again.

He was born Albert Lee Murray in 1916 and grew up in Magazine Point, Alabama, a hamlet not far from Mobile. His mother was a housewife, and his father helped lay railroad tracks as a cross-tie cutter. Everyone in the village knew there was something special about Albert. He knew it, too. After all, he'd overheard his mother say she'd raised him when his birth parents—middle class and educated but unmarried—couldn't. "It's just like the prince left among the paupers," Murray said cheerfully.

He earned his BS at Tuskegee Institute in 1939 and stayed on to teach. In 1941, he married Mozelle Menefee, his wife of more than seventy years, who, at the time, was a student at Tuskegee. Murray spent the last two years of World War II on active duty in the Air Force. Two years after his discharge, he moved to New York, where, on the G.I. Bill, he earned a master's degree in literature from New York University. It was also in New York that his friendship with Ralph Waldo Ellison, a former classmate at Tuskegee, took off. Ellison read passages to Murray from the manuscript that would turn into *Invisible Man*, and the two men explored the streets and sounds of Harlem together, hashing out ideas about improvisation, the blues, and literary modernism.

For a time, the life of the mind had to be tabled for the life of his family, and Murray rejoined the Air Force in 1951 to better support his wife and their beloved daughter Michele. He taught in Tuskegee's ROTC program for much of the '50s. In 1962, he left the military, took his pension, and moved back to Harlem. Despite his friendship with Ellison, at this point Murray was little known in New York's literary circles. His career in the military, which found him overseeing the administration of large-scale operations in North Africa and in the United States, obviously contributed to that. But upon his return to the Big Apple, his articles—commentaries, reviews, and observations on the civil rights movement—began to appear in magazines like *Life* and *The New Leader* and continued throughout the decade.

Then, in 1970, when I was a sophomore at Yale, with the Black Power movement ascendant, and the black ideological bullies, as I've called them, circling, some espousing the Black Panther program, some touting Black Cultural Nationalism, and still others preaching the Nation of Islam, Murray's *The Omni-Americans* hit the shelves, a collection of the articles he'd been producing during the previous decade. Secretly, many of us found the volume thrilling—transgressive, even. Murray wasn't interested in silos of black identity. We didn't need more sociological inquiry or separateness, he declared; what we needed was cultural creativity, nourished by but also transcending the folkways and traditions of black America.

It may seem ironic that the person who first urged *The Omni-Americans* on me was Larry Neal, one of the Black Arts founders. But Neal was a man of far greater subtlety than the movement he spawned, and he understood Murray's larger enterprise better than most. Where the black aesthetic movement had posited "the black experience" as a separate entity from white American culture, Murray argued that "American" and "black American" culture were mutually constitutive. There was no so-called American culture without the Negro American formal element and content in its marvelous blend, and no black American culture without its white American influences and forms.

Quite simply, Murray stood for complexity, and the black experience was—and is, and always will be—complex. What he was saying is that there is no prescription for being black, no program to conform to, despite what groups were calling for from their various corners. Like I said, transgressive.

During my visits with Murray, I loved to listen to his voice—grave but insinuating, with more than a hint of a singer's rasp. In *The Omni-Americans*, deploying the iterative jazzman's go-to form—theme and variation—he laid down the foundational melodies in his larger intellectual project and returned to them continuously. The melodies repeat and build upon each other, like movements in a composition. His words work their way into the mind but also through the senses —the way they sound, their arrangement on the page, the whirl of ideas "swinging" across the American landscape like a solo that seems improvised but is in fact the result of years of deep study and practice.

One overarching theme in Murray's *Omni-Americans* is the toxic mixture of "a folklore of white supremacy and a fakelore of black pathology," mutually reinforcing ideas whose theorists and propagators, in Murray's view, have conspired to define African Americans as lower-class citizens, mired in poverty, violence, and despair, despite the overwhelming evidence that black people and white people are more similar than different. "By any definition of race, even the most makeshift legal one," he argues, "most native-born U.S. Negroes, far from being non-white, are in fact part-white. They are also by any meaningful definition of culture, part-Anglo-Saxon, and they are overwhelmingly Protestant." No matter: "the deliberate debasement of the black image has been so viciously systematic and often times so exasperatingly casual that the scope of white malevolence is hard to exaggerate."

In seeking to determine why these ideologies of race and discrimination exist and persist, Murray indicts two seemingly unrelated groups for spreading the fakelore of black pathology: social scientists on the one hand, and black nationalists on the other. The first group he assails for spreading "social science fictions instead of scientific information" and for causing readers to "mistake the jargon of social science for insight into the nature and condition of man."

In particular, he skewers the most popular social scientists of the day for their embrace of this "social science fiction fiction." None was more prominent than Kenneth Clark, whose 1964 study for Harlem Youth Opportunities Unlimited, titled *Youth in the Ghetto: A Study of the Consequences of Powerlessness and a Blueprint for Change*, Murray describes as "a monument to social science nonsense and nonsensibility." To Murray, Clark "demonstrates again that other Americans, including most American social scientists, don't mind one bit what unfounded conclusions you draw about U.S. Negroes, or how flimsy and questionable your statistics, or how wild your conjectures, so long as they reflect degradation." Coming to Clark's *Youth in the Ghetto* after reading Murray, one can't help but read this theme into such lines as "Too many of these young people express their sense of personal defeat through stagnation, despair, and flirtation with narcotics as their means of developing social patterns of compensatory status which are compatible with ghetto modes."*

Equally damning in Murray's eyes is the late Senator Daniel Patrick Moynihan's *The Negro Family: The Case for National Action*, which Moynihan released while working in the Johnson administration in 1965. The Moynihan Report did little more than enhance the already prevailing view of black Americans' dim prospects. "The Moynihan Report is the stuff of which the folklore of white supremacy is made," Murray contends, "and providing such stuff is the role that the social science technicians and theorists all too often play in the extension of black degradation through the systematic oversimplification of black tribulations."

And then there were the black nationalists, whom Murray saw as too concerned with discrete power and telling other African Americans how to "be black." I saw it at Yale; he saw it everywhere. In Murray's view, militant African Americans had themselves fallen into the trap of the folklore of white supremacy—"over-responding to white norm/black deviation survey data-oriented conjectures and double-talk precisely because they are unprepared to identify it as the pseudo-scientific folklore of white supremacy it so frequently is. And by doing so they are likely to be reinforcing the very same condescending and contemptuous white attitudes toward black experience to which they are so vociferously opposed." Murray remained skeptical of the rising tide of black cultural protest: "Rhetoric of black militancy aside, what Negroes are obviously concerned, resentful, angry, and increasingly violent about is not too little identity or beauty or pride but too much exclusion from the power mechanisms and resources of the nation at

*HARYOU Organization, *Youth in the Ghetto: A Study of the Consequences of Power-lessness and a Blueprint for Change* (New York: Harlem Youth Opportunities Unlim-ited, Inc., 1964), 1.

large, including the publicity mechanisms which should acknowledge
and advertise black as being beautiful and as American as blackberry
jam."

Murray's critique also ventures into black literature, where "writers who are advertised as storytellers and artists produce pseudo-
scientific social theories" rooted in the fakelore of black pathology.
Notable black authors like James Baldwin and Richard Wright, he
argues, play to white people's desires to read about black people's
"moaning and groaning about black troubles and miseries." If these
writers resent their literature being viewed by white eyes as "incidental to protest," then "it is about time Negro writers began to wonder
why." These black writers "both profess great pride in Negroes, but in
practice seem to rate the theories and abstract formulations of French
existentialism over the infinitely richer wisdom of the blues," which is,
in fact, *the product of the most complicated culture, and therefore the
most complicated sensibility in the modern world."*

Ralph Ellison knew this, and Murray calls *Invisible Man "par excellence* the literary extension of the blues." He thought Baldwin and
Wright, however, had bought into the false idea that "political and
social absolutes . . . are the sine qua non of all human fulfillment."
Their work "[implies] that there are people who possess these political
and social absolutes, and that these people are on better terms with
the world as such and are consequently better people." Conversely,
Ellison, writes Murray, told "a prototypical story about being not
only a twentieth century American but also a twentieth century man,
the Negro's obvious predicament symbolizing everybody's essential
predicament. And like the blues, and echoing the irrepressibility of
America itself, it ended on a note of promise, ironic and ambiguous
perhaps, but a note of promise still."

Albert Murray was not a man to criticize without offering solutions, which, in his mind, were rooted in traditional black culture—
the blues, jazz, the spirituals, oral history, signifying, and vernacular
forms—a culture so complex and accomplished it could not possibly

be viewed as pathological by the disinterested eye. As he states in his praise of Ellison, the blues sensibility offers a way out. "The spirit of the blues," he writes, "moves in the opposite direction from ashes and sackcloth, self-pity, self-hatred, and suicide. As a matter of fact the dirtiest, meanest, and most low-down blues are not only not depressing, they function like an instantaneous aphrodisiac!" Murray's larger point is that the blues idiom allows black people to focus on what they like about themselves and their country, rather than wallowing in the degradation prescribed by the folklore of white supremacy and the fakelore of black pathology. Harlem, in Murray's view, is not the grim ghetto of Clark or Baldwin. Rather, it is better characterized by its people's "hard headed faith in democracy, its muscular Christianity, its cultural flexibility, . . . its universally celebrated commitment to elegance in motion, to colorful speech idioms, to high style, not only in personal deportment but even in the handling of mechanical devices," not to mention "the very existence of Harlem's fantastically knowing satire, its profound awareness and rejection of so much that is essentially ridiculous in downtown doings."

For Murray, Duke Ellington's Harlem reflected the neighborhood's complicated glory. Ellington "was well aware of the widespread hunger and filth and crime and political frustration in Harlem as long ago as when he wrote 'Harlem Airshaft.'" But the great jazzman, "whose music encompasses at least as much of the flesh and blood reality of life in the United States as do books like *An American Dilemma*," also understood "that Harlem for all its liabilities generates an atmosphere that stimulates people-to-people good times which are second to none anywhere in the world. (Life in Paris is better celebrated in story but not in song and dance.)" Murray drives the point home by predicting, "Someday, Ellington may well come to be regarded as the Frederick Douglass of most black artists. He is already regarded as such by most musicians."

Everything comes back to the title of the book, that people in the United States are omni-Americans, their culture "*incontestably mulatto*," where "ethnic differences are the very essence of cultural diversity and national creativity." He passionately defends this "*patently and irrevocably composite*" culture, "for all their traditional antagonisms and obvious differences, the so-called black and so-called white people of the United States resemble nobody else in the world so much as they resemble each other." Murray thus chose a quote from André Malraux as an epigraph: "The individual stands in opposition to society, but he is nourished by it. And it is far less important to know what differentiates him than what nourishes him. Like the genius, the individual is valuable for what there is within him. . . . Every psychological life is an exchange, and the fundamental problem of the living individual is knowing upon what he intends to feed."

These passages, then, surely make it no surprise that *The Omni-Americans* was both revered and reviled. There was little middle ground where the collection was concerned. *The Washington Post*'s *Book World* called it "an emancipating book" and placed it on its "Fifty Notable Books of 1970" list. To my mind, these were the readers who "got" it, who understood what Murray had to say. In the *Journal of Black Studies*, Daniel F. Collins identified Murray's "pluralistic vision of society." "In so doing," Collins wrote, "he picks a fine line between black narcissism and the danger of unconsciously urging assimilation of white values." Cleveland's *Call and Post* zeroed in on the same theme: the emphasis on "the formation of the national character as a whole" and the "[development of] citizens who are fully oriented to cultural diversity and who are not hung up on race."

In the *Boston Globe*, Carl Senna wrote of Murray's "courageous eloquence" and said the book "is about people who are called black because they were forbidden to do or express anything else which might change their identity." Black people had been locked into an identity for a long time. Murray himself had been born in the heart of the Jim Crow era, when reprehensible "Sambo" images permeated the advertising landscape. In the pages of magazines, on the backs of playing cards, on sheet music—in other words, everywhere—black people were bug-eyed, watermelon-eating clowns. Consider, also, the images put forth in the film *Birth of a Nation*, released just one year before Murray was born: black men alternately depicted as vile, incompetent buffoons stealing the legislature (and therefore the power) from honorable white men and, of course, as rapists. Murray articulated the limits put on African Americans (a term he despised, by the way, and refused to endorse or use) by the wider society, which had spent so many decades imbibing and internalizing such images.

Walker Percy suggested that "*The Omni-Americans* well may be the most important book on black-white relations in the United States, indeed on American culture, published in this generation." Other writers and critics, though, begged to differ, sometimes strenuously. Kenneth Kinnamon in *American Quarterly* questioned the book's veracity and therefore its validity: "[H]is book is not without its own exaggerations, distortions, and misrepresentations." Saunders Redding eviscerated the book in *The New York Times*, condemning it for its "mixture of pseudo-scientific academic jargon, camp idiom, and verbal play." He implied that Murray overcompensated for what was missing in "adduced facts—of which, incidentally, there is a notable lack," by wearing multiple hats, many of which turned out to be ill-fitting: "[T]he author is alternately, and sometimes simultaneously, sociologist, political scientist, psychologist, cultural anthropologist, musicologist, and literary critic." Redding continued: "Trying, or pretending to use the basic perceptions and the tools of so many intellectual disciplines compounds confusion." If one were to read this "non sense" at all, he warned, it should be "read one essay at a time with intervals of days or weeks duration between readings." Redding essentially saw no merit in the book: "The pieces never should have been brought together in a book."

Although a literary critic like Murray, Saunders Redding was eager to defend the dubious social science of Kenneth Clark's doll studies rather than give Murray's argument its full due. Redding was a remarkable man, a smart man, a pioneer. He was an English professor at Cornell, the first black professor at Cornell's College of Arts and Sciences, in fact, retiring a decade before I even got there. Before that, he had been appointed the first black faculty member at Brown University way back in 1949. I admire Saunders Redding greatly, but I disagree with him wholeheartedly. He was clearly rankled by Murray's contrariness. He just couldn't get past it, and it clouded his view.

No matter how polarizing, no matter the naysayers, the impact of Murray's book could not be dismissed. *The Omni-Americans* spelled the beginning of the end of the black aesthetic movement's mono-vocal dominance and helped give rise to the modernist and post-modernist artistic practices of writers such as Toni Morrison, Alice Walker, Maya Angelou, Leon Forrest, Ishmael Reed, Ernest Gaines, James Alan McPherson, Rita Dove, Elizabeth Alexander, and Colson Whitehead, who understood the task of the artist as finding the universal in the particularity of African American history and culture. "The last of the giants" McPherson called him.

This giant was also one of the first writers in the African American tradition, along with his close friend, Ralph Ellison, who based both his aesthetic theory and his literary practice on the belief that experiences of the Negro or the Afro-American, as he would have put it, were metaphors for formal expression of the human condition. Jean Toomer had achieved this effect in his experimental novel, *Cane*, at the beginning of the Harlem Renaissance in 1922, as did Sterling A. Brown in his book of poetry, *Southern Road* (1932), and Zora Neale Hurston in her masterpiece, *Their Eyes Were Watching God* (1937). This is why Murray valorizes the blues and jazz, and heralds his theory as an explication of "The Blues Idiom" rather than "The Social Science Fiction Monster," as Larry Neal nicknamed Murray's trope for documentary realism. For Murray, and for these other artists whose sensibility he shared and whose works informed his aesthetic theory—I'm thinking especially of his friends and alter egos Duke Ellington, Ralph Ellison, of course, and the painter Romare Bearden, among others—it would be as odd to read a black fiction writer's work as a sociological or anthropological *document* as to read Gustave Flaubert's *Madame Bovary* as a social scientific slice of life in mid-nineteenth-century France rather than as an imaginative work whose narrative method transformed the way authors wrote novels. In other words, language use—*form*—was far more important than a work of art's ostensible "*content.*" After all, if Flaubert, say, or Duke Ellington, or Bessie or Mamie Smith, or Toni Morrison, wanted their work to be interpreted primarily for its content, they would have written essays. Not to put too fine a point on it, but no one reads *Hamlet* as raw material for a dissertation on the history of the throne in Denmark. This is why Murray repeatedly refers to the blues as a mode of transcendence: because art transcends the specificity of its ostensible subject matter. Why, Murray asks again and again, should art by black writers and composers, singers and painters, be assumed to be any less complex—any less "artistic"—than the greatest works of art and aesthetics in the Western canon or, for that matter, in African sculpture and dance, which he often praises for their formal sublimity? The reason that Murray railed against the trope of the black experience in America as a repository of pathologies is that he saw that it was a social construction—whether in fiction or in social science (especially sociology and anthropology)—a norm sanctioned by custom, a convention with a life, a history of its own, propelled from text to text through imitation, repetition, and revision, rather than as a snapshot of reality.

At a time when many in our country are deeply divided over politics and distrustful of institutions across the board, we would do well to listen to Murray, who, produced by another century, spent a career *believing* in things, like the gospel according to Ma Rainey and Jimmy Rushing and Duke Ellington. More broadly, he believed in the sublimity of art, and he never was afraid of risking bathos to get to it. I learned a great many things when I sat with him in his New York apartment over the decades, and, summed up, they amounted to a larger vision.

That vision is even truer now, as the people of the United States grapple with and debate what it means to be American, with some even trying to put a physical wall around what that means. Surviving in this polarized, highly charged decade of the twenty-first century, we need Murray more than ever to teach us, as only he could, that the American *idiom* is not a collection of instruments but an irreducible composite built up over centuries and inherited from artists of every race and ethnicity. Not only is it dishonest and damaging to claim otherwise; it is folly.

Let us never forget what Albert Murray meant and still means to our "American story," which is in fact our *omni-American* story, or to the music animating it with a soul force he taught us to hear.

This foreword is a revised version of the article "The King of Cats," from the April 8, 1996, issue of The New Yorker.

THE OMNI-AMERICANS

To my wife Mozelle Menefee Murray
and for our daughter Michele,
a stage to dance on and
also some shoulders to stand on

The individual stands in opposition to society, but he is nourished by it. And it is far less important to know what differentiates him than what nourishes him. Like the genius, the individual is valuable for what there is within him. . . . Every psychological life is an exchange, and the fundamental problem of the living individual is knowing upon what he intends to feed.

—André Malraux

INTRODUCTION

I n a general sense perhaps all statements are also counter-statements. Even the simplest pronouncements, for example, whether of measurable fact or of a point of view, are also assertions to contradict something that is assumed to be otherwise. Perhaps even the most objective descriptions, definitions, and formulations (as well as being implicit protestations against subjectivity, imprecision, and fantasy) are in effect counter-actions against the void of the undefined, unformulated, and confusing. It may be, then, that such opening remarks as are found in the forewords to books are really answers before the questions; nay, replies, retorts, and refutations to exceptions that are not only bound to be taken but in a sense already have been.

In the same general sense statements may also be restatements. For instance, on close inspection, affirmation for one thing not only is an inevitable negation of something else but may also be a revision and extension. Seldom does unanimity stop with a simple yes or no. A concurring *yes*, that is to say, is not only a dissenting *no* to a different set of *yes*es but may also be a modification or adaptation that rephrases an implicit, perhaps unrecognized, question.

Even the most casual personal introductions are counter-statements of a sort. Names exist to counteract confusion of identity —*and intention*—in the first place. Thus even as an author, for example, tells you his name he declares his position (and involves himself in opposition!). Any name will do, of course, even the illiterate X de-signed as His Mark, for instance.

Nor are chance extensions of, or chance associations with, or puns upon any name without functional significance. (Martin Luther King *was* a Martin Luther, a reformer in rebellion against orthodoxy.) For example, at a time when an ever increasing number of writers seems to mistake the jargon of social science for insight into the nature and condition of man, if the name of a brown-skin U.S. Negro student of fiction and Americana reminds a few readers, by whatever chance, of Gilbert Murray, the great English author of *The Rise of the Greek Epic* and *Five Stages of Greek Religion*, and suggests, no matter how remotely, that the study of ritual might be a means of coming to terms with some of the ambiguities of human nature and conduct that may be outside the scope of current survey methodology, such an associa-tion might not be far from the intentions of that brown-skin student. If the juxtaposition further suggests to those who, perhaps unwittingly, have oversubscribed to social science, that interpretations of human behavior in the raw require at least as much respect for the complexity of human motives as the interpretation of a poem or play or a story, well, perhaps one might not even need to bother with saying anything other than one's name. But at the risk of being overly explanatory, let me be definite about the statements, counter-statements, restate-ments that have gone into the making of *The Omni-Americans*, a book whose very title is intended as no small counter-statement.

II

The essays, commentaries, and reviews out of which *The Omni-Americans* has been built, are all intended as counter-statements and restatements in the generic sense. Their most general significance should be suggested by the title. To race-oriented propagandists, whether white or black, the title of course makes no sense: they would have things be otherwise. But the United States is in actuality not a nation of black people and white people. It is a nation of multicolored people. There are white Americans so to speak and black Americans. But any fool can see that the white people are not really white, and that black people are not black. They are all interrelated one way or another. Thus the title *The Omni-Americans* is among other things an attempt to restate the problem formulated by the *Report of the National Advisory Commission on Civil Disorders* by suggesting that the present domestic conflict and upheaval grows out of the fact that in spite of their common destiny and deeper interests, the people of the United States are being misled by misinformation to insist on *exaggerating* their ethnic differences. The problem is not the existence of ethnic differences, as is so often assumed, but the intrusion of such differences into areas where they do not belong. Ethnic differences are the very essence of cultural diversity and national creativity.

In the context of the so-called national dialogue on the nature and implications of black experience, the counter-statements of *The Omni-Americans* are specifically forensic in intent. Each, that is to say, was written in an effort to make, so to speak, an affirmative rebuttal to negative allegations and conclusions about some aspects of Negro life in the United States. As a result they become not only somewhat argumentative from time to time, but also, and quite deliberately, polemical. Unlike the standard polemics of black American protest, however, they are immediately concerned not so much with political injustice as such as with inaccuracies and misconceptions that contribute to and even rationalize injustice. They question and dispute the reliability, validity, and comprehensiveness of information. They challenge and restate the issues. They suggest alternative points of view, and they seek to provide *a basis for action* which is compatible with those facts that in instances when Negroes are not involved are generally assumed to represent the universal element in all human nature.

In directing themselves toward action, these polemics, one would hope, are to be distinguished from the polemics of moral outcry, such for instance as are found in the well-known works of Richard Wright and James Baldwin, two of the most powerful exponents of protest/ accusation since the days of Émile Zola. The work of these writers (who will be the subject for further examination) seems to be designed to make those toward whom it is directed—i.e., white racists —feel guilty and fearful: white man, listen—or be damned. Take heed and mend your sinful ways because if you don't, I foresee fire and brimstone next time and believe me, you're going to get just what you deserve!

Producing guilt may or may not be fine, but stimulating intelligent action is better. And intelligent action always needs to have its way paved by a practical estimate of the situation. The immediate objective of the polemics in *The Omni-Americans* is to expose the incompetence and consequent impracticality of people who are regarded as intellectuals but are guided by racial bias rather than reason based on scholarly insight. *How is it that you white people who otherwise seem to be so knowledgeable and competent are suddenly so obtuse about something that is as obvious as the fact that human nature is no less complex and fascinating for being encased in dark skin? Don't you know that the direction of such stupidity is just the kind of general confusion that will destroy all of us? Don't you even know that prisoners sleep better than jailors? Get wise. As of now you are working against your own interest as much as that of your black compatriots! Furthermore, to the extent that your misdefinitions are picked up by Negroes, you are only aggravating the problem. This just simply is not the time for the politics of unexamined slogans.*

The prime target of these polemics is the professional observer/ reporter (that major vehicle of the nation's information, alas) who relies on the so-called findings and all-too-inclusive extrapolations of social science survey technicians for their sense of the world. The bias of *The Omni-Americans* is distinctly proliterary. It represents the dramatic sense of life as against the terminological abstractions and categories derived from laboratory procedures. Its interests, however, are not those of a literary sensibility at odds with scientific method.

Not by any means. On the contrary, a major charge of the argument advanced here is that most social science survey findings are not scientific enough. They violate one's common everyday breeze-tasting sense of life precisely because they do not meet the standards of validity, reliability, and comprehensiveness that the best scientists have always insisted on. As a result they provide neither a truly practical sociology of the so-called black community nor a dependable psychology of black behavior.

At any rate, the counter-formulations posed in *The Omni-Americans* are expressions of a sensibility structured, no matter how imperfectly, by science as well as literature. They are submitted as antidotes against the pernicious effects of a technological enthusiasm inadequately counter-balanced by a literary sense of the ambiguities and absurdities inherent in all human experience. To the literary sensibility, which is geared not to categorical jargon but to such universal patterns of human behavior as emerge from stories of suspenseful trials and instructive errors, the problems created by the misapplication of data are no less social than intellectual.

The overenthusiastic use of the highly specialized concepts of clinical psychology to define social conditions that are obviously beyond the controlled observation of the laboratory (and to do so without having established a "criterion" for normal limits) results in oversimplification. Like the glib pseudo-terminological use of such clichés as the ghetto, minority group, middle class Negro, and so on, it can never do justice to the facts of life. And as in the courtroom, doing justice to people goes hand in hand with doing justice to the evidence involved in their case.

The Omni-Americans is based in large measure on the assumption that since the negative aspects of black experience are constantly being overpublicized (and to little purpose except to obscure the positive), justice to U.S. Negroes, not only as American citizens but also as the fascinating human beings that they so obviously are, is best served by suggesting some of the affirmative implications of their history and culture. After all, someone must at least begin to try to do justice to what U.S. Negroes *like* about being black and to what they *like* about being *Americans*. Otherwise justice can hardly be done to the incontestable fact that not only do they choose to live rather than commit suicide, but that, poverty and injustice notwithstanding, far from simply struggling in despair, they live with gusto and a sense of elegance that has always been downright enviable.

But then perhaps only works of fiction on the scale of Tolstoy, Joyce, and Thomas Mann can truly do justice to the enduring humanity of U.S. Negroes, people who, for instance, can say of their oppressors, "Yeah, we got our troubles all right. But still and all, if white folks could be black for just one Saturday night they wouldn't never want to be white folks no more!" By which is not implied that white people necessarily should give up any wealth and power—but after all, the overwhelming majority of white people are neither wealthy nor powerful!

Maybe black assets are so seldom mentioned in books by most other U.S. Negro writers because such things are simply taken for granted. Underlying every allegation of *The Omni-Americans*, however, is the frank contention that the time for accentuating the positive and eliminating the negative is long overdue. This case for the affirmative is presented in three parts.

Part One, which consists of the title essay, begins with a discussion of the so-called question of black identity in terms of the cultural dynamics involved in the formation of the national character of the United States as a whole; moves on to an indictment of those theorists and social welfare technicians whose statistics-oriented interpretations of black experience add up to what functions as a folklore of white supremacy and a fakelore of black pathology; and concludes with a review, intended as a stimulus and rudimentary orientation for more extensive investigation and development by scholars and creative writers alike, of the actualities and potentialities of black

American experience as such elements are reflected in the blues idiom, one of the art styles most characteristic of U.S. Negro self-expression.

All of the reviews, articles, and pop-off exercises in Part Two, "The Illusive Black Image," were specifically intended as nonfiction counter-sketches, as it were—or indeed as sketch page erasures of images that were unlikenesses. (This material was written on various occasions between 1964 and 1969, and in some instances has been revised and expanded for inclusion here.) Together the selections are meant to define a continuing concern with the ways in which writers who are advertised as scholars produce social science fictions instead of scientific information—and how writers who are advertised as storytellers and artists produce pseudo-scientific social theories.

The reflections on black studies, black consciousness, and black heritage in Part Three represent extensions and applications of an assumption that is implicit in the definition of the Omni-American, that the function of education in the United States is to develop citizens who are fully oriented to cultural diversity—and are not hung up on race.

III

When issues engage widespread public attention, the so-called national dialogue becomes more of a verbal free for all than a formally (or informally) structured debate. As in a battle royal, everybody is out to get in his own punchline. In such a context, the literary intellectual or would-be intellectual assumes responsibilities and takes prerogatives somewhat similar to those of a piano player in a jam session. His relationship to the argument's overall frame of reference is very much like the relationship of the piano player to the chordal structure and progression of the piece of music being used as the basis for improvisation. Of all the musicians in a jam session, it is most likely the piano player who provides the point of reference in the score. He is not necessarily the best musician in the session, but his approach, like that of the apprentice to literature, is necessarily comprehensive. Thus he is not only authorized but obligated to remind the other participants what the musical "discussion" is about. Indeed, the most self-effacing accompanist did as much for Bessie Smith and for Coleman Hawkins.

These are the obligations assumed here. That few writers are likely to be able to exert the definitive authority of a Duke Ellington (who, the reader will see, is a hero of this book) is only too obvious. Nevertheless, once taking a position at the keyboard, even the novice on his first gig is required by the very nature of his responsibility to forget that he is not Duke Ellington. In any case, no matter what else he may be, the literary piano player is a would-be arranger-composer and maestro of discussions, who finds himself calling the soloists home in spite of himself. Sometimes he may even rap a knuckle here and there (almost as if he were also old Professor "Clinkscales"—which he definitely is not), but only in interest of the total sound and in accordance with his reading of the score, which of course is far from infallible but at least reaches for a sense of the whole.

In the context of a national dialogue, perhaps the only authorization required for "putting in your little two cents worth" is the constitutional provision for free speech. Moreover, the basis for the presumptions of dissent and counter-statement is the same as for popping off: the merest hint or suspicion that outrage is being committed against one's conception of actuality.

As for intellectual or scholarly authority, perhaps it is better never to claim more than one's ideas as expressed can make self-evident. By the same token, no more will be conceded to the opposition than, say, a Negro athlete would allow an opponent who has a Ph.D. in physical education from Harvard or Yale. There is simply too little difference between official certification and media promotion as things now stand.

Uptown Manhattan, 1969

PART I

The Omni-Americans

THE OMNI-AMERICANS

A NATURAL HISTORY: *E Pluribus Unum*

In the prelude to *Joseph and His Brothers*, Thomas Mann, whose awareness of context as a space-time continuum was as functional as it was comprehensive, refers to the historical background of things as being a bottomless well. He then goes on to suggest that it is bottomless indeed if what one has in mind is the background of mankind, which he describes as being a "riddling essence" encompassing one's own "normally unsatisfied" but quite "abnormally wretched" existence. The mystery of the bottomlessness past, he points out, not only includes one's own mystery but is in fact the beginning as well as the end of all inquiries and is thus also the mystery that gives immediacy to all statements and significance to all human endeavor.

According to Mann, a bottomless or formless quality is the essential nature of the space-time continuum of human experience. The deeper one probes into the background of mankind, the further the earliest foundations of culture recede into vagueness and myth. Moreover, as Lord Raglan corroborates in *The Hero: A Study of Tradition, Myth and Drama*, recent foundations have a way of receding in much the same manner. In any case, the ultimate sources of derivation almost always tend to defy scientific verification.

Nonetheless, writes Mann in a passage which suggests that the whole of history itself is largely mythological, "There may exist provisional origins, which practically and in fact form the first beginnings of the particular tradition held by a given community, folk or communion of faith; and memory, though sufficiently instructed that the depths have not actually been plumbed, yet nationally may find reassurance in some prehistoric period of time, and personally and historically speaking, come to rest there." As did the memory of Joseph himself, for instance, who for his part, as Mann goes to some lengths to show, regarded a certain occurrence in Babylonia as the beginning of all things, that is, of all that mattered to him—or more precisely, since such reassurance, whether national or personal, is always likely to be interwoven with strategic considerations, all that really mattered as an operational frame of reference. "In such wise," Mann adds later in his prelude, "are formed those beginnings, those time-coulisses of the past where memory may pause and find a hold whereon to base its personal history." And hence its national myths and symbols.

In other words, how far back into the past one goes in order to establish the beginnings of one's own tradition or cultural idiom is not only relative but even at best is also, on close inspection, very likely to be downright arbitrary and quite in accordance with some specific functional combination of desirable skills and attitudes in terms of which one wishes to project oneself. Thus there are some (many of whom are the makers of schoolbooks) who mark the beginnings of the American tradition from the time of the landings of the first Europeans in the Western Hemisphere, if not from the birth of Christopher Columbus (who never even saw the mainland). There are others for whom the settling of Virginia marked the official as well as the mythological birth of the nation. For still others it is as if nothing of significance happened before the landing of the *Mayflower*. And other "original beginnings" have been located in the Boston Tea Party, the Battle of Bunker Hill, the signing of the Declaration of Independence, the Constitutional Convention at Philadelphia. So it goes depending upon the orientation of the historian.

Constance Rourke (author of *American Humor: A Study of the National Character* and *The Roots of American Culture*), unlike many such historians, assumed quite accurately that there were "time-coulisses" in the pre-Columbian past that were relevant to the understanding of the American experience. Of the Boston Tea Party, for example, she wrote that "it may well be a question whether the participants enjoyed more dumping the tea in the harbor or masquerading in war paint and feathers with brandished tomahawks." "On the frontier," she goes on to say, "the whites had adopted Indian dress and used Indian weapons, among other things, keeping the names of villages, for instance, even when the original inhabitants had been ruthlessly expelled."

Nor did Constance Rourke overlook the Negro elements that have long been so deeply embedded in what she refers to as the "national character." "The Negro," she writes in a reference to a visit by a European to the America of 1795, "was to be seen everywhere in the South and in the new Southwest, on small farms and great plantations, on roads and levees. He was often an all but equal member of many a pioneering expedition. He became, in short, a dominant figure in spite of his condition, and commanded a definite portraiture." What is more, Rourke's acclaimed scholarly investigations of the origin and development of black face minstrels did not lead her to confuse elements of the national character with the folklore of white supremacy. Quite the contrary, her image of The American is a composite that is part Yankee, part backwoodsman and Indian, and part Negro. In tracing this composite, she was not unaware of the profound implications of *homo Americanus* as a vernacular adaptation, modification, and extension of *homo Europaeus*, whom Paul Valéry once described as a combination of ancient Greek, ancient Roman, and Judeo-Christian.

The three interwoven figures in the native fabric loomed large,

Constance Rourke explains, "not because they represented any considerable numbers in the population but because something in the nature of each induced an irresistible response. Each had been a wanderer over the lands, the Negro a forced and unwilling wanderer. Each in a fashion of his own had broken bonds, the Yankee in the initial revolt against the parent civilization, the backwoodsman in revolt against all civilization, the Negro in a revolt which was cryptic and submerged but which nonetheless made a perceptible outline." Such figures, she goes on, were the embodiment of a deepseated "mood of disseverance, carrying the popular fancy further and further from any fixed or traditional heritage. *Their comedy, their irreverent wisdom, their sudden changes and adroit adaptations provided emblems for a pioneer people who required resilience as a prime trait.*" (Italics added.)

So wrote Constance Rourke, whose richly informed observations on the texture of life in the United States seem to have exercised no significant influence on the so-called findings of the current crop of social science survey technicians. Nor is there any compelling evidence that her influence has been remarkably stronger among historians and literary intellectuals—most of whom, it turns out, are no less oriented to the folklore of white supremacy than are politicians. Nevertheless, so did she delineate the image and pattern of *homo Americanus*, and thus did she locate the taproots of contemporary style, and so in the process define "all that matters" in the national character. And however provisional as an historical coulisse or even a geographical coulisse, such is the composite wellspring from which the mainstream of American tradition derives.

Whence also, and no less directly or inevitably, is derived the U.S. Negro idiom, for all its distinctive nuances. There is, of course, no question at all that the ultimate source of the dance-orientation so central to the life style of most contemporary U.S. Negroes lies somewhere in the uncharted reaches of some region of prehistoric Africa. But for all immediate practical purposes, the blues tradition, a tradition of confrontation and improvisation—that is, to use Rourke's

word, of "resilience"—is indigenous to the United States, along with
the Yankee tradition and that of the backwoodsman.

Thus, though recognizing that the depths, which after all are bottomless, have not actually been plumbed, there is no truly urgent reason to trace the origin of U.S. Negro style and manner any farther
back in time than the arrival of a Dutch ship of war in Virginia with
a cargo of twenty black captives for sale in 1619—if indeed that far.
Negroes definitely were reluctant immigrants to the new world, but in
view of the life they had experienced in the land of their origin, they
could hardly have regarded it as a stronghold of individual freedom
and limitless opportunity. Nor could they have been unmindful of the
obvious fact that Africans "back home" were as actively engaged in
the slave trade as were the Europeans and Americans. Many contemporary Americans, both black and white, obviously assume that the
slave runners simply landed their ships and overpowered the helpless natives at will. Such was not the usual case at all. For the most
part, such entrepreneurs bartered for "Black Ivory" much the same as
for elephant tusks. "The whites," Negro historian Benjamin Quarles
points out, "did not go into the interior to procure slaves; this they
left to the Africans themselves. Spurred on by the desire for European
goods, one tribe raided another, seized whatever captives it could and
marched them in coffles with leather thongs around their necks to
coastal trading centers."

It is all too true that Negroes unlike the Yankee and the backwoodsman were slaves whose legal status was that of property. But it is also
true—and as things have turned out, even more significant—that they
were slaves *who were living in the presence of more human freedom
and individual opportunity than they or anybody else had ever seen before.* That the *conception* of being a free man in America was infinitely
richer than any notion of individuality in the Africa of that period
goes without saying.

That this conception was perceived by the black slaves is shown
by their history as Americans. The fugitive slave, for instance, was

culturally speaking certainly an American, and a magnificent one
at that. His basic urge to escape was, of course, only human—as was
his willingness to risk the odds; but the tactics he employed as well
as the objectives he was seeking were *American* not African. In his
objectives, he certainly does not seem to have been motivated by any
overwhelming nostalgia for tribal life. The slaves who absconded to
fight for the British during the Revolutionary War were no less inspired by *American* ideas than those who fought for the colonies: the
liberation that the white people wanted from the British the black
people wanted from white people. As for the tactics of the fugitive
slaves, the Underground Railroad was not only an innovation, it was
also an *extension* of the American quest for democracy brought to
its highest level of epic heroism. Nobody tried to sabotage the *Mayflower*. There was no bounty on the heads of its captain, crew, or
voyagers as was the case with all conductors, station masters, and
passengers on the northbound freedom train. Given the differences
in circumstances, equipment, and, above all, motives, the legendary exploits of white U.S. backwoodsmen, keelboatmen, and prai-
rie schoonermen, for example, became relatively *safe* when one sets
them beside the breathtaking escapes of the fugitive slave beating
his way south to Florida, west to the Indians, and north to far away
Canada through swamp and town alike seeking *freedom*—nobody
was chasing Daniel Boone!

Or to take another area of American experience. The pioneer spirit
of American womanhood is widely eulogized. But at no time in the
history of the Republic has such womanhood ever attained a higher
level of excellence than in the indomitable heroism of a runaway slave
named Harriet Tubman, who "kidnapped" more than three hundred
of her fellowmen out of bondage, and of whom William H. Seward
once said, "a nobler, higher spirit, or a truer, seldom dwells in human
form." Harriet Tubman was, like Sojourner Truth, already a legend in
her time. Ralph Waldo Emerson, Bronson Alcott, and Horace Mann,
among numerous others of that golden era of national synthesis,

immediately and eagerly acknowledged what the dynamics of racial oneupmanship have obscured for so many succeeding students of American civilization: Tubman was not only an American legend; she also added a necessary, even if still misapprehended, dimension to the national mythology.

Another example. In such an epochal figure as that of the mulatto fugitive, abolitionist, and statesman named Frederick Douglass, contemporary American Negroes can find all the fundamental reassurance as to their identity and mission as Americans that the Joseph of Thomas Mann found in the Man from Ur Kashdim. Indeed, not even such justly canonized Founding Fathers as Benjamin Franklin and Thomas Jefferson represent a more splendid image and pattern for the contemporary American citizenship of anyone. On balance not even Abraham Lincoln was a more heroic embodiment of the American as a self-made man. After all, Lincoln like Franklin and Jefferson was born free.

Not just the advantages of birth but also some aspects of his thought, rank Lincoln lower than Douglass. It was Lincoln who described the United States as man's last best hope on earth. It was also Abraham Lincoln who stated the case against secessionism most eloquently. But on the question of what to do about Negroes when they became free men, the Great Emancipator, who was not untainted with racism withal, and who was soft on segregation, was not above becoming involved with schemes to colonize American Negroes in Africa and South America. Needless to say, no such obscene compromise ever tempted Frederick Douglass, who incidentally did not hesitate to let the President know that Negroes were here to stay.

For all this, Lincoln himself did not allow the archetypal heroism of Frederick Douglass to go unremarked. The Reverend John Eaton, who arranged one of their several interviews, later reported that Lincoln had declared "that considering the condition from which he had risen and obstacles he had overcome, and the position to which he had attained that he [Lincoln] regarded him [Douglass] as one of the most meritorious men, if not the most meritorious man in the United States."

Thus, in the second and third quarters of nineteenth century America, Negroes can find adequate historical as well as mythological documentation for "all that really matters" in the establishment of their national identity. Not that they need to do so to meet any official requirements whatsoever. After all, such is the process by which Americans are made that immigrants, for instance, need trace their roots no further back in either time or space than Ellis Island. *By the very act of arrival*, they emerge from the bottomless depths and enter the same stream of American tradition as those who landed at Plymouth. In the very act of making their way through customs, they begin the process of becoming, as Constance Rourke would put it, part Yankee, part backwoodsman and Indian—and part Negro!

No one can deny that in the process many somewhat white immigrants who were so unjustly despised elsewhere not only discover a social, political, and economic value in white skin that they were never able to enjoy before but also become color-poisoned bigots. Indeed, an amazing number of such immigrants seem only too happy to have the people of the United States regard themselves as a nation of two races. (Only two!) Many who readily and rightly oppose such antagonistic categories as Gentile and Jew, gleefully seize upon such designations as the White People and the Black People. But even as they struggle and finagle to become all-white (by playing up their color similarities and playing down their cultural differences), they inevitably acquire basic American characteristics—which is to say, Omni-American—that are part Negro and part Indian.

The bitterness of outraged black militants against such people is altogether appropriate even if sometimes excessive. The militants' own insight into the pragmatic implications of the heritage of black people in America, however, is often only one-dimensional. Indeed, sometimes it seems as if they are more impressed by the white propaganda designed to deny their very existence than by the black actuality that not only motivates but also sustains them. In any case, when they speak of their own native land as being the White Man's country, they concede too much to the self-inflating estimates of others. They capitulate too easily to a con game which their ancestors never fell for, and they surrender their birthright to the propagandists of white supremacy, as if it were of no value whatsoever, as if one could exercise the right of redress without first claiming one's constitutional identity as citizen!

White Anglo-Saxon Protestants do in fact dominate the power mechanisms of the United States. Nevertheless, no American whose involvement with the question of identity goes beyond the sterile category of race can afford to overlook another fact that is no less essential to his fundamental sense of nationality no matter how much white folklore is concocted to obscure it: Identity is best defined in terms of culture, and the culture of the nation over which the white Anglo-Saxon power elite exercises such exclusive political, economic, and social control is not all-white by any measurement ever devised. *American culture, even in its most rigidly segregated precincts, is patently and irrevocably composite. It is, regardless of all the hysterical protestations of those who would have it otherwise, incontestably mulatto.* Indeed, for all their traditional antagonisms and obvious differences, the so-called black and so-called white people of the United States resemble nobody else in the world so much as they resemble each other. And what is more, even their most extreme and violent polarities represent nothing so much as the natural history of pluralism in an open society.

WHITE NORMS FOR BLACK DEVIATION

No other inhabitants of the United States have ever been subjected to the economic, social, legal, and political outrages that have been and continue to be committed against Negroes. Not even the Indians have been more casually exploited and more shamelessly excluded from many of the benefits of the material wealth of the nation. The overall social status of Negroes is such that even though the overwhelming majority are native born to multi-generation American parents, they do not enjoy many of the public services, normal considerations, and common privileges that are taken for granted not only by the most lowly of immigrants even before they become eligible for naturalization but also by the most questionable foreign visitors, even those from enemy countries.

The average law-abiding Negro citizen is constantly being denied such legal safeguards as are readily extended to the most notorious criminals, not to mention prisoners of war. It is a fact, for example, that Negro pilots of the 332nd Fighter Group who were captured during World War II preferred the treatment they received from the Nazis to that which they had endured at the hands of their fellow countrymen in Alabama, whose solicitude of German internees was beyond reproach! Qualified citizens of no other democratic nation in the world encounter more deviousness or nearly as much outright antagonism and violence when they attempt to participate in the routine process of local, state, and federal government.

Nor do Americans who are guilty of such atrocious behavior hesitate to add insult to injury. The very opposite is the rule. They hasten to *exaggerate* the damage they have perpetrated in the images of black depravity they advertise on every possible occasion and through every available medium. These images—which naive Negro spokesmen given to moral outcry seize upon as evidence of the need for reform—are all too obvious extensions of the process of degradation by other means, and have always functioned as an indispensable element in the vicious cycle that perpetuates white supremacy through the systematic exploitation of black people.

The negative image, for example, now permits decent white people to find satisfaction in the so-called norms—which would not exist but for the exploitation and exclusion of black people. These creatures, the logic-tight cycle begins, being non-white (the *negative* of white) are *less* than white, and being less than white are less than *normal* as human beings and are therefore exploitable; and having been rendered even *less* human as a result of exploitation, are thus *further* exploitable because less than human, and so on. (It is not at all unusual for some arrivistes to make casual references to Negroes as being unassimilable.)*

The cycle is no less vicious because philanthropy sometimes blurs its machinations. Indeed, American welfare programs for Negroes (and often for others too) increase the debasement they are supposed to ameliorate. Except in extremely unusual instances, the assistance afforded Negroes by philanthropic and governmental rehabilitation programs alike is not much more than a choice between contemptuous oppression and condescending benevolence. Not since the Reconstruction have there been any significant rehabilitation measures designed to accelerate the movement of Negroes toward equality. (The Reconstruction, of course, ultimately became the biggest betrayal in the history of the nation, but even so, no subsequent programs have approached, for one example, the achievements of the Freedman's Bureau.) In fact, even the best of the programs now in operation are more slapdash substitutions for justice and equality than anything else—and at worse, they are downright insidious.

The point is not simply rhetorical. In New York City, for example, the HARYOU-Act Program was ostensibly initiated as a measure to accelerate the movement of Harlem youth into the mainstream of national activity. But what its built-in racism has actually stimulated is a greater sense of alienation. HARYOU is a so-called community development program that bunches young Negroes even closer together in Harlem and provides even less contact with other areas of the city than they *normally* have. It also encourages them to think not like the many-generation Americans—which they are—who have as great a stake in this country as anybody else, but like Afro-Americans. As a

*A closer look at the uses and meanings of *non-white* is taken in a later essay, "Oneupmanship in Colorful America."

consequence of such programs, many Negroes who once proceeded in terms of the very concrete and immediate problem of coming to grips with themselves as native-born Americans, now seem to feel that because they are black (which most are not!) they must begin by establishing some symbolic identification with Africa, mistaking a continent for a nation as native-born "Africans" seldom do. But the riots across the nation since the summer of 1964 suggest that the self-segregation that seems so implicit in black racism is far less likely to lead to voluntary separatism than to a compression of resentment that explodes in violent rebellion.

The operating monograph for HARYOU, Kenneth Clark's *Youth in the Ghetto: A Study of the Consequences of Powerlessness and a Blueprint for Change*, is a monument to social science nonsense and nonsensibility. It demonstrates again that other Americans, including most American social scientists, don't mind one bit what unfounded conclusions you draw about U.S. Negroes, or how flimsy and questionable your statistics, or how wild your conjectures, so long as they reflect degradation. And anybody who thinks this statement is too strong, should try giving *positive* reasons for, say, Andrew Brimmer, General Davis, Carl Stokes, John Johnson, and see if most social scientists don't insist on *negative* ones, nor will their insistence be based on any celebration of the dynamics of antagonistic cooperation.

Another kind of "help" provided Negroes is exemplified in most of the plans and programs for the rehabilitation of places like Harlem and Watts. Such efforts begin with studies that find such places are "ghettos" which suffer as a result of being somehow blocked away from the rest of New York and Los Angeles. Every failing of man and beast is attributed to the inhabitants of such places; *and then the programs promptly institute measures that could only have been designed to lock the inhabitants even further away from the center of things*. Suddenly, programing experts begin discussing ways to make Harlem and Watts *self-sufficient*. Nobody ever explains why Harlem should be self-sufficient but Inwood not. In concocting such plans, no social

scientists seem to remember anything at all about the natural principles of centralization that underlie the existence of garment districts,
financial districts, theater districts, shopping districts, manufacturing
complexes, and so on. For some reason, when it comes to Negroes,
the planners seem to forget all about the desirability of keeping residential areas free of commercial congestion.

But ill-conceived and condescending benevolence seems to be the
way of American welfare-ism when dealing with Negroes. It is all of
a piece with the exasperating convolutions of an immense number
of social science theorists and survey technicians who, consciously
or not, proceed on assumptions equivalent to those which underlie
the rationalizations of intentional white supremacy and black subju-
gation. Moreover, not only are the so-called findings of most social
science surveyors of Negro life almost always compatible with the allegations of the outright segregationist—that is, to those who regard
Negroes as human *assets* so long as they are kept in subservience—
they are also completely consistent with the conceptions of the technicians who regard Negroes as *liabilities* that must be reduced, not in
accordance with any profound and compelling commitment to equal
opportunities for human fulfillment but rather in the interest of domestic tranquility.

The statistics and profiles of most contemporary social science surveys also serve to confirm the negative impressions about Negroes
that the great mass of "uninvolved" white people have formed from
folklore and the mass media.

What such universal concurrence actually reflects, however, is far
less indicative of the alleged objectivity, comprehensiveness, validity,
and reliability of the methodology employed than of its preoccupation with the documentation of black shortcomings. There are, to
be sure, many social science theorists who question and reject the
motives of the segregationist. But few seem to find it necessary to
register any insistent dissent to his assessment of Negroes as being
generally backward—except perhaps to disavow any suggestion that

such backwardness is inherent in black racial origins. (Of course no contemporary American social science theorist and technician of any professional standing would endorse racism in any form!) And yet no other survey makers in the world seem to have a greater compulsion to catalogue human behavior in terms of racial categories.

The widely publicized document that became known as the Moynihan Report (*The Negro Family: The Case for National Action*) is a notorious example of the use of the social science survey as a propaganda vehicle to promote a negative image of Negro life in the United States. It has all the superficial trappings of an objective monograph of scientific research and has been readily accepted by far too many editors and teachers across the nation as if it were the final word on U.S. Negro behavior. Many white journalists and newspaper readers now presume to explain the conduct of Negroes in the United States in terms of the structure of Negro family life as described by Moynihan. And yet Moynihan did not initiate his research project as a comprehensive study of family life at all. He set out to compile such data as would advertise Negro family life in the worst possible light in order to make, as he insists even in his title, "The Case for National Action."

In these terms, the report certainly has not achieved its purpose. The sensational nationwide attention the report has generated has not been in response to the case it makes for action. Not even the most generous do-gooders have made very much of that. Some black wailing-wall polemicists have in their usual quasi-literate intellectual bankruptcy grab-bagged it as "useful to the cause." But to most white people, sympathetic and antagonistic alike, it has become the newest scientific explanation of white supremacy and thus the current justification of the status quo.

Moynihan insists that his intentions were the best, and perhaps they were. But the fact remains that at a time when Negroes were not only demanding *freedom now* as never before but were beginning to get it, Moynihan issued a quasi-scientific pamphlet that declares on the flimsiest evidence *that they are not yet ready for freedom*! At a time when Negroes are demanding freedom as a *constitutional right*, the Moynihan Report is saying, in effect, that those who have been exploiting Negroes for years should now, upon being shown his statistics, become *benevolent* enough to set up a nationwide welfare program for them. *Not once does he cite any Negro assets that white people might find more attractive than black subservience.* Good intentions notwithstanding, Moynihan's arbitrary interpretations make a far stronger case for the Negro equivalent of Indian reservations than for Desegregation Now.

The source of this document, strange to say, was not the Department of Health, Education, and Welfare but the Department of Labor. Yet the report does not concern itself at all with any of the extremely urgent labor problems that Negroes are forever complaining about, and it includes no data on the extent of noncompliance with local, state, and federal policies and laws against racial exclusion in employment. What it cites are numerous figures on illegitimate Negro children, broken homes, lack of education, crime, narcotics addiction, and so on. It charts Negro unemployment, but not once does it suggest national action to crack down on discrimination against Negroes by labor unions. Instead, it insists that massive federal action must be initiated to correct the matriarchal structure of the Negro family!

Even if one takes this point at face value, nowhere does Moynihan explain what is innately detrimental about matriarchies. In point of fact, there is nothing anywhere in the report that indicates that Moynihan knows anything at all either about matriarchies in general or about the actual texture of Negro family relationships in particular. And if his sophomoric theories about father figures were not being applied to black people, they would no doubt be laughed out of any snap course in undergraduate psychology. They most certainly would be questioned by any reasonably alert student of history and literature. Was Elizabethan or Victorian England a matriarchy? What about the Israel of Golda Meir? No father figure ranks above that of epic hero, and yet how many epic heroes issue from conventional families?

As for Moynihan's glib but predictably popular notions about the emasculation of the Negro male, not only do they have all the earmarks of the white American male's well-known historical trait of castrating black males by any means but the report's own statistics on illegitimate births among Negroes would seem to contradict any neat theories about the cycle of black female dominance at the very outset. For if males are generally emasculated and the women are well-established matriarchs, it is very curious, to say the least, that it is the women who get stuck with the illegitimate children and most of the problems of raising them while the men run loose. There was a time when you could bag Negro males for being diseased rapists. Moynihan now represents them in terms of complete emasculation and, as his figures on child-birth show, prodigious promiscuity at the same time.

The fact of the matter is that Moynihan's figures provide for more evidence of male exploitation of females than of females henpecking males. Instead of the alleged cycle of illegitimacy-matriarchy and male emasculation by females, which adds up to further illegitimacy, the problem of Negro family instability might more accurately be defined as a cycle of illegitimacy, matriarchy, and female victimization by gallivanting males who refuse to or cannot assume the conventional domestic responsibilities of husbands and fathers. In any case, anybody who knows anything at all about Negro women knows very well that what they complain about is not the lack of masculine authority among Negro men either as husbands or as father figures but the lack of employment and the lack of interest in conventional domestic stability. *Black women, who seem to be more aware of the instability of the white family than apparently is Moynihan, are forever referring wistfully to the white woman's ability to make the white man pay and pay and pay!*

But then if Negro males were as thoroughly emasculated as the Moynihan consensus insists they are, there would be no current racial crisis. White people would not feel so hysterically insecure about the

resentment of those whom they are convinced have lost their manhood. White men would not feel that they needed a lynch *mob* to
take revenge on *one* uppity Negro. White policemen would not go
berserk at the slightest sign of black resistance. White teachers in Harlem would be able to handle Negro pupils at least as well as the great
majority of Negro teachers have always handled them elsewhere. Nor
would white people ever have felt the need to enact or defend any laws
against interracial marriages.

Further, though images of black masculinity may simply be invisible to Moynihan, it does not follow that they are also nonexistent for
Negroes themselves. Thus, while white supremacists were responding to Uncle Toms, Old Black Joes, and Stepin Fetchits, Negroes were
celebrating John Henry, Stagolee, Jack Johnson, and Joe Louis. While
white people promote wailing-wall spokesmen, black people are committed to numerous "unknown" local leaders. For all his rhetorical
resonance, the late great Reverend Martin Luther King was much
more highly regarded among Negroes when he *did* more and *talked*
less, not that they didn't love the way he talked. The mass media provide unheard of publicity for empty-handed black hot-air militants
but the truth is that while Negroes obviously enjoy making white people nervous, they much prefer to keep them guessing.

The Moynihan Report is the stuff of which the folklore of white
supremacy is made, and providing such stuff is the role that the social science technicians and theorists all too often play in the extension of black degradation through the systematic oversimplification
of black tribulations. There was a time when the white supremacist
ideologized his conduct in terms of the divine rightness of the status
quo: "If the good Lord had intended all people to be equal, he would
have made everybody the same." In the current age of liberal enlight-
enment, however, even some of the most reactionary segregationists gear their prejudices to the methodology of scientific research.
The situation now is that the contemporary folklore of racism in the
United States is derived from social science surveys in which white

norms and black deviations are tantamount to white well being and black pathology.

That most social science technicians may be entirely unaware of the major role they play in the propagation of such folklore can be readily conceded. But the fact that they remain oblivious to the application of the material that they assemble neither reduces the degree of their involvement nor mitigates the distortion, oversimplification, and confusion that they aid and abet. As a matter of fact, their innocence, which is not altogether unlike that of certain ever so nonviolent munitions experts, allows them to function with a routine detachment that is even more deadly than deliberate underhanded manipulation of facts, figures, and interpretations. The forthright white supremacist, after all, must often contend with matters of conscience, if only to rationalize them away (which accounts for much of his need for folklore in the first place). The unwitting survey technician has no such problem. Believing himself to be free of ulterior motives, he assumes that his studies are disinterested.

As even the most casual examination of his actual point of departure and his customary procedures will reveal, however, such a technician's innocence is not nearly so innocent as it is intellectually irresponsible. Nor should his lack of concern with consequences be mistaken for scientific objectivity. When the technician undertakes any research project without having become thoroughly familiar with its practical context and with the implications of his underlying thesis, his action does not represent the spirit of scientific inquiry at all. *It is the very embodiment of traditional piety.* And it permits him to substantiate the insidious speculations and malevolent preconceptions of the white status quo as readily as it allows him to do anything else.

Ordinarily American intellectuals, like those elsewhere, are profoundly preoccupied with the abnormally wretched predicament of contemporary Western man in general. Ideas derived from Karl Marx (who was convinced over a hundred years ago that modern white society was so hopelessly corrupt that its only cure was violent revolution) like those derived from Sigmund Freud (who came to view the personality structure of contemporary European man as a tangle of pathology) occupy a central position in all intellectual and cultural deliberations. Furthermore, almost every significant work of art of the twentieth century contains some explicit and often comprehensive indictment of the shortcomings of contemporary society and the inadequacies of contemporary man. There is very little indeed in the texture of the existence reflected in *The Waste Land*, "The Hollow Men," *The Great Gatsby*, *The Sun Also Rises*, or *U.S.A.*, that anybody can interpret as a glorification of white excellence in the United States. And matters are hardly improved by including such masterworks of contemporary Europe as *Ulysses*, *The Magic Mountain*, and *The Castle*.

As soon as any issue involving Negroes arises, however, most American social science theorists and technicians, the majority of whom are nothing if not Marx-Freud oriented, seem compelled to proceed as if Negroes have only to conform more closely to the behavior norms of the self-same white American middle class that writers like Theodore Dreiser, Sinclair Lewis, and Sherwood Anderson had already dissected and rejected long before the left wing political establishment of the nineteen thirties made it fashionable for even the average undergraduate to do so. Somehow or other, the minute the social science technician becomes aware of Negroes having fun "stomping at the Savoy" and enjoying luxuries (of say, Cadillacs) in spite of bad housing and low incomes and injustice, he begins to insist that they should cut out the apathy and escapism and join the all-American rat race—blithely ignoring the fact that there are in almost every Negro community domestic servants and relatives and friends of domestic servants who often have infinitely more first-hand experience with and inside information concerning the social structure and existential texture of white "middle class" life in the United States than is likely to be represented in any survey. In fact, it may well be that few psychiatrists have either more intimate contact with or more functional understanding of the effects suffered by white people from trying to keep up with the Joneses—or with the whims of Madison Avenue.

Some of the omissions and self-contradictions of white norm/black deviation folklore reveal the most appalling intellectual hypocrisy. Whereas the rate of illegitimate births among Negroes is represented as being catastrophic, for instance, the implications of the fantastically lucrative abortion racket among white Americans is conveniently overlooked—as are the procedures that deliberately obscure the rate of white illegitimacy. When the "high rate of crime" among Negroes is featured as cause for alarm, the universally conceded anti-Negro double standards of most white police, judges, and juries somehow become irrelevant! At that point, they apply only a single standard. When problems of drug addiction are under consideration, the very same Harlem that otherwise is always assumed to be suffering from the most abject poverty immediately becomes the main market for the multi-million dollar international cash-and-carry trade in narcotics. (References to crime can hardly explain this last inconsistency —not even if surveys could show that one half of Harlem burglarized the other half every night.)

The Moynihan Report, which insists that Negro men are victims of a matriarchal family structure, makes no mention at all of the incontestable fact that aggressiveness of white American women is such that they are regarded as veritable amazons not only in the Orient but also by many Europeans and not a few people at home. But then the Moynihan Report also implies without so much as a blush that all of the repressions, frustrations, and neuroses of the white Organization Man add up to an enviable patriarchal father image rather than the frightened insomniac, bootlicking conformist, "The Square," which even those who are too illiterate to read the "Maggie and Jiggs" and "Dagwood" comic strips can see in the movies and on television. Shades of father Jack Lemmon and Tony Randall.

Similarly those white Americans who express such urgent concern when the reading test scores of Harlem school children do not

conform to white-established norms seem to forget that some Negroes know very well that all the banality and bad taste on television
and the best seller lists comes from and is produced for those same
norm-calibrated whites. But Sancho Panza was far from being the last
man of the people who had to go along with the pedantic foolishness
of cliché-nourished bookworms. Nobody in his right mind would
ever seriously recommend illiteracy as a protection against brainwashing, to be sure; but still and all it may well have been his illiterate
immunity from the jargon of the fashion magazines that enabled the
little boy in Grimms' fairytale to see that the emperor's fancy new
clothes were nothing more than his birthday suit.

There may or may not be something to be said for being an unenthusiastic black sheep in a school system that emphasizes conformity to the point of producing a nation of jargon-and-cliché-oriented
white sheep. Nevertheless, one factor that is always either overlooked
or obscured in all interpretations of the low academic performance
of Negro pupils is the possibility of their *resistance* to the self-same
white norms that they are being rated by. What some white teachers
refer to as being the *apathy* of Negro pupils, competent black teachers
are likely to describe as lack of interest and motivation. Black teachers know very well that *when there is genuine Negro interest there is
seldom any complaint about Negro ability*. And yet most social science
technicians persistently interpret low Negro test scores not in terms
of the lack of incentive but in terms of a historic and comprehensive
cultural deprivation.

But then nowhere are the omissions and contradictions of white
norm/black deviation folklore more operative than in matters of formal education. Indeed, the establishment of the notion of a so-called
"culture gap" seems to have been the ultimate function of norm lore
from the outset. By ignoring the most fundamental definitions of anthropology and archaeology along with the most essential implications of the humanities, the contemporary American social science
technician substitutes academic subject matter for culture. He then

misrepresents deficiencies in formal technical training as cultural deprivation, a very neat trick indeed.

Such is the procedure that enables the folklore technician to provide statistical evidence as proof to show that Negroes are not like other Americans. But why is it that no widely publicized social science surveys ever measure conformity and deviation in terms of norms of citizenship, which are based on the national ideals as established by the Declaration of Independence and the Constitution? The Constitution not only expresses principles of conduct that are valid for mankind as a whole; *it is also the ultimate official source for definitions of desirable and undesirable American behavior.*

The major emphasis in the large surveys is never placed on the failure of white Americans to measure up to the standards of the Constitution. The primary attention repeatedly is focused on Negroes as victims. Again and again the assumption of the surveys is that slavery and oppression have made Negroes *inferior* to other Americans and hence less American. This is true even of such a relatively fair-minded study as *An American Dilemma.*

In point of fact, however, slavery and oppression may well have made black people more human and more American while it has made white people less human and less American. Anyway, Negroes have as much reason to think so as to think otherwise. It is the political behavior of black activists, not that of norm-calibrated Americans, that best represents the spirit of such constitutional norm-ideals as freedom, justice, equality, fair representation, and democratic processes. Black Americans, not Americans devoted to whiteness, exemplify the open disposition toward change, diversity, unsettled situations, new structures and experience, that are prerequisite to the highest level of citizenship. Black not white or even somewhat white Americans display the greatest willingness to adjust to the obvious consequences of those contemporary innovations in communication and transportation facilities whose networks have in effect shrunk the world to one pluralistic community in which the most diverse people are now neighbors. It is Negroes, not the median of the white population, who act as if the United States is such a world in miniature. It is the non-conforming Negro who now acts like the true descendent of the Founding Fathers—who cries, "Give me liberty or give me death," and who regards taxation without representation as tyranny. It is the norm-oriented white American who becomes the rednecked progeny of the Red Coats, and yells, "Disperse, ye rebels." It is the white American who, in the name of law and order, now sanctions measures (including the stock piling of armor piercing weapons to be used against American citizens) that are more in keeping with the objectives of a police state than those of an open society.

There is little reason why Negroes should not regard contemporary social science theory and technique with anything except the most unrelenting suspicion. There is, come to think of it, no truly compelling reason at all why Negoes should not regard the use of the social science statistical survey as the most elaborate fraud of modern times. In any event, they should never forget that the group in power is always likely to use every means at its disposal to create the impression that it deserves to be where it is. And it is not above suggesting that those who have been excluded have only themselves to blame.

PALEFACE FABLES, BROWNSKIN PEOPLE

It seems altogether likely that white people in the United States will continue to reassure themselves with black images derived from the folklore of white supremacy and the fakelore of black pathology so long as segregation enables them to ignore the actualities. They can afford such self-indulgence only because they carefully avoid circumstances that would require a confrontation with their own contradictions. Not having to suffer the normal consequences of sloppy thinking, they can blithely obscure any number of omissions and misinterpretations with no trouble at all. They can explain them away with terminology and statistical razzle-dazzle. They can treat the most

ridiculous self-refutation as if it were a moot question; and of course
they can simply shut off discussion by changing the subject.

The self-conception in terms of which most Negroes have actually
lived and moved, and had their personal being for all these years, however, has always been, as they say, something else again. Perhaps self-
indulgence causes white people to overlook the most obvious fact in
the world: Negroes are neither figments of bigoted imaginations nor
academic abstractions. They are flesh-and-blood organisms and not
only do they possess consciousness, they also enjoy self-awareness.
They are, that is to say, purposeful human beings whose existence is
motivated by their own self-centered interests.

There are, no one should be surprised to find, a number of prominent Negro spokesmen and black ideologists of welfare-ism who
employ, repeat, and even extend the imagery of white supremacy. In
most instances, they appear to have been far more thoroughly victim-
ized by the current popularity of social science than by the system of
oppression itself. In any case, what they say about how Negroes have
been damaged by slavery and oppression is almost always restricted
by Marxian and Freudian dialectics. But what many of them do often
evokes nothing so much as the irrepressible spirit of '76—without so
much rag tag and bobtail to be sure: the Negro revolution is certainly
one of the most fashion conscious uprisings of all times. (Even the
protest hair-dos, to the extent that they are protest, are geared to high
fashion, often misguided, no doubt, and sometimes disastrous, but
high fashion nonetheless.)

The nature of Negro moral outcry polemics, it should also be remembered, is now such that the most glibly self-confident and even
the most smugly chauvinistic black spokesmen and leaders readily
and frequently refer to themselves as being fear-ridden, emasculated,
and without self-respect. No wonder white Americans continue to be
so shocked and disoriented by the intensification of the civil rights
struggle. Instead of relying on what is now known about the nature of
social uprisings, white Americans keep allowing themselves to expect

the theoretical Sambo promised, as it were, by Stanley M. Elkins in *Slavery: A Problem in American Institutional and Intellectual Life*, implicitly confirmed by the pronouncements of Kenneth Clark in *Dark Ghetto*, and conceded by so much self-deprecating rhetoric. But what these same white Americans keep running up against is such bewildering, outrageous, and (to some of them) terrifying behavior as the intransigent determination of leaders like Charles Evers in Mississippi; the mockery and high camp of media types like H. Rap Brown on all networks; and people like those in Watts, Newark, and Detroit, who respond to the murderous hysteria of white police and national guardsmen with a defiance that is often as derisive as it is deepseated.

The compulsions nourished by the folklore of white supremacy seem to be such that white Americans are as yet unable to realize that they themselves are obviously far more impressed by their own show of brute force than black insurgents ever seem to be. They still do not seem to realize that what they actually see on television during all of the demonstrations and, as the saying goes, civil disruptions is not a herd of wall-eyed black natives cringing before white authority. What they see are heavily armed, outraged, and slaughter-prone white policemen and soldiers smoldering with rage and itching to perpetrate a massacre, confronting Negroes who are behaving not only as if the whole situation were a farce and a carnival but who also have time to grant television interviews in which there is as much snap-course social science jargon as street-corner hip talk: "Like it's either upward mobility, or burn, baby, burn!" As one character in *For Whom the Bell Tolls* who, shaking his head, kept saying of the Spanish during the Civil War, "What a people!" Indeed, as Negroes are forever saying in delighted puzzlement of each other, "My pee-pul, *my people*. Ain't nothing *like* 'em. Man, when you talking about *us*, you talking about something *else*."

On the other hand, perhaps it is easy enough to see why so many white Americans who are more puzzled than delighted are always so eager to cite quotations from books like *Black Rage* and *Dark Ghetto*.

When *Dark Ghetto*, a good example of how a book by a black writer may represent a point of view toward black experience which is essentially white, insists that slavery and oppression have reduced Negroes to such a tangle of pathology that all black American behavior is in effect only a pathetic manifestation of black cowardice, self-hatred, escapism, and self-destructiveness, these white Americans evidently assume its author is corroborating their own notions of black inferiority. Many treat *Dark Ghetto*, which in point of fact reveals very little if any meaningful, first-hand contact with any black community in the United States, as if it were an official document. As yet not one white social science theoretician or survey technician of national prestige has made any significant public outcry against the fact that a document whose statistics are at times clearly ridiculous and whose central assumptions and embarrassingly sloppy conclusions make a travesty of scientific methodology is by way of becoming a veritable handbook of race relations in some parts of the country. But then, not very many Negro social science technicians have come forth to take issue with *Dark Ghetto* either. Not even those ever so prideful black nationalist spokesmen who otherwise display so much suspicion about becoming victims of brainwashing (whitewashing) and who express so much militant concern about improving "the black man's image in America," seem in the least aware of the fact that almost every chapter of *Dark Ghetto* not only supports the stereotypes that Negroes have always been extremely sensitive about, but also provides a quasi-scientific refutation of the very elements of Negro American history upon which contemporary Negro leaders must build.

Dark Ghetto, which is strong on political indictment but, as will be seen, weak on psychological insight, represents Negroes as substandard human beings who subsist in a sick community. Its image of Harlem is, in effect, that of an urban pit writhing with derelicts. According to the impression the author creates (even if his figures do not), black despair has driven most of its inhabitants either to crime, narcotics addiction, prostitution, and the like, or to obsessive imitations of something which he calls "the white man's society." "Few if any Negroes," he goes so far as to claim, "ever lose that sense of shame [of being dark skinned] and self-hatred." "The obsession with whiteness," he adds later, "continues past childhood and into adulthood. *It stays with the Negro all his life.*" (Italics added.) It is extremely difficult to believe that the evidence that *Dark Ghetto* presents in support of such a sweeping generalization would meet the scientific standards of, say, Talcott Parsons, who cannot fail to note that Clark's overestimation of white well being is almost worshipful. *Dark Ghetto* actually indicts Negroes for having a low suicide rate. It also confuses the personal motives of homicide with the socialized motives leading to warfare. It is all part of the game for a polemicist to denounce a murderer for not being a soldier, but just how scientific is it for a psychologist to do so?

The emphasis on black wretchedness in *Dark Ghetto* easily exceeds that in most of the books written by *white racists to justify segregation.* And yet Gunnar Myrdal, for instance, does not regard its author as a man who hates both himself and other Negroes for being black. Myrdal seems quite certain that Clark is an ideologist of social welfare measures much like himself. In the foreword to *Dark Ghetto,* Myrdal describes the author as being "desperately anxious that the ugly facts of life in the Negro ghetto become really known to the ruling majority." But Myrdal, who is anything but a de Tocqueville, then ever so hastily equates "the balanced view" with *false objectivity* (!) and so implies that *ugly* facts are more important and more useful than *plain* or even *beautiful* facts, not to mention *comprehensive* facts.

But thus have wailing-wall spokesmen almost always confused the politics of philanthropy with the *real politik* of municipal, state, and national government. The exaggeration of black suffering or "putting on the poor mouth" may be a time-hallowed means for obtaining benevolent handouts, but it is hardly the best method of developing rugged political power. In fact, many of the white politicians who back stop-gap poverty appropriations bills do so because they assume that this is the surest and smoothest way of delaying active and equitable participation in the power mechanisms.

Social science folklore-oriented black ideologists of welfare appropriations are seldom guilty of deliberate duplicity. They simply do not realize that their one-sided featuring of black pathology might frighten white Americans into an easier tolerance of anti-Negro police tactics. They really think that their exaggerations will gain white sympathy for black grievances. As incredibly naive as it may sound—and in point of fact is—they seem to think their emphasis on black mistreatment will make comfort-seeking but easily rattled white people react charitably to black threats and disruptions. Thus, when the author of *Dark Ghetto* came out for the integration of Manhattan schools, he overlooked the fact that he was trying to browbeat "powerful" white people into intermingling their norm-secure children with Negroes whom he himself had described as powerless hoodlums, addicts, and prostitutes. No thinking person really expects white people to do such a thing, certainly not if they accept the findings of books like *Dark Ghetto*. (There is good reason to believe that Clark is sincerely appalled by the current trend toward "black separatism." But when he takes militant separatists to task, he seems to forget that a book like *Dark Ghetto* gives them no alternative except militant self-pity!)

Many welfare spokesmen engage in such wholesale debasements of the image of their fellow Negroes not because they want to sell them out, for their commitment to social betterment is as unquestionably sincere as the form it takes is politically infantile. They do so because somehow or other neither their common understanding nor their formal education has yet to come to terms with that which the folk wisdom of the fugitive slave and the Reconstruction freedman took for granted long ago: *The Declaration of Independence and the Constitution are the social, economic, and political heritage of all Americans.*

Unfortunately, it seems that such spokesmen, like most other Americans, have been conditioned by school systems and communications media that have overpromoted the methodology and the categories of social science at the expense of the more comprehensive wisdom of the humanities and the arts—leaving thereby their sense of context deficient. In any case, they appear to have become so fascinated by pretentious terminology and easy oversimplifications that they no longer remember what experience is really like. If so, perhaps it is only natural that they no longer realize how complicated human life is, even at its least troubled and freest. Which, of course, means that they are not likely to realize how rich and exciting its possibilities are either. And yet such people, who confuse metaphorical ghettos with real ones, are often regarded as expert planners and programers! They are not. They are polemicists, and often third-rate polemicists at that. Or worse. Their propaganda is often more useful to the other side than to their own.

The obsessive preoccupation of the white people of the United States with the folklore of white supremacy makes one thing all too obvious: *White Americans do not take the privileged status of white people for granted. They work at it.* They pretend that it is natural to their social inheritance. So would they impress others and so perhaps do they reassure themselves, somewhat. But in reality they leave little to nature, and what they inherit is the full-time obligation to keep up social appearances without ever seeming to do so. As with all other forms of oneupmanship, however, nothing is more clearly indicative of the depth of their watchful concern than is their never quite casual indifference.

In other words, beneath the ever so carefully structured surface of solipsistic complacency and seemingly thoughtless condescension, there is almost always the anxiety of a people who live in unrelieved anticipation of disaster. For, people who really feel secure in their status just simply do not expend all of the time and energy, not to mention the ingenuity, that white colonialists have always been convinced is necessary to "keep Negroes in their place." There is no denying that as a result of constant practice, some white smugness becomes quite habitual. But that is not all the same thing as becoming natural;

and in truth, as Negro slaves found out long ago, the vaguest hint of black hostility is more than enough to throw the most arrogant white Americans into a frenzy of trigger-happy paranoia. Some white Americans seem to regard every hostile black remark as if it were an official declaration of war.

After all, white people in the United States are not simply explaining anti-Negro atrocities of police by attributing them, as they seem ever so eager to do, to high-handed inhumanity and moral callousness. When white people wink away the hot-headed murder of a fourteen year old Harlem schoolboy by an experienced, six foot, white New York policeman, or excuse a Los Angeles patrolman for the instant execution of a cantankerous but unarmed black husband for running traffic signals en route with his pregnant wife to the maternity hospital, it seems clear that they do so out of a sympathy born of their own very simple human terror at the prospect of having to confront an angry Negro on "equal" terms! Over a century and a quarter after Nat Turner's revolt, even the most highly certified white American intellectuals reviewing William Styron's *Nat Turner*—which will be examined in some detail later—still insist that such a black thrust forward toward freedom could only have been a form of fantasy, if not insanity. They still seem to find *comfort* in the fact that more than two hundred unarmed Negro slaves were killed in retaliation for the liquidation of less than sixty white slavocrats. Also, whenever the possibility of anti-white violence is mentioned, white intellectuals (whose conception of military demography, incidentally, is not only obsolete but tribal) keep reminding every body that white people enjoy a ten-to-one population majority. *But they keep acting as if such odds were not enough.*

Norm deviation folklore, mass media images, and wailing-wall polemicism notwithstanding, Negroes have always lived in full, even if somewhat inarticulate, awareness of the fact that whenever there are circumstances which suggest the possibility of black and white person-to-person or group-to-group confrontation, to say nothing of antagonism, white Americans almost always react as if they have only the highest regard for black capacity and potential. Most police forces seem to feel that they cannot handle black disorders without super weapons! Negroes have always noted with wry satisfaction that white Americans rarely if ever display even the slightest condescension or disdain in such situations. They beef-up the police force, organize rifle clubs and combat schools, stockpile arms and incendiary tanks.

But then, regardless of the obsequious rhetoric of so many of their outcry-oriented spokesmen, only the most inattentive Negroes have ever really assumed that white Americans have been unmindful of black Americans as human beings the consequences of whose self-interest is something to be reckoned with. As so much of their secretiveness goes to show, most Negroes have always suspected that white Americans only *pretend* to be misinformed about black motives and aspirations. Nor is their traditional black distrust of white people ever likely to permit many Negroes to accept anybody else's dehumanized images of black people. So far as most Negroes are concerned, the so-called problems of the Black Image have always been a matter of calculated misrepresentation. Much goes to show that the so-called problem of black identity is essentially a problem of bad publicity. Time and again it turns out that when Negro spokesmen refer to the lack of black identity, they are really complaining about the lack of public recognition, appreciation, and acclaim.

In any case, most Negroes are not likely to believe that white Americans do not really know that there is an obvious difference between the drive to acquire more of the material benefits of the United States and the desire to be white. Consistent with their own traditional secretiveness and idiomatic abstruseness, they concede that white people could only be confused about many Negro motives and hence do not appreciate a great number of nuances in Negro style and manner. But they are also consistent when they accuse the same white Americans of being dishonest about what they really do know and how they actually do feel about Negroes.

Most Negroes, far from believing that white Americans have only the lowest opinion of black Americans, are forever revealing the fact that they are firmly convinced that even those white people of wealth and power spend a highly significant amount of time emulating Negroes while pretending not to. No conviction is more indicative of Negro self-esteem, the appreciation Negroes have for other Negroes, or the ambivalence of which their response to white Americans is seldom free. Nor does anything contradict all of the current pseudo-psychiatric nonsense about black self-hatred and self-rejection more profoundly than the arrogant bitterness with which Negroes complain that ruthless, mechanically efficient, but essentially provincial white Americans prosper on pale dilutions and hopelessly square commercial vulgarizations of the music of the Negro idiom. The catalogue of elements that make up the so-called mainstream of American culture but which Negroes claim were appropriated from the Negro idiom is endless. And of course, what is significant is not the accuracy of the enumeration but rather what the existence of such a belief reveals about how Negroes really feel about white "supremacy."

Nowhere, incidentally, do the curious notions about Negro "self-hatred" and "group hatred" become more preposterous than when race-oriented psychopolitical technicians and theorists insist on drawing sweeping pathological inferences from fads in fashions and cosmetics. Seldom do "scientists" show such an exasperating tendency to draw such far-reaching conclusions from such "evidence." *Dark Ghetto*, as might be expected, provides a good example. "The preoccupation of many Negroes with hair straighteners, skin bleaches and the like," runs one wrong-headed passage, "illustrates this tragic aspect of American racial prejudice—Negroes have come to believe in their own inferiority."

But the book makes nothing whatsoever of the traditional and undisguised *contempt* that Southern Negroes have always displayed toward "poor white trash." *Dark Ghetto* manages somehow to ignore the implications of Negro distaste for almost every aspect of the hillbilly life-style; it doesn't even hint at the self-regard implicit in the seething resentment that Northern Negroes have always felt because the system permits so many white immigrants whom Negroes regard as being the European equivalent of rednecks to get ahead of Negroes who are clearly more deserving. *Dark Ghetto* makes no mention at all of the black *snobbishness* so explicit in the epithet *ofay*, which is not only a condemnation of whiteness as being synonymous with "square" but is also accepted as such by countless "middle class" white Northerners as being justifiably contemptuous. Almost any Negro seems to feel that he can call any white person square and get away with it.

The implications of fashion fads are anything but as simple as the typical one-dimensional conjectures in works such as *Dark Ghetto* would make them out to be. To begin with, dark-skinned Negroes, it should be obvious to anyone interested in such matters, do not apply skin bleaches to all parts of their bodies as white people anoint themselves with suntan oil. Such bleaching agents as *Nadinola* and *Black and White* normally come in two-ounce containers and frequently last for months because they are used primarily to remove facial splotches. But who knows! Perhaps some determined race-oriented psychologizer will interpret this as a form of schizophrenia, white faces or masks but black bodies. That sort of thing. It makes, as they say, jolly good theory but no more tenable than the one that could be made from the symbolic self-mutilation involved in the nose jobs that are so popular among many Jewish Americans, who as any Negro country club dishwasher knows, already have white skin, straight hair, status employment, and even wealth.

As for the hair styles of Negro women, perhaps the best thing to do is to leave all female head decorations to the fashion magazines. It does seem, however, that Negro women can often do things with wigs and hair colors that could hardly have been dreamed of by the white people who manufacture them and who, by the way, did not originally design them for Negroes.

Incidentally, a number of "natural texture" promoters notwithstanding, in African culture there is much less emphasis on naturalness than on design and stylization. Traditional African sculpture, for example, is not representational but abstract. And certainly no one regards ornamental face and body cicatrices, filed teeth, Ubangi lip extensions, the wearing of nose rings, and so on, as accentuations of the natural. Indeed, the marvelous masks, the prevalence of mask-like makeup, and the exuberant inventiveness found in the personal adornments of tribe after tribe would seem to indicate that the African ancestors of U.S. Negroes have hardly ever been so excited about "The Natural Look" as the editors of *Vogue* and *Harper's Bazaar* become from time to time. And of course one can only guess what the self-hatred specialists will make of evidence that indicates not only that some Africans have always gone in for wigs (and blond wigs at that) but that others were also slicking their hair down with mud and other ingenious pomades including cow dung long before white Europeans arrived as agents of oppression. (The chances are that Africans were extending their human characteristics by appropriating such animal features as they admired—say, like Richard the Lion Hearted, or the Detroit Lions.)

With male hair styles, perhaps what is most often overlooked by those who insist that the Negro man's process or conk is an imitation of the straight-haired, pale-faced "oppressor," is the fact that those Negro men who are clearly most interested in integration and assimilation, who have gone to interracial schools, who work in integrated employment, live in interracial communities and whose speech and dress (whether naturally or deliberately) most closely resembles that of the so-called white middle class, *seldom if ever have processed hair.* Indeed they have always been the major opponents of the process. On the other hand, those who do—and there never has been a time when the majority did—are almost always unmistakably Negro-idiom oriented.

Survey technicians who take the time to do the necessary historical research will probably find that the conk was much more directly influenced by the dark-, sleek- (or wavy-) haired Latin type dandy than by the pale- (or ruddy-) faced, straight- (or shaggy-) mopped

Anglo-Saxon of the power elite. Modish Negro men seem to feel closer affinity with the "dark and handsome" movie smoothies who go at least as far back as Rudolph Valentino and the young George Raft, than with the lighter all-American squares like Gary Cooper and James Stewart. Nor should careful research fail to take into account the completely "normal" influence of curly-headed mulatto-type relatives, friends, and heroes, who are admired and imitated not simply because they resemble the "oppressors" but for any number of other reasons that are no less operative among other people than among U.S. Negroes.

But perhaps of even greater immediate relevance to current questions of identity and Negro self-regard is the likelihood that truly insightful students of culture will upon reflection come to concede that no matter what its origins were, the conk has long become a U.S. Negro "thing," and that therefore a young man sporting a Sugar Ray Robinson or Nat "King" Cole process, say in the mid-fifties, was not copying someone who was trying to be like white people but rather copying a very special Negro whom he rated above *all* other people in the world. When pop singer James Brown switched from his patent-leather glossy coiffure to Brillo, he made a number of statements about black identity and pride, but those who followed him already knew precisely who he was all the time as well as what he represented, and they were already as proud of him as they could possibly be.

Actually, when most Negroes who have not been "faked out" by social science jive artists see a conk, they are almost certain to assume the person wearing it is either in show business or identifies with Negroes in the world of show business—which, of course, includes stylish prizefight promoters, gamblers, pimps, racketeers, and so on. For most Negroes the process goes with certain manners in clothes, speech, music, and even movement, which are anything but ofay oriented.

Processed hair, in other words, implies no less emphasis on black identity than the *au naturel*, Afro-Brillo. Nor should the role of show business in the development of the current natural texture fad be forgotten either. In fact, to do so would be to omit a key element in the *American* image-making process. For just as certain popular post-bop musicians have given beards chic status among certain black hipsters, so had the neo–Paul Robeson image of Harry Belafonte and Sidney Poitier begun to popularize the so-called natural texture-do, which the bop era had already initiated among hipsters long before the promoters of *negritude* began trying to philosophize it or the late Malcolm X to politicalize it.

The truth is, as Negro beauticians (who are mainly hair dressers) are forever reminding their customers, some people look marvelous in wigs while others are every bit as stunning when processed and still others are equally as wonderful looking with the Afro-Brillo. (Some of course are just fine looking in any style and some, alas, are not.) Thus, perhaps the most realistic thing to point out about Negro hair styles—as about styles in general—is the altogether fascinating fact that in contemporary America the cosmetics and fashions industries have so expanded the possibilities of makeup and make believe that all questions of image and identity are now matters of some personal choice for all Americans of all racial derivations. If you don't like the hair texture or hair color you were born with, you can now buy what you like on installment plan if necessary.

But even more fundamental and no less obvious is another fact which the racism that underlies most discussions about American identity almost always obscures: In spite of the seemingly hypnotic spell that updated versions of the Huck Finn or Norman Rockwell plug-ugly and the shirt collar ad Anglo-Saxon and Gibson girl images exercise over so many self-effacing, assimilation-bent European immigrants, *there is no standard melting pot mold for the American Image. The only official national image is the eagle.* There never has been a standard image, and currently, for all the emphasis on norms, nothing seems to change more than the points of conformity. Meanwhile, although they are most often referred to (even by many of their own spokesmen) as if they were all jet black natives only recently arrived from the dark land of Africa, U.S. Negroes represent a composite of all images. No other segment of the population of the United States encompasses more of the nation's limitless variety, whether in physical appearance or in behavior. Indeed, perhaps the most significant and scientifically supportable observation to be made about native-born U.S. Negroes as a *race* is that they may well be by way of becoming a new racial (i.e., physical) type, perhaps the only one that is truly indigenous, so to speak to contemporary North America. But this is just an aside: as stated before *race* is hardly as useful as an index to human motives as is culture.

As for behavior or life style, no other people in the land have as yet evolved a characteristic idiom that reflects a more open, robust, and affirmative disposition toward diversity and change. Nor is any other idiom more smoothly geared to open-minded improvisation. Moreover, never has improvisation been more conditioned by esthetic values—or at the same time been more indicative of the fundamental openness that is the necessary predisposition for all scientific exploration! Improvisation after all is experimentation.

When such improvisation as typifies Negro music, dance, language, religion, sports, fashions, general bearing and deportment, and even food preparation is considered from the Negro point of view, there is seldom, if ever, any serious doubt about how Negroes feel about themselves or about what they accept or reject of white people. They regard themselves not as the substandard, abnormal *non-white* people of American social science surveys and the news media, but rather as if they were, so to speak, fundamental *extensions* of contemporary possibilities.

That much of the blackest frustration grows out of being excluded goes without saying, but much of it also comes from having to witness others making a mess of something you are convinced you can do better. The white press notwithstanding, Negroes do *not* regard successful Negroes as proof that black people can do as well as white people; they regard them as proof that given only half a chance black people can do better than most white people who have had all the advantages. *Arrogant? Oh, but yes! The topic is self-esteem.*

The whole world defers to the supremacy of American political and economic power mechanisms. Negro attitudes toward the so-called white cultural establishment, however, are entirely consistent with the pragmatic improvisational irreverence that most Negroes display toward so many other established patterns and values. As a result, many things that most other Americans seem to accept as models for reverence and emulation, Negroes, not unlike jam session–oriented musicians, use mainly as points of departure. Even when Negroes set out to make literal imitations of white people, they often seem to find it impossible not to add their own dimensions.

THE BLUES IDIOM AND THE MAINSTREAM

The creation of an art style is, as most anthropologists would no doubt agree, a major cultural achievement. In fact, it is perhaps the highest as well as the most comprehensive fulfillment of culture; for an art style, after all, reflects nothing so much as the ultimate synthesis and refinement of a life style.

Art is by definition a process of stylization; and what it stylizes is experience. What it objectifies, embodies, abstracts, expresses, and symbolizes is a sense of life. Accordingly, what is represented in the music, dance, painting, sculpture, literature, and architecture of a given group of people in a particular time, place, and circumstance is a conception of the essential nature and purpose of human existence itself. More specifically, an art style is the assimilation in terms of which a given community, folk, or communion of faith embodies its basic attitudes toward experience.

And this is not all. Of its very nature, an art style is also the essence of experience itself, in both the historical and sensory implications of

the word. It is an attitude, description, and interpretation in action—
or rather, perhaps most often, in reaction. For needless to say, action
is seldom gratuitous or unmotivated. Not only does it take place *in* a
situation, it also takes place *in response to* a situation.

Kenneth Burke has equated stylization with strategy. To extend
the military metaphor, one can say stylization is the estimate become
maneuver. In such a frame of reference, style is not only insight but
disposition and gesture, not only calculation and estimation become
execution (as in engineering), but also motive and estimation become
method and occupation. It is a way of sizing up the world, and so, ultimately, and beyond all else, a mode and medium of survival.

In current social science usage, the concept of "survival technique"
has somehow become confused with technology and restricted to
matters of food, clothing, and shelter. (Incidentally, the most transparent fallacy of almost all white norm/black deviation folklore is
its exaggeration of the *cultural* implications of the control by white
people of the production and distribution of the creature comforts
required for subsistence in the Temperate Zone.) Human survival,
however, involves much more than biological prolongation. The human organism must be nourished and secured against destruction, to
be sure, but what makes man human is style. Hence the crucial significance of art in the study of human behavior: *All human effort beyond
the lowest level of the struggle for animal subsistence is motivated by the
need to live in style.*

Certainly the struggle for political and social liberty is nothing if
not a quest for freedom to choose one's own way or style of life. Moreover, it should be equally as obvious that there can be no such thing
as human dignity and nobility without a consummate, definitive style,
pattern, or archetypal image. Economic interpretations of history
notwithstanding, what activates revolutions is not destitution (which
most often leads only to petty thievery and the like) but intolerable
systems and methods—intolerable styles of life.

*

Most Americans know very well that the blues genre which in its most elaborate extensions includes elements of the spirituals, gospel music, folk song, chants, hollers, popular ditties, plus much of what goes into symphonic and even operatic composition, is the basic and definitive musical idiom of native-born U.S. Negroes. But few if any students of America seem either to understand or even to have any serious curiosity about the relationship of art style to Negro life style. None seems to consider the blues idiom a major cultural achievement. Not even those writers who have referred to it as being perhaps the only truly American innovation in contemporary artistic expression seem able to concede it any more significance than of some vague minor potential not unlike that of some exotic spice.

As for the contemporary American social survey statistician, his interests seem never to extend beyond social pathology and the need for revolutionary political reform or community rehabilitation. Seldom do any of his all too comprehensive evaluations of Negro cultural phenomena reflect either anthropological insight into the dynamics of ritual or stylization, or even a rudimentary appreciation of the functional role of esthetics. What the blues represent in his view of things is a crude, simpleminded expression of frustration and despair. Thus, so far as he is concerned, swinging the blues achieves only an essentially pathetic therapeutic compensation for the bleak social and economic circumstances of black people in the United States.

Obviously most American social survey technicians see no connection at all in this context between swinging the blues and the fact that the pronounced emphasis on rhythm-oriented improvisation in U.S. Negro creative expression is derived from dance-oriented antecedents in African culture (although in other contexts, everyone is quick to talk about the African roots of this and that). But worse still they are thus also oblivious to the fact that the same basic improvisational stylization (with its special but unmistakable overtones of what Johan Huizinga, discussing man as *homo ludens*, refers to as the play element in all cultures) applies to positive as well as to negative situations. As a result, they consistently misconstrue what is really the dynamics of confrontation for the mechanics of withdrawal, escape, and relief!

The blues ballad is a good example of what the blues are about. Almost always relating a story of frustration, it could hardly be described as a device for avoiding the unpleasant facts of Negro life in America. On the contrary, it is a very specific and highly effective vehicle, the obvious purpose of which is to make Negroes acknowledge the essentially tenuous nature of all human existence.

The sense of well being that always goes with swinging the blues is generated, as anyone familiar with Negro dance halls knows, not by obscuring or denying the existence of the ugly dimensions of human nature, circumstances, and conduct, but rather through the full, sharp, and inescapable awareness of them. One blues ballad after another informs and keeps reminding Negro dance couples (engaged, as are all dance couples, in ritual courtship) of the complications and contradictions upon which romances are contingent: *Now, don't be coming to me with your head all knotty and your nose all snotty; if you don't know what you doing you better ask somebody.*

As an art form, the blues idiom by its very nature goes beyond the objective of making human existence bearable physically or psychologically. The most elementary and hence the least dispensable objective of all serious artistic expression, whether aboriginal or sophisticated, is to make human existence *meaningful*. Man's primary concern with life is to make it as significant as possible, and the blues are part of this effort.

The definitive statement of the epistemological assumptions that underlie the blues idiom may well be the colloquial title and opening declaration of one of Duke Ellington's best-known dance tunes from the mid-thirties: "It Don't Mean a Thing if It Ain't Got That Swing." In any case, when the Negro musician or dancer swings the blues, he is fulfilling the same fundamental existential requirement that determines the mission of the poet, the priest, and the medicine man. He is making an affirmative and hence exemplary and heroic response to that which André Malraux describes as *la condition humaine*. Extemporizing in response to the exigencies of the situation in which he finds himself, he is confronting, acknowledging, and contending with the infernal absurdities and ever-impending frustrations inherent in the nature of all existence *by playing with the possibilities that are also there*. Thus does man the player become man the stylizer and by the same token the humanizer of chaos; and thus does play become ritual, ceremony, and art; and thus also does the dance-beat improvisation of experience in the blues idiom become survival technique, esthetic equipment for living, and a central element in the dynamics of U.S. Negro life style.

When the typical Negro dance orchestra plays the blues, it is also *playing with* the blues. When it swings, jumps, hops, stomps, bounces, drags, shuffles, rocks, and so on, its manner not only represents a swinging-the-blues attitude toward the "bad news" that comes with the facts of life, it also exemplifies and generates a riffing-the-blues disposition toward the "rough times" that beset all human existence.

The blues-idiom dancer like the solo instrumentalist turns disjunctures into continuities. He is not disconcerted by intrusions, lapses, shifts in rhythm, intensification of tempo, for instance; but is inspired by them to higher and richer levels of improvisation. As a matter of fact (and as the colloquial sense of the word suggests), the "break" in the blues idiom provides the dancer his greatest opportunity—which, at the same time, is also his most heroic challenge and his moment of greatest jeopardy.

But then, impromptu heroism such as is required only of the most agile of storybook protagonists, is precisely what the blues tradition has evolved to condition Negroes to regard as *normal procedure*! Nor is any other attitude towards experience more appropriate to the ever-shifting circumstances of all Americans or more consistent with the predicament of man in the contemporary world at large.

Indeed, the blues idiom represents a major American innovation of universal significance and potential because it fulfills, among other things, precisely that fundamental function that Constance Rourke ascribes to the comedy, the irreverent wisdom, the sudden changes and adroit adaptations she found in the folk genre of the Yankee-backwoodsman-Negro of the era of Andrew Jackson. It provides "emblems for a pioneer people who require resilience as a prime trait."

Obviously those who are conditioned by the folklore of white supremacy would have it otherwise. They insist that political powerlessness and economic exclusion can lead only to cultural deprivation. One unmistakable objective of white norm/black deviation survey data is to show how far outside the mainstream of American culture Negroes are. Another may well be to insinuate that they are unassimilable. The blues idiom, however, represents the most comprehensive and the most profound assimilation. It is the product of a sensibility that is completely compatible with the *human* imperatives of modern times and American life. Many white composers, unlike most white social technicians, are already aware of the ease with which the blues idiom sound track can be extended from the cotton fields and the railroad through megalopolis and into outer space.

So far, incredible as it may be, no Negro leader seems to have made any extensive political use of the so-called survival techniques and idiomatic equipment for living that the blues tradition has partly evolved in response to slavery and oppression. Even more incredible is the fact that most Negro leaders, spokesmen, and social technicians seem singularly unaware of the possibility of doing so. (There are many spokesmen whose fear of being stigmatized as primitive is so hysterical that they reject out of hand any suggestion that U.S. Negro life style is geared to dance-beat improvisation. As far as they are concerned, such a conception is inseparable from the racism behind the old notion that all Negroes have natural rhythm.) In any case, the riff-playing or vernacular inventiveness that is so fundamental to the way Negroes react otherwise is conspicuously absent from their political behavior. In other situations they play by ear, but for some curious reason they seem to think that political problems must be solved by the book, which in most instances only a few seem to have read and not that many have digested.

No self-respecting Negro musician would ever be guilty of following the stock arrangements of white song writers as precisely as Negro leaders adhere to the Tin Pan Alley programs of white social technicians! Nor is bravado an adequate substitute for efficiency. Nor should riff-style be confused with the jive-time capers of second-rate con-men. White squares are always being "taken" by such small-time hustlers—but only for peanuts!

Part of the political failure of most Negro leaders, spokesmen, and even social technicians is that they really have been addressing themselves all these years to moral issues and not the actualities of local, state, and national power. Perhaps as more of them become more deeply and intimately involved with the practical requirements of government in action and hence more personally familiar with the chord structure and progression of official maneuvers, the extension of the riff-style into politics is inevitable. Perhaps when this happens even the young black radicals will move beyond their present academic reverence for radicalism per se and begin playing improvisations on the gospels of Marx, Mao, Guevara, and Fanon. Perhaps even they will begin to realize that when great Negro musicians like Armstrong, Basie, Ellington, Parker play by ear, they do so not because they cannot read the score but rather because in the very process of mastering it they have found it inadequate for their purposes. Nor should it be forgotten that they often find their own scores inadequate. (Harold Cruse's *The Crisis of the Negro Intellectual* represents a heroic attempt of one Negro writer to establish his own context and perspectives.)

As yet, however, most Negro social technicians seem unable to realize that the civil rights movement has now entered a stage that requires them to shift their primary emphasis from protest to practical politics. Such an obvious cultural lag may grow out of the fact that the most widely publicized black spokesmen are preachers, heads of organizations sponsored by white liberals, and student idealists, for all of whom a preference for moral outcry over the dirty business of wheeling and dealing with political machines is only natural.

Meanwhile, it is no less natural, or at least predictable, that Negroes in general continue to function in terms of extensions and elaborations that enabled their ancestors not only to endure slavery but also to sustain an unexcelled sense of human worth and possibility in the process. In spite of the restrictions and atrocities of the plantation system, the personal and social intercourse among slaves was so fabulous in the richness of its human fellowship, humor, esthetic inventiveness, and high spirits that the masters—who, ironically, lived in constant fear of black uprisings—could only pretend to shrug it off as childishness! It was not infantilism, however, that girded fugitive slaves for the ordeals of the Underground Railroad and conditioned so many of them to become productive and responsible citizens and men of their time as rapidly as the means became accessible and white resistance would allow.

Nor is it otherwise for contemporary Negroes. It is not cultural lag that creates the major obstacle for those who migrate from the farms and small towns of the South into the industrial and commercial web of the Northern metropolis. It is racism, much of it official, that prevents them from obtaining adequate employment, decent housing, and equal protection under the law. As for their ever so widely publicized lack of preparation in, for instance, specific job skills, such deficiencies, which are hardly greater than those of thousands of white immigrants, are more than offset by Negro eagerness to receive the technical training required. Nor are Negroes from the South any less teachable than any other erstwhile peasants. For the rest, sensibilities formed in the blues tradition seem uniquely equipped to withstand the dislocation traumas that usually result from such an abrupt and radical shift in environment and mode of existence.

Indeed, someday students of machine-age culture in the United

States may find that Negro slaves in the cotton field had already begun confronting and evolving esthetic solutions for the problems of assembly line regimentation, depersonalization, and collectivization. After all, the so-called Industrial Revolution had as much to do with the way personnel was used as with machinery as such. In any event, Harlem and Detroit Negroes, for example, are neither terrified by the intricacies of contemporary technology nor overwhelmed by the magnitude of megalopolis. On the contrary, they seize every opportunity to get into the swing of things, almost always contributing vitality and new dimensions of elegance when they succeed.

It is also possible that the time will come when students of U.S. life styles will regard the so-called abnormal structure of the Negro family not as the national liability that the Moynihan Report depicts but as a positive force! They may find that it is an institution with a structure that has always been remarkably consistent and compatible with the structure of modern society, and produces personalities whose rugged flexibility is oriented to cope with the fragmented nature of contemporary experience. Further investigation may discover that the actual family of many contemporary Negroes, like that of plantation slaves, is the neighborhood. Much goes to show that among U.S. Negroes parental authority and responsibility have always been shared by neighborhood uncles and aunts of whom sometimes none are blood relatives. *White Southerners were not the only people who benefited from the magnanimity of the black mammy*. Nor have all Negroes been as inattentive to the worldly wit and wisdom of Uncle Remus as most of the current crop of civil rights spokesmen seem to have been.

The cultural deprivation from which Negroes in general suffer is not their own but rather the deprivation that makes for the incredible provincialism of those white social science technicians (and their Negro protégés), who when they report their observations and assessments of Negro life, invariably *celebrate* the very features of American life that the greatest artists and intellectuals have always found most highly questionable if not downright objectionable. But come to think of it, what usually seems to matter most in all findings and evaluations made by American social science survey technicians are indices of material affluence and power. In fact, sometimes it seems that even the most comprehensive social science assessments are predicated upon some indefinite but ruthlessly functional theology involving the worship of wealth and force. In any case, it almost always turns out that whoever has acquired money and power—by any means whatsoever—is assumed to be blessed with everything else, including the holiest moral disposition, the richest sense of humor, creative genius, and impeccable taste.

Of course the mechanics (or machinations) of white supremacy permit white Americans in general to presume themselves the natural heirs and assignees to a median legacy of such qualities. But for the rest, so barbarous is the anthropological value system to which contemporary American social science seems to be geared that so far as the technicians who survey Negro communities are concerned people without affluence and power are only creature-like beings whose humanity is measured in terms of their potential to accumulate material goods and exercise force with arrogance.

Alas, not even the most fundamental human value that democratic societies are specifically designed to guarantee seems to count for very much once such technicians become involved with Negroes. On the contrary, far from revealing any significant preoccupation with or even appreciation for personal freedom and self-realization in any intrinsic sense, the technicians now proceed in an alarming number of instances as if statistical measurements of central tendencies—for all that they may have been initiated in the interest of programing the greatest good for the greatest number—have become a means of justifying an ever increasing standardization, regimentation, and conformity. In so doing, they tend to condemn the very elements in U.S. Negro life style that other non-totalitarian cultures seek and celebrate:

its orientation to elastic individuality, for one, and its esthetic receptivity, and its unique blend of warmth, sensitivity, nonsense, vitality, and elegance.

There is, as no man of good will would ever dispute, everything to be said for the high priority that most Negro leaders and spokesmen have always placed on emergency measures to counteract poverty, exclusion, and injustice. But in giving so much emphasis to the moral aspects of the case, they often seem to neglect the fundamental nature of the hardheaded pragmatism that underlies so much American behavior. Sometimes Americans are disposed to fair play and sometimes they are not. But they almost always invest their time, money, and enthusiasm in assets with promise, not liabilities. Even those who become involved in salvage operations have been sold on *inherent potential.*

There should never be any relaxation of the pressure for national fair play. But even so it may well be that more emphasis on the discovery, development, and assimilation of things that the so-called black community may contribute to the welfare of other Americans (who are not nearly so well off as advertised) may make the best sales pitch for the cause of black people precisely because it will offer investment possibilities that will best serve the immediate as well as the long term interests of the entire Republic. The so-called population explosion does not alter the fact that there never has been a time when the United States did not need all of the human ingenuity it could muster.

Nor are the people who evolved the blues idiom likely to restrict their ingenuity to the proliferation of technological innovations. As would be entirely consistent with their tradition or life style, they are far more likely to regard all mechanical devices as truly significant and useful only to the extent that such devices contribute to the art of living, the art, that is to say, of human enjoyment—without which there can be no such thing as human fulfillment no matter how rich the nation's natural resources or how refined its technology.

PART II

The Illusive Black Image

INTRODUCTION

Providing the American public with images of black experience has become over the past decade a major source of income and public and sometimes academic status for both the survey technicians who are oriented to tabloid journalism and the tabloid journalists who spout the jargonistic conjectures of social science survey technicians. While the quest for the illusive black image may never provide the sort of dependable data that can be of practical significance to the well being of the total national community, it already seems to have created a new job category: the Two-Finger Pig-Latin Swahili Expert, an image technician who files survey-safari reports on Ghettoland, U.S.A.

This new and very special type of white or somewhat white hunter is an American not an African phenomenon. He makes survey data safaris into the deep, dark, torrid-zone interior of the Eight Ball. He is regarded as an expert on U.S. jungle manners and mores, but his natives are no longer referred to as savages. They are "culturally deprived [i.e., non-white!] minorities." And the natives are no longer thought of as cannibals who eat *other* people. As now reported, they are people who spend most of their time eating *their own hearts out* (and being generally self-destructive) because they are not white.

The self-styled, publicly proclaimed friendship of this very special white hunter for U.S. Negroes, whom he has recently taken to calling the blacks in the old white African manner (but also with overtones of Jean Genet's *Les Nègres*), is quite like the friendship of his prototype in Kenya in that it seldom extends beyond the requirements of the safari. When he brags that, "Malcolm X said I was one of the few whites he . . ."; or that "Eldridge Cleaver accepted me and said . . .", he is really taking care of several bits of the very urgent business of self-promotion at once: (1) He is consolidating his one-up status over those base-camp white people (who subsidize his reports because they are interested in reading about Negroes but are terrified at the mere notion of entering the Eight Ball) and also over other white reporters; (2) he is up-grading his credentials and bargaining power with white editors and publishers; and (3) he is making a public presentation of his black passport to such Eight Ball tribal chiefs as might figure in future safari assignments.

The Two-Finger Swahili Reporter and Image Collector never makes it clear as to which Eight Ball creatures are the natives and which are the animals. He is out to get them all into his black notebag of white supremacy folklore anyway. This section considers some of these image collectors and their techniques—and some of the literary counterparts of both—and the realities they are trying to capture. It begins with a short look (so as to set the focus) at one of the realities, Harlem, and at one of its images, the so-called ghetto, and then turns to techniques, collectors, and other reports and "students" of U.S. Negro life.

IMAGE AND UNLIKENESS IN HARLEM

Mass media images of contemporary Harlem reveal only a part of the actual texture of the lives of the people who inhabit that vast, richly varied, infinitely complex, and endlessly fascinating area of uptown Manhattan. Those who create such images almost always restrict themselves to documenting the pathological. Thus not only do they almost always proceed in terms of the liabilities of Harlem but what they record more often than not also leaves the entirely incredible but somehow widely accepted impression that there are no negotiable assets of any immediate significance there at all.

But not only do the human resources of Harlem exceed the liabilities, even the existing material assets and possibilities do. There are thousands of rundown, poverty-ridden, vermin-infested tenements in Harlem which have long been unfit for human habitation and which are not only overpriced but also overcrowded. But even so, far from being one sprawling and teeming network of endless shambles, Harlem is an industry-free, ideally situated residential area with broad avenues and well-planned streets, and the convenience of its transportation facilities is unexcelled by any other residential community in Manhattan. Nor do many other areas match the charm and elegance of its architecture. (Some of the least interesting buildings in

This article, which first appeared in *The Urban Review*, was written to accompany a group of fine photographs by Fred McDarrah.

Harlem, such as those in Delano Village near where the Savoy used to be, were constructed comparatively recently. They provide modest urgently needed comfort but little else.)

There may or may not be such a thing as a Moynihan Report image finder, a *Dark Ghetto* image finder, and so on, but there most certainly are focused viewpoints that exclude almost everything except that which substantiates Moynihan's Victorian notions about broken homes, Clark's (self-excepted) descriptions of black powerlessness and black self-hatred, and various pop art constructions of juvenile delinquency and uptown camp. But what is there to see if one lifts away these blinders?

Much has been made of the Harlem dweller's response to rats, discrimination, and poverty (but no more, incidentally, than Richard Wright made of Bigger Thomas' response to the same rats and the same discrimination and poverty in the Chicago of *Native Son*). What most observers almost always seem to be unaware of for some strange reason, however, is the incontestable fact that Negroes in Harlem, like those elsewhere, also respond to beauty, style, and elegance—even as their wonderful ancestors found delight in the magnolias and honeysuckles, the crepe myrtles and cape jasmines, the terrain, the fabulous thickets, woodland streams, and verdant hillsides, the gourd vines and trellis work near the cabins, the graceful lines of plantation mansions and even the deep richness of the soil they tilled during the darkest and most oppressive days of slavery.

It is true that most people in Harlem have little interest for articles in, say, *Vogue* or *House Beautiful* about the grillwork on wrought iron gates, the ornamental griffins, period-piece bay windows, splendid archways, and charming courtyards to be found in the area. But after all, there are other and perhaps better ways of responding to such things. One can assimilate them, for instance, and simply live in terms of them, which is largely what they were made for in the first place. Obviously, there is much to be said for the conscious cultivation and extension of taste, but there is also something to be said for the functional reaction to artistic design (and honeysuckles) as normal elements of human existence. And there is, of course, also quite a bit to be said against fastidiousness and academic pretentiousness. (Not that Harlem can't use all the art history it can get.)

As James Weldon Johnson noted years ago, not very many New Yorkers in other parts of town seem to have as much involvement with their immediate neighborhoods as do the people of Harlem. Nor is the Harlemite's involvement a mark of oppression. It is a mark of openness. Most other New Yorkers seem to spend so much of their time hustling from one interior to another that they don't ever seem to see very much of their affluent and antiseptic neighborhoods except on the run, and they seem to see even less of the neighbors whose status locations they pay such high rents to share. On the other hand, weather permitting, the sidewalks and the brownstone doorways and steps of most of the streets of Harlem always hum and buzz with people in familiar contact with other people. The need for better housing and more adequate community services in Harlem is a national scandal, but what many Harlemites do with what they have is often marvelous all the same.

The life style of Harlem Negroes of all levels, in fact, goes with the very best esthetic features not only of Harlem but of New York at large. Harlem Negroes do not act like the culturally deprived people of the statistical surveys but like cosmopolites. Many may be indigent but few are square. They walk and even stand like people who are elegance-oriented. They talk like people who are eloquence-oriented. They dress like people who like high fashion and like to be surrounded by fine architecture. The average good barber shop and tailor shop in Harlem is geared to a level of sartorial sophistication that is required only from the best elsewhere. There is no telling what outside image makers think of the amount of formal wear sold and rented in Harlem, but one thing it suggests is that many of the social affairs sponsored by Harlemites scintillate. Not even the worst dressers in Harlem are indifferent to high fashion. They are overcommitted to it!

It is very curious indeed that at a time when Harlem Negroes encounter fewer restrictions, exercise more political power, earn more
money, and have more involvements elsewhere than ever before, media reporters (following a writer like Clark) describe them as denizens
of a ghetto, who are all but completely ostracized from the mainstream
of American life—which media reporters refer to as the white world.
The term ghetto does not apply to Harlem, if indeed it applies to any
segregated housing area in the United States. Perhaps it applies to this
or that Chinatown. It *does not* and *never has* applied to segregated
areas where U.S. Negroes live. The overwhelming majority of the residents of Harlem, along with most other native-born U.S. Negroes,
are part-white Anglo-Saxon Protestants, and Southern at that, with
all the racial as well as cultural ramifications that this implies. Harlem
contains a vast network of slum areas which are an ambitious social
worker's absolute delight, but Harlem itself is no ghetto at all. No matter how rotten with racial bigotry the New York housing situation is, it
is grossly misleading to imply in any way that the daily involvements,
interests, and aspirations of Negroes are thereby restricted to the so-
called black community.

Harlem Negroes are New Yorkers. (The mainstream is not white
but mulatto.) Harlemites have their special cultural distinctions, as
do New Yorkers who live in the Bronx, Queens, Greenwich Village
and so on, but a Harlem Negro looking down Fifth Avenue from Mt.
Morris Park is not nearly so cut off from the center of things as the
word "ghetto" implies. He is looking toward midtown and downtown, where most people in Harlem work, and he feels as intimately
involved with Macy's, Gimbels, Saks, and Bloomingdale's as his income and his credit card will allow. He, like most people in Harlem,
is also aware that midtown is, among other things, Lena Horne at
the Waldorf, Ella Fitzgerald at the Royal Box, Diahann Carroll at the
Plaza, Jackie Wilson at the Copa, Count Basie at the Riverboat, and a
wide choice of Negro prizefight champions and basketball players at
Madison Square Garden. Nor is Leontyne without uptown followers

—and competitors. The Harlem Negro knows very well that there are uptown lawyers and judges in the downtown courts, and that the Manhattan Borough President is almost always a Negro. After all, he probably helped to put him (or her) there. Segregation in New York is bad enough, but it just isn't what it used to be. The national headquarters of the NAACP is at 57th Street on Broadway, and the office of the NAACP Legal Defense Fund is at Columbus Circle.

But what useful purpose is really served by confusing segregated housing in the U.S. with the way Jewish life was separated from the gentile world in the days of the old ghettos? After all, in addition to physical segregation, the real ghettos also represented profound differences in religion, language, food customs, and were even geared to a different calendar. It is grossly misleading to suggest that segregated housing anywhere in the United States represents a cultural distance that is in any way at all comparable to the one that separated a Jewish ghetto from the life styles of various European countries.

Duke Ellington, whose music encompasses at least as much of the flesh and blood reality of life in the United States as do books like *An American Dilemma*, was well aware of the widespread hunger and filth and crime and political frustration in Harlem as long ago as when he wrote "Harlem Airshaft" (he had already written "The Mooch"), and so was William Strayhorn when he wrote "Take the A Train." But Ellington and Strayhorn and most of the other Harlem musicians, including the old rent party piano players, were—and still are—also aware of something else: that Harlem for all its liabilities generates an atmosphere that stimulates people-to-people good times which are second to none anywhere in the world. (Life in Paris is better celebrated in story but not in song and dance.)

The music of Harlem makes people all over the world want to dance. It makes the rich, the poor, the powerful and weak alike clap their hands and tap their foot in celebration of the sheerest joy of human existence itself. Not only that, but it disposes them toward affirmation and continuity even as, with the blues, it reminds them of their infernal complexity. (Incidentally, musicians and athletes are far more numerous, more symbolic, and more influential in Harlem than are the criminals and addicts.)

Images of Harlem that could have been derived only from the current fad in psychopolitical gossip about Negro self-hatred, only serve to charge an atmosphere already at the point of explosion. The system of racial exclusion in employment forces most people in Harlem to function far below their minimum potential even as it enables recently arrived white immigrants with no better qualifications than Harlemites to exceed their wildest dreams. Not even the most degenerate rituals of the South are more infuriating to multigeneration U.S. Negroes than the pompous impertinence of those European refugees who were admitted to the U.S. on preferential quotas, who benefit by preferential treatment because of the color system, and who then presume to make condescending insinuations about the lack of initiative, self-help, and self-pride among Negroes.

Meanwhile the least that is required of those who would help Harlem achieve its aspirations (some of which may very well be higher than many of those held in the most self-satisfied and self-restricted white communities and which are, if anything, even better for the nation at large than for Negroes) is that they disentangle themselves from the folklore of condescension and approach the people of Harlem with the attitude that good photographers seem to take when they aim their cameras at the streets and the buildings.

ONEUPMANSHIP IN COLORFUL AMERICA

One way of not seeing U.S. Negroes for what they are is to call them non-white. But the mystery is that when people define Negroes this way, as do especially those people who are given to reading and quoting the behavioral sciences, it is extremely difficult to know for sure whether they are being incredibly naive or deliberately so— or both. It is easy enough, however, to see that such people, whatever their avowed commitments, are very much involved, knowingly or not, in at least one version of the all-seasons game of U.S. color oneupmanship.

The indications are unmistakable. One American classifies another as non-white. He does so with a straight white face to indicate that such a classification is the most obvious, objective, and scientific thing in the world. However, if the second American, whose face may be every bit as white as the first American's or not quite as black as the ace of spades, classifies the first as non-Negro, the first immediately becomes apoplectic white and then red-white. Then he smiles. But it is a serious smile, and it gives the whole grim game away. Because it is also a powerful smile, and he does his best to make it as powerful as the power structure itself. It is an establishment smile, of the sort that tolerates the likes of Black Muslims and other news media types, but behind it is all the vicious compassion the one who suddenly and unexpectedly has been upped has for the audacious, the unthinkable, and the pathetically outrageous.

The implications of this by now classic but somewhat unsportsmanlike game are even less mistakable. In spite of all the well-known honestly admitted, widely lamented, all too human, and of course self-declared shortcomings of those who, as it were, are yes-white, am-white, is- and are-white, those who are classified as non-white are somehow, as has been noted, all too naturally assumed to be non-this, non-that, and non-the-other. Thus are all the fundamental assumptions of white supremacy and segregation represented in a word, in one key hyphenated and hyphenating word.

One hears endless talk and sees much hand wringing and head shaking about the problem of race and racism in America, most of it by people who always confuse race with culture. But the real key to understanding the actual dynamics of segregation in the United States is not *race* and certainly not culture as the social sciences would define it and have it, but COLOR. When your yes-am-is-are-white U.S. citizen says non-white, he has said it all and given away the game. What he forgets, however, and much too easily, is the fact that, as the self-chosen model from which the non-white variant is a bad departure, he himself, more often than not, is self-identified, self-certified, and self-elected. He also forgets that he is self-esteemed—and for the most part only self-esteemed. Or does he ever really forget this? *What is the U.S. system of segregation if not institutionalized paranoia?*

As for U.S. Negroes being non-white, nothing could be further from scientific accuracy. Indeed, no classification was ever less accurate. By any definition of race, even the most makeshift legal one, most native-born U.S. Negroes, far from being non-white, are in fact part-white. They are also by any meaningful definition of culture, part-Anglo-Saxon, and they are overwhelmingly Protestant. And not only are they more often than not Southerners, they tend to be Southern aristocrats! (Aristocratic is the only word for their basic orientation to sports, style, leisure, luxury, and even money and power. In such matters, seldom are they middle class; many may be ignorant but few are that square. Poor often, but *poor whites* never: what with all those yard children for relatives, they were one up on the poor white even during the days of slavery.)

None of this is really news. It is really quite obvious, at some level of consciousness, even to the most casual observer. And yet it is perhaps the second most persistently overlooked flesh-and-blood fact of everyday life in the United States. The first of course is the all but unmentionable but equally undeniable fact that an infinite and ever-increasing but forever hidden number of assumed white Anglo-Saxon Protestants are among other parts part-Negro. Off-white and not-very-white Negroes seem to know more about this than anybody else. (They always knew, for instance, which assumed-white movie stars used to be Negroes, and they have said all along that Jackie Robinson was not the first Negro to play major league baseball, only the first dark one.)

There is no need to make any claims for any of this or to stake any claims on it. Nor is there any reason, the mail-order psychoanalysts to the contrary, to feel any special pride, shame, or confusion about any of it. It is a fact, and it is incontrovertible, even by law. It exists both in men's hearts and in their genes, although it is most "marketable" when it shows white in their faces. It exists for something, for nothing, or for everything, but whatever, it is just the sort of demographic detail that characterizes an open society.

Nevertheless, color gamesmanship is as American as apple pie, credit cards, the Ku Klux Klan, Miami Beach, peroxide blondes, sun lamps, and suntan lotions. And it finds expression in many ways. Many be-white, passing-for-white, or occasional-white Americans sport the deepest tans for the express purpose of emphasizing the primordial extremeness of their whiteness, a whiteness not one degree less white than the whiteness of Herman Melville's white whale. And of course not-very-white Negroes are always suspicious of those assumed-white people who make compulsive complaints about getting sunburned and those who are forever referring to how ghastly and ghostly pale they always get in mid-winter.

Political, social, and economic colormanship or rather colorless-manship, requires other techniques. Some of them are amusing, but some are without any humor whatsoever. The key to everything is the people who belong to the all-white establishment. These are yes-am-is-are (or assumed-) white Anglo-Saxon Protestants, or, for short, yes-Wasps. Some of these have blood that is said to be blue. This means that one of their ancestors might have been a blue-eyed tennis player on the *Mayflower* or might have been a convicted base stealer released to Oglethorpe in Georgia or might have been the blue-eyed illegitimate son of some blue-eyed somebody well off enough in England to stake him to forty acres and a mule in Colonial Virginia. Such blue-blood can be certified several shades bluer if subsequent ancestors engaged in the slave trade or owned slaves, and another shade of blue is added for any lingering guilt about this last, provided the guilt be philanthropic. The ironic thing about the establishment, however, is that your yes-Wasp has more part-white, off-white, and assumed-not-white blood relatives than everybody else.

Be that as it may, your yes-Wasps make up the am-white establishment. They determine color validity and color symbols. All other Americans gear their color machinations to the yes-Wasp system.

Now, your sheet-white Anglo-Saxon Protestant, or sheet-Wasp, regards his identification with the yes-Wasp establishment as a matter much too serious for gamesmanship of any kind. It is a matter that is not only sacred to him, it is his one and only reason for being. He shakes and trembles at the very thought of his sheetness. It is so sacred indeed that it must be ritualized with flaming crosses and human sacrifices. But it is still gamesmanship, a gory game of up-black-man-ship.

Currently, of course, there are the increasing number whose color-manship comes in the guise of what is called "social science." The one place U.S. Negroes have always found themselves most rigidly segregated is not in the inner sanctum of the is-white family but in the insistent categories of behavioral science surveys, studies, and statistics. It was none other than social science that contributed the "nonwhite" category to the modern American vocabulary in the first place —and this, despite the fact that there is no scientific method by which one can establish that a measurable percentage of any given trait or given number of traits, racial or otherwise, makes some people only part-white and others all-white. As things stand now nobody really knows which person has how much of what. And if you cannot determine who is all-white, it is perhaps a bit unscientific to claim that you already know who is non-white. But social scientists seem not to have given this simple line of reasoning much thought.

The key question to ask a social scientist is why he fools with these categories in the first place. Ask him that. Why does the social scientist make so many studies about the differences between yes-whites and non-whites? Why does he want to know so much about these two? Why is the need for information about the *differences* between yes-whites and non-whites so much more urgent than information about the differences between, say, U.S. Christians and U.S. non-Christians; U.S. Germans and U.S. Scandinavians; U.S. Irish Catholics and U.S. Italian Catholics; U.S. synagogue Jews and U.S. non-synagogue Jews; or, say, native-born U.S. Negroes and West Indian-born U.S. Negroes. Yes-whites apparently assume that all these yes-white/non-white surveys are made in the interest of behavioral science. Alleged non-whites assume that they are a matter of color politics and blackman-outmanship.

But still and all your social science oneupman is always right in there, and he has some significant results to show for his highly subsidized efforts: *Many book reading Negroes read social science and nothing else.* They read all those negative things about themselves, wrapped in all that educated terminology, and become convinced for the first time that to be non-white is to be inferior after all.

But that is only half of it. The minute they accept the idea of white supremacy, they proceed to become more be-white than everybody else! Which of course is easy enough, what with social science providing a yes-white checklist which contains nothing that anybody didn't already know. So what really happens? Nobody was ever more devoted to white middle class norms than social science Negroes! But luckily they are few. And in recent months, many of these have taken to acting like middle class Africans.

There are, of course, people who are white, and there are those who are not, and some of both live in the United States, and of course there are many differences between them. That is not the point. The point is that social science as an intellectual discipline has yet to deal with those differences in suitable terms, many of which have much more to do with esthetics than with science. And as for equality—it is a scandal that one must raise this point again and again—who needs social science to say who is equal and who is not? This is the issue that was solved some time ago by the Declaration of Independence and the Constitution.

There are many other U.S. color techniques and technicians. But no such technicians are more worthy of note than the not altogether or somewhat white liberal Intellectual, that watchdog of the do-good establishment. He is almost always a self-advertised revolutionary or radical of some kind, although most of the time his Marxism, Freudianism, or Reichianism gets so mixed up, it is hard to say whether he is really interested in world revolution or world revenge (or as some one has said, even sex revenge), but that is another game. Whatever his motives and purposes, most of the methods he uses in the color game involve the use of intellectual confusion—and even intellectual chaos. This complicates matters all right, but there are times when it is not at all difficult to see that the confusion is designed to ingratiate the not-altogether white with the yes-white establishment, at the (incidental?) expense of the alleged non-white.

For instance: the yes-Wasp knows very well that most U.S. Negroes are part-Wasp. He pretends to ignore it and confronted with the fact, he hysterically denies it, and of course, he absolutely refuses to think about how many assumed-yes-Wasps are part-Negro. But he knows all this because he brought it all about.

And although he was in Europe or somewhere (sometimes China or Japan) when it all happened, your not-altogether white intellectual is having none of that, and in he moves with commentary after commentary, and reams of scholarly propaganda reassuring everybody that nothing of the sort ever happened or ever could have happened, and he invents the black ghetto or ebony chinatown or muslim medina to prove it. Thus the U.S. Negro becomes the all-black dweller in the all-black ghetto and the somewhat white, one-time immigrant, now full-time expert on blackness becomes simply (but not quite purely) white!

Among all other U.S. color gamesmen, the liberal intellectual is the one who insists most urgently on being accepted as the U.S. Negro's very best yes-white friend. Sometimes he even comes begging forgiveness for the slave trade, which his peasant ancestors (well, they may have been seamen) had very little to do with indeed. It is hard to say whether all this goes to show that he has no sense of humor and irony at all, or that he has far too much.

But what always seems to get overlooked in all the color-prestidigitation is the fact that the United States goes right on being an open society. Not yet open in enough ways, to be sure, but open enough to make future improvements always likely. And perhaps this is another practical way of looking at the U.S. Negro side of the black rebellion, as many alarmed but intransigent people call the civil rights movement. Negroes are already integrated in many long standing but unacknowledged ways, but they are not yet desegregated nearly enough in some other ways, especially in some bread and butter ways that they feel are their natural due—as flesh and blood members of the great American family.

THE ILLUSIVE BLACK MIDDLE CLASS

Perhaps the most illusive of all black images is that of the so-called middle class Negro. Safari technicians are forever accusing their brown-skin peers and betters of being Middle Class, insinuating thereby that because such Negroes are literate and employed they are somehow not only betrayers of their black fellow men but also traitors to blackness. Moreover, the safari theoretician almost always seems to visualize middle class Negroes as being lighter-skinned, that is to say, whiter than "the real Negro" (the black Blacks!) so much so in fact that when he actually finds himself in the presence of a very dark Negro who displays professional competence and is well to do, the ghetto safari expert seems compelled either to regard him as a pretentious black-face comedian or simply to ignore what is happening and insist that here is another pathetic black victim in need of white charity.

But nowhere is the sneaky hostility of some friendly white ghettologists, and their antagonism to the Negro middle class, more transparent than when they become involved in what amounts to the promotion of a black intramural class struggle. Only such a sinister objective could induce the pseudo-academic publicity the ghettologists have given to the off-the-cuff Marxist notion that there is a historical basis for such a struggle in the house slave/field slave structure of the plantation system.

Students of life in the antebellum South agree that there was indeed such a thing as a plantation hierarchy and that field hands as a rule were at the foot of the scale. Historians also agree that the domestic servants, such as the butlers, maids, nurses, and cooks, enjoyed certain "advantages" by living in the master's household. But some highly publicized contemporary historians seem to forget that there was also a "class" of skilled and semi-skilled artisans who were neither house slaves nor field slaves.

In *From Slavery to Freedom*, black historian John Hope Franklin writes about the functional class structure of slavery as follows:

> In 1850 there were 400,000 slaves living in urban communities. It may be assumed that not only a majority of these were engaged in non-agricultural pursuits, but that their number was augmented by those plantation slaves whose owners hired them out to townspeople. There is no way of knowing how many such slaves were hired out, but there must have been thousands, especially in the period between the harvest and the new planting. It was in the non-agricultural pursuits that the slaves displayed the greatest variety of talent and training. Many plantations had their slave carpenters, masons and mechanics; but the skilled slaves were to be most frequently found in towns. Indeed, a large number of town slaves possessed some kind of skill. In the Charleston census of 1848, for example, there were more slave carpenters than there were free Negroes and whites. The same was true of slave coopers. In addition, there were slave tailors, shoe makers, cabinet makers, painters, plasterers, seamstresses and the like. Many owners realized the wisdom of training their slaves in the trades, for their earning power would be greatly enhanced; and if the slave was ever offered for sale he would perhaps bring twice as much as a field hand of similar age would bring.

But then some Class Struggle–prone historians seem to proceed from an oversimplified hypothesis of slavery rather than from historical documentation in the first place. The following description in *Life and Labor in the Old South* by conservative old U. B. Phillips (perhaps the most famous apologist for slavery), provides much more

accurate information about the circumstances of slavery than does
the image evoked by the misguided house Negro/field Negro dialecti-
cians: "At all times in the South as a whole *perhaps half* [italics added]
of the slaves were owned or hired in units of twenty or less, which
were too small for the full plantation order, and perhaps half of this
half were on mere farms or in town employment, rather as 'help' than
as a distinct laboring force. Many small planters' sons and virtually all
the farmers in person worked alongside any field hands they might
possess; and indoor tasks were parceled among the women and girls
white and black." The point is, anyone who talks in terms of two antagonistic "classes" among American Negro slaves is talking incorrect
theory not fact.

Not even the long-standing, widespread employment of the
present-day HNIC—Head Negro (mispronounced Southern style)
in Charge—who derives from the figure in charge of the black compound in the temporary absence of the white boss-man, can be used
in support of the pseudo-Marxist house slave/field slave hypothesis.
For the HNIC is most often likely to be (as was his forerunner) a man
not from the big house but from the compound itself. (Contrary to
the cliché image, the domestic slave, whose position was not hered-
itary by the way, was admired, envied, emulated, and respected by
less favorably placed slaves, but the domestic did not automatically
exercise the authority of a black overseer over field hands. Nor is there
reason to believe that he placed the master's interests above the liberation of his fellow bondsmen. There were Judases as well as snobs
among the domestics to be sure; but as a general rule, the house slave
seems to have brought infinitely more tactical information *from* the
big house to the cabins than any information about subversive plans
he ever took back.) The HNIC, then as now, is a man of the people
become black foreman, black strawboss.

Perhaps the most important thing to remember about the HNIC is
that he is selected by white people. Nor should it be forgotten that he

may often be selected primarily because he *symbolizes* militancy. Part of his job is to be tough, and of course he may brag about what he is going to do to whitey. But consistent with his main function as black foreman, which is to keep Negroes in line, his physical acts of violence are most often committed not against *white* people but against *black* people! It is seldom the loudmouth spokesman who tees off on whitey. The cool non-leaders do that. Remember who triggered the "riots" in Watts, Newark, Detroit, and elsewhere.

The main objective of the HNIC is obviously *to be in charge*. Currently there are those who are status quo conservatives, those who are welfare gradualists, those who are syndicate-controlled cynics, others who are verbal rebels and others who are one vague type of left-wing revolutionary or another. Some HNICs are outright separatists and some are not. But desegregation in any form is a threat to the very existence of the HNIC, whatever the type. It is pretty hard to control a black student who takes all that education jive seriously enough to become an engineer, earn, say, $35,000 a year, move his family out of a tenement district and into a more comfortable suburban subdivision—so you accuse him of being a deserter to the cause! A charge which is seldom brought against dropouts, dope addicts and murderers!

And naturally the friendly white theoretician agrees. A main part of *his* job seems to be to support the White Man's Black Man by building up the image of the HNIC as the Black Man's White Man! The white dialectician loves black revolutionary rhetoric and TV side-show heroics, but black revolutionary action scares the hell out of him. So much so that he spends much of his time staving it off by trying to convince "the real Negroes" that all black achievement is really a token dispensation from the all-powerful, all-white power structure. Regardless of what is said, however, it is extremely difficult to believe that white athletes, for instance, *permitted* Willie Mays, Bob Gibson, Big O, and O. J. Simpson to become superstars; or that the white people of Massachusetts are so charitably disposed towards Negroes that they elected a Negro senator in order to placate black militants in Roxbury—not to mention the citizens in the South Side of Chicago!

In all of this nonsense about black good guys and bad guys—in their varying shades of militancy and class origin and status—what is most often forgotten is the nature of the problem. *So far as white people are concerned, the most revolutionary, radical, and devastating action any U.S. Negro can engage in is to compete with other Americans for status, employment, total social equality, and basic political power.* Even more obvious (one would have assumed) is the fact that it is the so-called middle class Negro (or Negro with so-called middle class aspirations) who represents the most fearsome revolutionary threat to the white status quo. White Americans are forever expressing their concern about the poverty and ignorance of the black "masses" and about crime in the streets. But they know very well that the police are not really worried about the essentially routine transgressions of the poor and the ignorant. Nobody knows better than the police that there is all the difference in the world between the random violence of individuals during an upheaval and, what is not characteristic of the poor and the ignorant, the tactics and strategies of revolutionary activists.

Attentive students of the actual dynamics of modern revolution re-alize that revolts are seldom initiated by the so-called masses. They are engineered by the disgruntled "middle class" ideologists who know how to inspire and organize (and manipulate) the masses. Such was certainly the case in the American, French, and Russian revolutions, and it is also the case in the civil rights struggle. The highly literate college-oriented young people of SNCC, CORE, SLCC have seldom been any less "middle class" than the good gray NAACP—which, in-cidentally, probably has more grass roots members and activities than any other civil rights organization of national scope—and the spruce, buttoned-down Urban League.

Not only is it the so-called middle class Negro who challenges the status quo in schools, housing, voting practices, and so on, he is also the one who is most likely to challenge total social structures and value systems. Black proletarians do not seem to embrace radical doctrines or become members of such mass revolutionary organizations as the Communist party any more readily than do theory-oriented black "middle class" types. And certainly the black masses don't go around theorizing about culture, identity, hair texture, and the like (while sticking with *Vogue* and *Apparel Arts* on most other details!). To the extent that the so-called black masses become involved in such matters, they seem most likely to be following the fashions of the day which have been popularized if not initiated by the so-called middle class whom they seem to admire and emulate much more than they envy. The one thing they don't tolerate from successful Negroes is arrogance. Adam Clayton Powell is arrogant toward white people and other successful Negroes not the masses of black people.

It should not be at all difficult for students of social power to see the dynamics of the so-called middle class at work in the civil rights movement over the past decade. Thurgood Marshall for example was every bit as "middle class" when he was winning epoch-making decisions, as when he penetrated the most exclusive power sanctum of all, the U.S. Supreme Court. The Reverend Doctor Martin Luther King (who as clergyman was really an aristocrat) would certainly qualify as middle class by the cliché standards of most white reporters, and no black leader in the history of the United States developed a greater and more active and trustful following among the black "masses" in all sections of the nation. Malcolm X, whose role as spokesman and leader was also geared to the inherently elite status of clergyman, first came to national attention, not as a hustling criminal but rather as the most articulate intellectual of the Black Muslim movement. Moreover, his phenomenal prominence, which is not to say power, went hand in hand with his increasing preoccupation with books, theories, and college lectures, as well as dialogs with TV intellectuals, who as a rule are nothing if not "middle class" oriented. During his actual lifetime, however, Malcolm X was never able to exercise either the institutional power or the widespread mass influence of such "middle class" activists as James Farmer, Robert Moses, Floyd McKissick, and Stokely Carmichael. Dedicated man that he was, Malcolm was on the scene during a number of historic confrontations, but the "masses" on such occasions had been mobilized and the contentions had been defined, not by Muslims but by SNCC, CORE, SCLC, or the NAACP.

It is also worth noting that many of the most vocal of Malcolm's present-day followers were not old enough to be active when he was alive. The heroic influence that he exercises over them has most likely been through his posthumous *Autobiography*, a book whose collaborator was a "middle class" professional, a magazine writer, and a book that was edited, published, and promoted by the avant garde–oriented (!) Grove Press. Further, although the young people seem to forget it, *they* themselves are book reading, theory-oriented, "middle class" student-types. They are not the food, clothing, and shelter-oriented black masses. Nor would the masses want them to be. The masses want leaders who are educated as well as trustworthy. Nor do the black masses regard "middle income" Negroes as tokens. They regard them as people who got the breaks—or who were able to make the most of the breaks.

All this is so much news to most white reporters who, when they concern themselves with U.S. Negroes, seem to blind themselves wilfully to the obvious fact that no matter how lowly the birth of a leader, any man automatically becomes upper class when he becomes a leader because he automatically becomes a member of the power elite. If Whitney Young and Adam Clayton Powell are middle class, who is above them? If Eldridge Cleaver is lower class, what then is the class status of the Ivy League and *Ramparts* magazine types who follow and look *up* to him? In point of fact, top Negro leaders enjoy functional as well as protocol rank far superior to that of most of the white Americans who are ever so much richer but whose social power is either only local or regional, or of a lower order.

Perhaps the supreme irony is the fact that white reporters always seem to be taken in by precisely those so-called middle class Negroes who actually do exploit black causes for personal gain. But such black operators, who are loud-mouthed and poor-mouthed by turns, are nothing if not pros at their trade. They know very well that manipulating condescending but unhip white reporters is the first step towards the do-good-foundation budgets and the appropriations committees of the federal government, which is where the real con game begins. To such black con artists the reporter is as incidental as is the Black Cause. (No special skill is needed to be such an artist. All you have to do nowadays is put on a costume and pretend to be a racist.)

But then the class struggle hypothesis of black experience ignores what should be the most obvious weakness of the class structure approach to American society: social science has never been able to establish a meaningful cut-off point between class levels. Certainly income is not a reliable index to class status among U.S. Negroes. (A large income is not a primary requirement for membership in black organizations that carry the highest social prestige.) Nor is residence a dependable key, for many Negroes who are exceptional in every other respect, who are leaders, educators, people of highly refined taste, of high standing in the arts and so on, earn middling incomes and reside in mid-range or even welfare-range buildings and neighborhoods because of discrimination in employment and housing. And in many cases, their conduct as well as their outlook is infinitely more comparable to the white upper or elite class than to the essentially mediocre middle class white people of the statistical surveys.

Nor is education a valid index. After all, many white journalists and survey technicians tend to regard any brown-skin or light-skinned American who speaks grammatically and enunciates carefully as educated and therefore middle class. But is Claude (Manchild) Brown of Howard and Rutgers middle class? If not, why not? And if so, is he more or less middle class than, say, the eloquent James Baldwin of no college, or than Richard Wright of no high school? What about the semi-literate parents who live on a Connecticut estate with their son, a wealthy electronics engineer whom they put through M.I.T. by working as menials? Where do they fit into the class structure with reference to, say, a very articulate brown-skin welfare officer, a Columbia M.A., the son of a highly successful Harlem doctor, who for the past ten years has been residing in a labor union housing project on the Lower East Side of Manhattan with his Jewish wife (by whom he has two children) and her widowed mother, a former semi-skilled garment district worker who speaks with a heavy Warsaw ghetto accent?

Is being a public figure an adequate index? If so, is rich folk singer Harry Belafonte more middle class than millionaire "soul" singer James Brown? Is Ray Charles more middle class than the conductor of the glee club at Yazoo City high school? Is Stokely Carmichael more middle class than Muhammad Ali? What about such well-known public figures as O. J. Simpson, Willie Mays, Sidney Poitier, LeRoi Jones, Robert Hooks, and, oh yes, Leontyne Price? Where do they stand or fall status-wise beside Jervis Anderson, Harold Cruse, Martin Kilson, Archie Epps, and the editorial board of *Freedomways* magazine?

But finally is not the term "black middle class" or "black bourgeoisie" now used more often as a political epithet than as an objective sociological category? Can specific people actually be classified as middle class in accordance with any existing scientific yardstick? Perhaps *black elite* would be a more accurately comprehensive and less contradictory term. The people it suggests are no less illusive to be sure, but that is exactly the point. The status or rather the *influence* of such people is too mobile and is based on too many different things to be easily and precisely defined in terms of class dialectics. In any case, the term *black elite* will allow black polemicists as well as white Eight Ball experts to place Eldridge Cleaver beside Julian Bond without contradicting themselves and confusing their readers.

As for those militant, and in truth somewhat envious, black rhetoricians who (to the delight of white do-gooders and do-badders alike) accuse affluent black inhabitants of the "integrated" suburbs of having deserted the cause, they should take a more careful look. The minute a Negro moves into any integrated situation in the U.S. he becomes blacker than ever before. Ever so friendly white suburbanites almost always insist that their black neighbors identify themselves as a part of black suffering everywhere. White integrationists are far more likely to condemn and reject their clean-cut, professionally competent black neighbors for not being black enough than to congratulate or simply accept them for not being problems. "Man," said one middle-aged black resident of Westchester County, a man who has spent his whole life working for better Negro education, job opportunities, and civil rights, "you go to one of those parties and fail to show the proper enthusiasm for Malcolm, Rap, and Cleaver, and then some ofay millionaire and his wife will call you an Uncle Tom to your face! And you know who will back them up? Almost every establishment editor present. Man, it's getting so that if you don't go in there pissing and moaning and making threats, they'll call you a moderate and drop your butt fifty times faster than Malcolm ever would. You got to cuss them out, or you're out of it, buddy. But damn, man, the minute you sound off, you realize that they've tricked you into scat singing and buck dancing for them; because there they are, all crowding around, like watching you masturbate, like they are ready to clap their hands and yell, 'Go, man, go. Get hot, man.' But Goddamnit, you know what they really want you to be? A blind man with a guitar!"

TWO CASE HISTORIES

hat follows are comments on two books that purport to be personal memoirs but which in fact are much closer to being social science case histories and which have more to do with the fakelore of black pathology than with the texture of everyday experience. Black actuality is no less illusive in these and similar case histories than in the statistical surveys that some readers obviously assume such histories corroborate.

CLAUDE BROWN'S SOUL FOR WHITE FOLKS

Being black is not enough to make anybody an authority on U.S. Negroes, any more than being white has ever qualified anybody as an expert on the ways of U.S. white people. It simply does not follow that being white enables a Southern sheriff, for instance, even a fairly literate one, to explain U.S. foreign policy, air power, automation, the atonality of Charles Ives, the imagery of Wallace Stevens, abstract expressionism, or even the love life of Marilyn Monroe.

If it did, then it would also follow that the oldest and blackest Negro around would be the most reliable source of information about Africa, slavery, Reconstruction politics, the pathological effects of oppression, the tactics and strategies of civil rights organizations, the blues, championship sports competition, and the symbolic function of the stud horse principle (and the quest for the earth dark womb!) in interracial sexual relationships.

Neither does it follow that because somebody lives or even works in the garment district, he has authentic inside information on the labor problems of the needle trades. Nor does it follow that the best diagnostician at Bellevue is somebody who has personally suffered the most serious diseases.

Nothing in the world could be more obvious. And yet this seems to be precisely the sort of thing that no longer goes without saying. A book like Claude Brown's *Manchild in the Promised Land* (The Macmillan Co., 1965), for example, is recommended all-around as if it were a profound, knowledgeable, and even comprehensive account of life in Harlem because its author is a Negro who grew up there and had a rough time doing so. An astonishing number of book reviewers and U.S. social critics actually insist that *Manchild* reveals what it is really like to be a Negro.

It does no such thing. It tells them absolutely nothing about Willie the Lion Smith, Sugar Ray Robinson, Adam Clayton Powell, Constance Baker Motley, the chief of maintenance at Lenox Terrace, the barman at Smalls Paradise, the society editor of the *Amsterdam News*, and so on. There's hardly anything in the book about how it feels to help run the most complicated transport system in the world—which is what quite a few New York Negroes do. As a matter of fact *Manchild* (a title that probably makes some white people think they know how chitterlings and collard greens taste), like so many other books written for white people by Negroes, is so full of the fashionable assumptions of the social sciences that little of what its young author has to reveal about what it is like to be one very special Harlem Negro named Claude Brown really represents his own insights. Perhaps one of the most significant things this book actually reveals is how difficult it is to be a serious writer when you've been interviewed, advised, rehabilitated, and structured by social workers, liberals, and other do-gooders year after year.

Many U.S. social critics or whatever they are, seem to be every bit as innocent as those newsmen and opinion-surveyors who interview the man-in-the-street but never catch onto the obvious fact that the man-in-the-street mostly knows what he reads in newspapers, hears on the radio, and sees on TV. And even when he knows more, he is likely to express only what he thinks will grind his own special ax or will make him appear especially informed (and in this, he is not unlike the average U.S. college student).

Thus do so many samples of ordinary public opinion turn out to be so many big fat jokes on the gullability of both the opinion-surveyor and the reader of surveys. But perhaps the most outrageous joke of all is the one on the reporter who doesn't recognize his own half-dashed news item when it is fed back to him by some Negro standing on Lenox Avenue or sitting in a hamburger joint in the Watts section of Los Angeles. And more exasperating than outrageous is the fantastic number of sociologists and psychologists who go out and allow themselves to get sucked in on their own conjectures and rumors!

When a U.S. Negro, whether his name be Martin Luther King, James Farmer, Whitney Young, slum dweller 45, or narcotics case 46, begins talking in terms of the ghetto, culturally deprived minorities, disadvantaged youth, middle class norms, upward mobility, self-rejection, alienation and so on, you are listening to a very pretentious and confused American displaying his stylish vocabulary—and very little else. There was a time, one likes to think, when any ordinary reporter could spot the difference between sidewalk savvy and newsstand erudition. But perhaps there were not so many newsstands in those days. Or perhaps there was just more common sense.

Personal experience, one hastens to concede, is a fundamental element in all writing. It is indispensable. But so are several other elements. Personal experience is a very fine thing to have indeed, the richer the better, but what one is able to make of it in a book is something else again. This is likely to be determined by one's sensibility, one's imagination, one's perspective, the depth and keenness of one's insights, one's linguistic precision and eloquence. The would-be writer's complexion, his street address, and police record can never really make up for the absence of any of these.

Only to the extent that Claude Brown, James Baldwin, James Joyce, Wright Morris, or anybody else has a rich enough awareness of many things other than his complexion, street address, and police record is he as a writer likely to be able to reveal very much about himself that one can't come by just as easily from his case history. Indeed, if these things are all that a writer knows, what he is most apt to produce is precisely a personal case history, and one of limited documentary value at that. The fact that somebody assures you that the incidents in a book really happened in the flesh does not add to the credibility or validity of the book. It is more often than not only an excuse for bad writing.

But then this whole thing about somebody revealing what it is really like to be black has long since gotten out of hand anyway. Not even the autobiography of Sigmund Freud reveals what it is really like to be Jewish, for instance. Nor do the memoirs of, say, J. William Fulbright reveal what it is really like to be a white Southerner. Does anybody actually believe that, say, Mary McCarthy reveals what it is really like to be a U.S. white woman, or even a Vassar girl?

It is all but impossible for one to imagine a U.S. Negro, no matter how substandard his formal educational background, telling anybody white or black that any one book reveals what it is really like to be a white man. Nevertheless a white Negro like Norman Mailer, a part-time Negro like Nat Hentoff, a non-Negro like Norman Podhoretz, and a non-Jewish New York know-it-all like Tom Wolfe, the trick typist from Virginia by way of Yale, have all engaged in promoting *Manchild* as the raw truth and excusing its shortcomings, as if the raw truth didn't require just as much writing skill as the refined granulated or confectionalized truth.

It sounds like the old jazz situation all over again. *White reporters write about jazz for other white people.* Although most jazzologists and record liner scholars can't even pat their feet in the presence of Negroes without embarrassment, they write about the Negro idiom in U.S. music as if U.S. Negro readers don't exist. (Which incidentally goes to show the difference between most white jazz *reporters* and white jazz *musicians*. During a rehearsal for the Newport Jazz Festival several years ago, a white piano player complained that his white trumpet player was not swinging enough on a certain up-tempo blues number. Aghast, the white trumpet player turned and coolly looked the white piano player up and down and then replied, "And how would *you* know?" They stood glaring at each other, and then suddenly they both realized that the veteran Negro bass player was waiting, somewhat impatiently, for them to get the hell on with the rehearsal. Both turned without another word and resumed their playing positions and nodded for *him* to give the downbeat.)

Perhaps the white negrologists could learn something about intellectual and artistic sincerity as well as American culture from the more serious white jazz musicians. These jazzmen sound as if being closely interrelated with Negroes were the most natural thing in the world. Unlike the white negrologist (not to mention the white writer, who rarely endows black people with dreams and heroic aspirations that in any way approach his own), white jazz musicians eagerly embrace certain Negroes not only as kindred spirits but also as ancestral figures indispensable to their sense of purpose and to their sense of romance, sophistication, and elegance as well. Negroes like Duke Ellington, Louis Armstrong, Bessie Smith, Billie Holiday, Chick Webb, Coleman Hawkins, and others too numerous to enumerate, inspire white Americans like Woody Herman, Gerry Mulligan, and countless others to their own richest sense of self-hood and to their highest levels of achievement. As for the white jazzologist, he is forever celebrating the authenticity of this or that white musician, but he never seems to realize how you get that way.

Young Brown himself, it must be said, seems to have a much clearer conception of the practical significance of his first and somewhat less than brilliant book than do most of his downtown boosters and ad-mirers. He is, no doubt, delighted at how famous it is making him, astonished at all the easy money, and he also hopes quite frankly that all the publicity will add up to the kind of usable popularity that will bring him political power.

Brown may well outgrow the autobiographical social science fic-tion of *Manchild in the Promised Land*. Some day he will probably be able to see just how superficial all of those welfare department as-sumptions really are—and maybe at that time he will also begin to understand why so many U.S. Negroes with much more wisdom than they're usually given credit for, don't put too much stock in books as such although they have the greatest respect in the world for the kind of education and training that "qualifies" other people and may some-day qualify them to exercise so much power.

And if he follows his announced intention and enters Harlem pol-itics one day, Brown is almost certain to outgrow the role of the black boy who tells white folks dirty stories about Negroes. The mass-media-made Negro spokesman is one thing, but a duly elected representative is something quite different indeed. No Negro media-spokesman re-ally needs to be anything more than a very special kind of entertainer who uses charts, graphs, and monographs as his stage props. All he ever has to do is keep his gossip obscene and irrelevant enough, his rumors ridiculous enough, and then pretend (with a militancy nice enough) to be upset about the miserable plight of his white-ridden or his black-ridden "brothers," and he can make himself a fairly sizable income and keep himself in a limelight of sorts as long as this kind of thing pleases enough white people enough.

The Harlem politician, however, like most other vote seekers else-where, must please his constituents. He just flatly cannot afford to waste his time representing the precious misconceptions of self-righteous non-resident kibitzers. They can write all the contemptu-ous editorials they want to so long as the people in his district think he is taking care of business. Once Brown enters politics he will no doubt discover very soon that Harlem voters have their own notions about how they want to be represented. Outsiders refuse to believe this, in spite of the fact that Congressman Adam Clayton Powell has a twenty-odd year re-election record to prove it. But then, as any con artist knows very well, outsiders always prefer social science fiction to the black and white, flesh and blood facts of everyday life among U.S. Negroes—in Harlem or elsewhere.

GORDON PARKS OUT OF FOCUS

Gordon Parks, as is well known and seldom disputed, least of all by his peers, is one of the finest photographers in the world. He is also, any way you look at it, a very remarkable man. He is indeed, one delights to say, the kind of well-rounded twentieth century human being the best U.S. schools have been trying to turn out for all these years. He is well adjusted, as they say in the seminars on developmental psychology, exceptional in his chosen profession, well above average in a number of others, and has a high potential in still others. In fact, it is hard to imagine him below average in anything he really puts his mind to.

Parks also has the kind of personal style, cosmopolitan taste, beautiful manners, charming wit, and sophisticated connections that not even the most exclusive schools catering to the richest and most ambitious families can guarantee. And as if all that were not enough, he is also solidly grounded in the kind of all-round efficiency that only the self-made man can fall back on when the going really begins to get rough.

As a matter of fact, Gordon Parks not only updates most of the old Horatio Alger success stories; he also up-ends most of the superficial nonsense about those marks of oppression one encounters in print everywhere these days—some of which, one is scandalized to say, his own writing is not always free of. And finally, not the least fabulous thing about this remarkable man of so many parts is the fact that for all his already widely recognized accomplishments, he is at fifty-plus even more promising than he was at nineteen. Few characteristics are more representative of life in the United States.

Parks has been a member of the photographic staff of *Life* magazine for some twenty years. During this time he has done photographic essays on subjects that have taken him into almost every region on the globe. Today he is a contributing photographer, which is just about as "in" one can get to be in that field. No photographers on any staff anywhere get more choice assignments, are better paid, and have their work more expertly showcased, taken more seriously, or distributed more widely.

He has also done outstanding pictures, both artistic and commercial, for a number of the leading fashion magazines, including *Vogue* and *Harper's Bazaar*. And not only has work by him been included in most of the major exhibitions representing photography as a fine art, there was an outstanding one-man show in the gallery on the ground floor of the Time-Life Building. It was called "The Works of Gordon Parks: Images, Words, Music," and outside, facing Sixth Avenue at 50th Street, there was a dramatic newsprint shot which shows him to be a strikingly handsome and dashingly romantic U.S. Negro man of action. Inside, in addition to the arresting excellence of the photography itself, one was immediately impressed by the extraordinary range of interest that the subject matter revealed. There were studies that captured the mobility of Alexander Calder's sculpture, portraits of women of wealth and fashion, compositions that blended old paintings with still life objects, abstract color études comparable to good contemporary painting, landscapes, skyscapes, seascapes, natural studies, sporting events, and so on. Among the fine black and white enlargements, which included selections from a documentary study-in-depth of a South American family and a wide variety of shots taken on news assignments, was one smoggy and sooty Harlem rooftop panorama which might have been the work of a Manhattan Piranesi.

In addition to the photography, there was music. His piano concerto, which had a premiere with some fanfare in Venice in 1952, was used as the background sound track for the show. One heard nothing that reflected the composer's early years as a honky tonk piano player; instead of Kansas City for getting with it, what one heard was rather like Honegger for the Darkroom. However, it sounded thoroughly professional, if a bit ofay when one thought of Count Basie.

There were also words, galley proofs, and copies of his books. During the past several years, Parks has become a part-time writer. A number of his articles have appeared in *Life*, and in 1963 he published a novel about early adolescence in the Midwest. One also learned that Parks was planning to make a motion picture based on this novel, *The Learning Tree*. Meanwhile his current book is *A Choice of Weapons* (Harper & Row, 1966).

Some of the sequences of *The Learning Tree* were written with professional competence, and from time to time, there are some details that are expertly rendered. But on the whole, it must be said, one was left with the impression that the author was really much more interested in turning out a fictionalized memoir to illustrate the "meaning" of certain experiences of his own childhood than in telling a story about Newt Winger, the book's young hero, and his friends and competitors, who have such wonderfully nostalgic names as Beansy, Jappy, Earl, Marcus, and Skunk.

A Choice of Weapons is a nonfiction memoir, which begins in a sense where *The Learning Tree* ends. There is a prologue, but the story begins in Kansas with the death of Parks' mother when he was sixteen. It covers his coming of age in Minnesota in the nineteen thirties, his struggle to put himself through high school, his experiences as busboy, dining car waiter, basketball player, piano player, song writer, and Civilian Conservation Corps worker. It also relates his adventures in and around pool rooms, bars, whorehouses, and flop houses; his travels to Chicago, the far West, New York; and there are accounts of his early marriage and family life and of how he came to be a photographer. The book ends with him returning to Harlem after having been promised and then denied an overseas assignment as a combat cameraman with the all-Negro 332nd Fighter Group during World War II.

Given the author's subsequent success in his line of work, *A Choice of Weapons* is a newsworthy book. It is also, given the action it encompasses, an occasionally interesting book. But on balance, it is not really in itself a very good book. Sometimes, for all the details that are supposed to tell it like it really is, it is not even a very convincing one. Not, one hastens to add, because one questions the accuracy of the facts but because unfortunately they too often are so artificially structured that they just simply do not ring true enough.

To begin with, the book does not "sound" at all like Gordon Parks talks, walks, looks, and certainly not the way he operates. Parks, as his career suggests, is a man who has always been on easier terms with the everyday world than are most other people. The *facts* in his narrative make this clear enough. One has only to remember how well he handled himself and maintained his personal integrity and his ambitions throughout all the difficulties of his first days in Minnesota, to say nothing of the days that followed. But his insistent interpretations are often so stilted and self-conscious that, more often than not, they project a false naiveté on the one hand and a totally uncharacteristic pretentiousness on the other. His sentiments upon hearing the news of Pearl Harbor, for instance, are so noble that they would put Douglas MacArthur himself to shame. "Self-concern at such a time was petty, I told myself, but I could not still my anxiety." Man, how you sound!

Gordon Parks functions easily enough in almost any situation almost anywhere in the world. He can get along very well in the slums or in the most elegant drawing rooms. A street fight doesn't faze him, and neither does an occasion of state. He is hip in a crap game, cool at the swankiest race tracks, gone in the world of high fashion, with it in the world of the intellectuals, a pro in Hollywood, cagey in the political capitals, smooth on the dance floor, and canny in combat. He tools on land, by sea, and in the air, as they used to say during World War II. But *A Choice of Weapons* seems deliberately designed to read like the story of a very lucky little black boy who somehow or other did not become a social problem but rather has made an astonishing breakthrough into the great wide wonderful white world of milk and money—has made it but not quite, or something like that.

Most of the time the author of *A Choice of Weapons* is so busy try-ing to show that his actions are conditioned by a background of U.S. Negro experience that he becomes confused and misleading not only about the nature of his own life and the lives of other U.S. Negroes but also about the nature of human motives as such. Sometimes, in fact, *A Choice of Weapons* reads for all the world as if Gordon Parks, a classic U.S. son of a gun if there ever was one, is trying to pass himself off as the son of social science fiction, Flash Gordon, the upward mobile kid from the (segregated) twilight zone of inner space!

Yes. *Of course* his actions are conditioned by the experience of his U.S. Negro background. What the hell else is he going to operate out of? Even when he is applying some esthetic insight which he learned roaming alone through the Chicago Art Institute, he is responding out of it. The trouble is that his conception of U.S. Negro experience, in this book at any rate, tends to be more abstract than real. He just simply will not let enough of the encounters stand on their own, with-out commentary; and ironically, like most U.S. Negro writers these days, he seems most convinced that he is laying on the heroic com-plications when he is only piling up the academic oversimplifications.

The background experiences of U.S. Negroes is a rich source of many things. But many people insist that it is only the source of frus-tration and crime, degradation, emasculation, and self-hatred. But then most of these people are headlong do-gooders who, for all their good will, are too hopelessly superficial to realize that all human cir-cumstances are the source of these very same things. That is just too much for them to think about. Nevertheless, it is patently ridiculous to assume that there is automatically more frustration and crime in a segregated slum area than there is in power politics or high finance. Nor is there necessarily more personal compensation in Scarsdale than Lenòx Terrace, not if neurotic behavior is any indication!

The background experience of U.S. Negroes includes all of the negative things that go with racism and segregation; but it also includes all of the challenging circumstances that make for ambition, integrity, and transcendent achievement. And anyway, nobody who is really and truly interested in the perpetually fascinating mystery of human motive and conduct is ever likely to ignore the fact that many of the non-Negroes who infest Greenwich Village, the Bowery, and the narcotics dens of the Upper West Side often come from a background of freedom and even wealth and power. Nor will anyone with a reliable sense of human potential ever fail to realize that an obviously well-heeled and cultivated U.S. Negro sitting in a Paris café speaking charming French to a countess may well be operating out of a background of an Alabama cotton picker who once averted his eyes (or pretended to) every time a barefooted red-headed, red-neck girl spoke to him. It should be no news to anyone that a large number of the smoothest city slickers come from the country. That many U.S. Negroes have never lived anywhere except the city should be no news either.

And of course, any truly serious student of American culture should know that segregation for all its brutal restrictions never has blocked U.S. Negroes off from the essential influences of the public school system. Nor has it screened them against the educational fallout from the mass media. Thus, in spite of all the substandard test scores, anybody who assumes that the average white U.S. schoolboy is really closer to the classics, for instance, than the average U.S. Negro schoolboy is either talking about the relative percentage of literary snobs or is simply kidding himself. A white schoolboy *may* be persuaded to bone up and pass a formal exam on, say, metaphysical poetry, but that doesn't actually mean that he gives a damn about it. A Negro boy, on the other hand, might well have a genuine feeling for the blues, which certainly represent an indigenous "substitute" for certified high-culture poetry.

One assumes, of course, that Gordon Parks is well aware of all this. At any rate he operates with it, and he tries very hard to show its relevance to his development. But unfortunately he does not succeed very well. Thus he has not done himself justice in *A Choice of Weapons*. The result is that sometimes it is as if he himself doesn't quite know what to make of what he has in fact *already* made of himself.

Nevertheless, many people who are otherwise extremely careful about the books they rate noteworthy may not only make a fuss over this one but will be prepared to give all kinds of essentially sentimental excuses for its obvious shortcomings. And one suspects that many will be doing so because Gordon Parks is a successful U.S. Negro and because everybody is for encouraging the Negro this year. This is a hell of a reason to excuse anybody for not writing well enough. But then many of these people never did expect to see a poor little black boy write as well as Parks already does.

But white supremacists will be white supremacists, it seems, some without ever actually becoming aware of it. But they are. These "friendly" ones are the benevolent white supremacists, who are forever forgiving Negroes for something. As a matter of fact many are all too eager to forgive all sorts of sins that Negroes were never guilty of in the first place. And there are, to be sure, those doubly innocent U.S. Negroes who actually accept such totally irrelevant forgiveness—and then go around fuming about the crocodilia they put up with from white folks.

Gordon Parks is not that kind. He is never very likely to accept anybody else's excuses for anything he has ever flubbed. This is why he got where he is today, as the Southern Negro high school principals say. And in this he is not unlike the U.S. Negro prizefighter. Nobody ever heard of a Negro fighter excusing himself for a poor showing in the ring because he comes from a low income family and never got enough to eat. And one reason a fighter knows better than to try to pull this kind of old thin stuff is that there are too many other hungry Negro fighters (many of them fatherless—anti-matriarchists please note) winning championships.

The makers of sentimental excuses always seem to overlook the most obvious facts of everyday life. Nothing, for example, could be more obvious than the fact that anybody who has a life that merits an autobiography has had to overcome one sort of obstacle or another, just one hog ass thing *after* the other, as the saying goes. Thus, when one refers to Gordon Parks as having had an unpromising beginning and reports that his life has been beset with obstructions, one is really only indicating that Parks' life has the makings of a good story. Everybody knows that there can be heroes without walls and dragons. But people who substitute psychological or psychiatric theory for experience go right on pretending and perhaps even believing that nobody ever actually survives any adventure or reaches the enchanted castle.

There are others whose confusion about all this even leads them to write as if no one can enjoy a spring rainscape unless he also has the right to vote, a passionate night of love unless he has executive status, or even a succulent prime steak unless he has a seat on the New York Stock Exchange—even though he has the price of the bill of fare.

When one says that there was little in his early environment to indicate that young Gordon Parks would someday grow up to become such a magnificent photographer, one should also remember that there could hardly have been more in the environment of young Mathew Brady either. And furthermore, if becoming a member of the photographic in-crowd of *Life* magazine represents a very special breakthrough for Negro Gordon Parks, it is no less a breakthrough for every other in-crowd member and not one bit less special. One has only to remember all the unsegregated white boys squinting into view finders all over the country and dreaming of taking pictures for *Life*. It is, when one stops and thinks about it, absolutely impossible for Negro Gordon Parks to be more gratified by his progress than non-Negro Carl Mydans is by his or non-Anglo-Saxon Mark Kauff-man is by his.

Gordon Parks is aware of all this also, and there is every reason to assume that he is aware of a good many other things as well. But he has been unable to get them into sharp enough focus in *A Choice of Weapons*. Thus this book, like *The Learning Tree*, cannot be ranked beside his best photography. One wishes that Parks had worked closer to the theme suggested by the highly evocative title and had made more of the implications of the storybook hero forging his sword. This may even have given all of the insistent political overtones a much deeper resonance. But perhaps in the actual process of recording the events involved he found the military metaphor too restrictive, or perhaps, as often happens, the title came afterwards. In any case, a camera is not only a magic weapon to be used against chaos. In the hands of someone as gifted as Gordon Parks, it becomes something even better, something that works miracles with form and gives both insight and delight.

WHO THAT SAY, WHAT DAT, EVERY TIME US DO THAT?

A well-known New York newspaper pundit, a somewhat reconstructed but sometimes sentimental Southerner out of Virginia
through Maryland, once wrote that he had never met a Negro
who didn't trust white people too much and that he had met very
few who really understood what white people were really doing to
them. This is perhaps all too true of far too many of the Negroes this
well-meaning but sometimes condescending white maverick's maverick has actually met or allows himself to remember ever having
met. Nevertheless, one cannot help wondering about the company he
keeps.

There are, after all, Negroes, and still other Negroes, not all of them
naive, nice nonentities, non compos mentis—or even non-white.
There are, to be sure, many who give little evidence that they have
any understanding of anything, except how to survive by hook or
by crook; and not a few of these are the ones publicized by the mass
media as leaders and spokesmen. Sometimes, however, it is hard to
tell whether the mass media establishment regard some of them as
leaders or as disguised replacements for Amos and Andy and Lawyer
Calhoun.

But there always have been many others who not only have always
understood all too well what other people have been doing to them
all these years, but have also been doing a few things of their own on

their own in the meantime. These others are part of that enduring U.S. tradition of self-control, wisdom, courage, and commitment to human freedom and individual fulfillment, which few other native traditions, in this country or elsewhere can equal and none excel—and of which the Underground Railroad was a part. For a long time the tradition has also been represented by the educational, inspirational, and political role of the Southern Negro doctor. People who are more interested in highly tenuous theories of social class than in everyday Negro life have long ignored and denied the key role of the Negro doctor as community leader. But Southern Negro educators (another overlooked type) cannot, nor can any grass roots worker in the civil rights movement.

It is incredible that none of the mature, knowledgeable or just plain shrewd Negroes one sees not only surviving but also laughing about it seems to have made any significant impression on the white intellectuals of these nothing if not academic times—perhaps least of all on those most given to explaining the meaning and mysteries of black experience, which many usually confuse either with *bleak* experience or *psychedelic* experience.

An ever increasing number of U.S. intellectuals these days seems absolutely convinced that all knowledge and certainly all guidelines for the perplexed are found only in books, and that all wisdom comes engraved in sacred terminology with reverent references to other books, especially those based on the gospels of Karl Marx and Sigmund Freud. But it is a mistake to assume that people have no knowledge or understanding of their circumstances because their reactions may not be conventional or because their verbalization does not fit neatly into somebody else's value system or some commonly accepted highfalutin frame of reference.

No Negro intellectual who really keeps his eyes and ears open at home, on the street, and in the barber shop and then goes on to college, is likely to underestimate the accuracy of the insights of other

American Negroes, no matter how many formal intellectual disciplines he himself may master. Nor are most black people unaware of another completely obvious phenomenon: They themselves may be essentially *invisible* to most other people, but a whole lot of other people are in turn all too *transparent* to the black people all around them everywhere every day.

It is also a mistake to forget that there are always those people who are not going to tell other people what they really think about anything. They just do not trust other people that much. There is also, one should not forget, something to be said for the *prudence* of a domestic servant, a day laborer, or even a managing editor who does not reveal that he knows something crooked is going on and who does not tell his boss what he really thinks of him—and it would hardly make sense to tell the boss's friends and spies. Neither should one forget that there are also those people who find out that other people will believe anything, and so they tell them anything, *anything at all.*

Perhaps it has been extremely difficult for many Northern-born Negroes to realize what their white liberal friends have been doing to them behind all those interracial handshakes and brotherhood smiles. Only recently have they begun to realize the extent of the double dealing. But although some Southern Negroes have also been confused by Northern do-gooders from time to time and some for a long time were overimpressed with Northern Negro tales about unsegregated buses and hamburgers, many have always realized what Southern white people—solid, moderate, or extreme—were up to. They have always been on to Southern courthouse hoaxes, and white gentlemen's shady agreements. Sharecroppers, for instance, have never really been fooled by all that phony bookkeeping. Trapped, to be sure, but fooled by no means. And, of course, everybody knows what all those laws against intermarriage, as the saying goes, are all about. Since they hardly ever see anybody being put in jail about all those mulatto children, Southern Negroes know very well that those laws are never intended to be used against race mixing, or commingling, as the white preachers sometimes say. Everybody has always known that these laws are really against shotgun weddings, *as nobody ever says*!

There just simply never was a time when most U.S. Negroes trusted any white people too much or did not really understand what was going on. The captive Africans, who never had trusted any enemies to begin with, certainly had no illusions at all about the white slave traders. The only thing that really surprised them about it all, so one old barber shop version goes, was that these Europeans, who were clearly the most savage foes any Africans had ever encountered, did not intend to eat them. Some comb and scissors historians trace all of that wonderfully complicated U.S. Negro laughter and mockery back to that realization. There is absolutely no evidence, however, that U.S. Negroes have ever lost their suspicions about other things.

Perhaps the New York news prophet has allowed himself to be misled by his contacts with too many social science Negroes. These Negroes often seem to regard themselves as The-Black-Man's-New-York-Intellectuals because they read monographs subsidized by the philanthropic foundations and know all about footnotes, bibliographies, and cross references (but who, unlike real New York intellectuals, who are truly people of the book, also regard themselves as down to earth pragmatists because they read only earthy fiction and have no interest in any art that goes beyond fashionable entertainment). And then there are the social workers, a breed slightly apart, who often seem to regard themselves as The-Black-Man's-White-People (or Middle Class Establishment, as it were), but who more often than not are themselves regarded by other Negroes as being The-White-Man's Negroes, or Strawboss Negroes.

It should be easy enough for no-nonsense newsmen, or anybody else for that matter, to spot both these types at interracial confabs, their natural habitat. Both speak with a profoundly pretentious sense of long-standing cultural deprivation and a fairly generously under-written commitment to moral outrage. The social science type on one side of the drawing room usually smiles at *his* white interracialists and says something like, "Do you dig Odetta?" in a carefully decontaminated Ivy-accented voice. (*He* digs Joan Baez!) Also for the benefit of *his* white people he responds to any statement by other Negroes with, "Define your terminology." On the other side of the room the welfare or power structure type either nods his head murmuring, "Progress," or shakes it sadly, muttering, "No progress," with just the right overtones of black militancy to make *his* white folks feel safely hip. When he wants to shake them up, he looks away, shrugs his shoulders, and refers to "Moll-com" (Malcolm X) as if to an old billiards drinking friend. When either one of these types says, "Now we are getting down to the nitty gritty," he does not mean the basic human implications of the social issues under discussion. He means money for a welfare project.

As American as they are, neither of these apple pie people represents the complex mass of U.S. Negroes, not to be confused with The Negro. Both types, for example, are forever referring to white middle class norms as if they were talking about the greatest good for the greatest number. But most other Negroes, whether down-home or up here, know all about the "squareness" and mediocrity of those norms and the hypocrisy of middle class values.

After all, integrated or not, Negroes have always been in a position to observe almost everything that has been doing and undoing in this country. Other people always seem to forget it, but Negroes are almost always behind the scenes, whether they are on camera or not. And for inside news, no U.S. press club could ever really compare with the good old Negro barber shop (and beauty parlors) where all the old doormen, waiters, pullman porters, valets, chauffeurs, ex-shoe shine boys (and maids and cooks) go to swap lies and to signify about the state of the nation.

Most Negroes have always had enough inside information about the history of this great hit-and-miss republic to know that other people have been deliberately writing Negroes out of the history books, even as the same people permitted newly arrived immigrants to write themselves in. Even the social science and welfare elite know this (but unfortunately all they seem to be able to do about it is to suggest that black history be taught to black people who already know it— or to pretend that U.S. Negroes are all descendents of African kings, queens, and Hottentot potentates). Other U.S. Negroes, however, realize that as long as white Americans are misinformed about the actualities, the history of the United States is going to cause even more confusion among white citizens than among black ones.

Sentimental friends and self-styled benefactors of The Cause were flabbergasted when so many Negroes went along with the nomination of Lyndon Johnson for the vice-presidency. Negroes themselves, however, had been saying all along that if they ever found a Southern politician (politician, mind you, not liberal) who really felt concerned about what white people have been doing to Negroes, they would finally have somebody in the White House who would really try to do something about it. On the other hand, they have seldom felt that any Northern political humanitarians really *could* feel bad enough about it. And besides, they also know only too well that many Northerners turn up trying to become honorary Confederate drummers or something. Negro voters and political bird watchers had some hopes for FDR and JFK, felt stuck with Ike, are still philosophical about Truman; *but they put their money on LBJ*—and were somewhat saddened to find how many of their Northern liberal friends insisted that LBJ's civil rights record counts for nothing and that Negroes should *hate* him because of his blunders in Vietnam. Many suspected that much of the opposition to Johnson's foreign policy was really another sneaky Northern backlash trick to weaken his *domestic* policy!

The mass media may continue to give a lot of wrongheaded publicity to a few noisy, headline hunting–hype artists, but many U.S. Negroes know that the people who are really being taken in are not always black and exploited but perhaps most often white and sometimes rich and powerful. With all due respect to overzealous police surveillance and researchers at Harvard, Yale, and the Lemberg Center for the Study of Violence, one must remind people like that nice if somewhat proprietary newsman that they probably meet very few *white* people who do not trust all *Negroes* too much and hardly any who even begin to understand what *Negroes* are really doing to *them* and making them do to themselves. At this very moment, for instance, Negroes have thrown the whole white world, as the saying goes, into a state of shock, confusion, and almost suicidal exasperation with a simple little black magic trick like insisting that the Constitution is really nothing more or less than the Golden Rule. The best white minds, as the IQ experts say, are having trouble figuring that one out! And yet there are intellectuals who still insist that power and intelligence go hand in hand. Perhaps such is the case. But there are at least a few Negroes who have their own ideas about the keys to the handcuffs. These have always insisted that while white supremacy may sometimes be devious, it is not really predicated upon intelligence but on ruthlessness.

A CLUTCH OF SOCIAL SCIENCE FICTION FICTION

O nly a few American writers since the twenties have been able to create fiction with implications beyond the most obvious and tiresome of the clichés derived from social science. Even the most existentialistic and psychedelic avant-garde experimentalists seem as often as not to be circumscribed by assumptions that are essentially only Marxian or Freudian. Moreover, most book reviewers, no less than American readers in general, now seem to regard fiction as being little more than a very special extension of the social science case history.

Unlike the stories and novels of Hemingway, Fitzgerald, and Faulkner, which, like those of Melville, Mark Twain, and Henry James, embody the writer's insight into the poetic and dramatic dimensions of the human situation (man's aspirations and his possibilities), those of more recent American writers frequently read like interim research reports and position papers. Indeed, what most American fiction seems to represent these days is not so much the writer's actual sense of life as some theory of life to which he is giving functional allegiance, not so much his complex individual sensitivity to the actual texture of human experience as his intellectual reaction to ideas *about* experience.

Fiction about Negroes offers an obvious example. Instead of the imaginative writer's response to the infinitely fascinating mysteries, contradictions, and possibilities of human existence, what fiction about U.S. Negroes almost always expresses is some very highly specialized and extremely narrow psycho-political theory about American *Negro* existence. And what is even worse, these are the theories that, for the most part, only add up to the same old bigoted assumptions that underlie the doctrine of white supremacy.

Accordingly, although Negro life in the United States has always been the incarnation of the "very essence of adventure and romance" (Henrietta Buckmaster's phrase), most often fiction about it is specifically concocted as a documentation of U.S. Negro wretchedness. Seldom do American writers celebrate U.S. Negroes as heroes in fiction. There was William Faulkner, to be sure, who created Lucas Beauchamp, Dilsey, Sam Fathers, and Ned William McCaslin, but the best most other white American writers seem to be able to do by the Negro is show that he deserves economic and political assistance. Nor do many U.S. Negro writers do any better. (But that is another story —one about wailing-wall polemics.)

Here are three reviews of novels which deal with the subject of U.S. Negroes in various mixes of social science and fiction. The novels range from middlebrow ladies' entertainment to very serious efforts at fictional re-creation indeed.

STAR-CROSSED MELODRAMA

Perhaps the most significant thing about *Five Smooth Stones* (Crown, 1966), a first novel by Ann Fairbairn, is the fact that it represents a consistent and positive attitude toward the so-called U.S. Negro middle class. The author does not confuse middle income Negroes with white Americans who represent the middle class "norms" of the statistical surveys, and she avoids most of the other usual condescending clichés about educated middle and upper income Negroes. By and large she seems much more concerned with creating people who have human interest and historical resonance than with forcing some theory of class conflict into the interpretation of the behavior of people who make up what is perhaps the most open and intimately inter-related social class structure in the United States.

The career of her hero is nothing if not a testimony to the fluid nature of Negro life in America. David Champlin, who was born in poverty and segregation in New Orleans during the Depression, grows up with ever extending horizons of aspiration, graduates with honors from an integrated college in the Midwest, finishes Harvard Law School, becomes successful in his profession, and moves with assurance in the integrated social circles of Boston and London without ever losing contact with any area of Negro life he has ever known. Moreover, the higher he rises, the more his respect for the rich humanity of his "uneducated" grandfather increases. There are scientific studies and surveys, usually based on over-simplifications, that would have it otherwise, but in this case at least, it is the subjective observations of the fiction writer that come closest to the complexity of actuality.

Still, *Five Smooth Stones* has some curious inconsistencies in its treatment of Negro subject matter. In spite of the author's obvious personal and intellectual freedom from bigoted thinking, she is given to an exasperatingly sloppy overemphasis on race as a social category. Time and again as the omniscient narrator, she uses such expressions as "people of his own race," "one of his own race," "she was of his own race," when "Negroes," "Negro," and "she was a Negro" would be smoother as well as more accurate. And besides, her book demonstrates at every turn how Negroes are racially *interwoven* with other Americans. That U.S. Negroes make up a very distinct sociopolitical group with discernable cultural features peculiar to itself goes without saying, but by no ethnological definition or measurements are they a *race*.

Also Ann Fairbairn is all for intermarriage, as the saying goes, and illustrates her case in terms that are as human as you please. And her conception of the hero's grandfather reveals a rare understanding and magnificent feeling for the role of the older generation Negro as a source of "faith and courage." And yet the minute she has to consider Negroes in terms of "social problems," she becomes as cliché-ridden as a survey technician, and her writing degenerates to the level of the most irresponsible tabloid journalism. She obviously thinks she is making a big fat plea for social rehabilitation when she has one of her most dedicated do-gooders describe the Negroes of the Chicago South Side, East Philadelphia, Watts, and Harlem as being "gangsters at ten, addicts at fourteen, killers at seventeen and dead inside at twenty." But the best that can be said for such glib nonsense is that it reflects an incredibly stupid approach to polemics. It should take a certified imbecile less than fifteen seconds to realize that if the main problem of Negro children in Harlem and Watts is that they are gangsters, addicts, and killers, there would be no overcrowded classrooms and no serious agitation for school desegregation in these places. In fact, there would be no Northern civil rights movement at all! And besides, the Negro youths who are most troublesome to white people these days are not the hoodlums but the social reformers!

In many ways, then, *Five Smooth Stones* is another book of social science fiction despite its virtues. It has implications of an epic and overtones of tragedy, but it never gets beyond the platitudes of melodrama, which just might be the literary fate of such fiction at best. In any event, *Five Smooth Stones* is a melodrama with an unhappy ending. The good guy, in this instance, is David, who has the nicest and most humane white friends and benefactors in the world. The bad guys are the ugly, snarling segregationists and the sneaky reactionaries. The great chase, of course, is the civil rights movement. And the girl the good guy gets is Sara, an apple pie of a white girl, who, as tiny as she is, just has too much of the pioneer spirit of her ancestors in her to be restricted by the kind of people who would not want their sisters and daughters "to marry one." The climax, however, is only as American as a hysterical mob of white backlashers and a Mississippi redneck with a sniper's rifle. But the momentum for constructive nonviolent social action is there, and Negroes are bound to show up better on social science surveys hereafter.

Without denying any of David's obvious and often charming differences, the author of *Five Smooth Stones* can accept a Negro hero as being as American as anyone else. The author of *Mojo Hand* (Simon & Schuster, 1966), Jane Phillips, cannot. Not only does she insist that middle income Negroes are as dull and as square as she finds or imagines the white middle class to be, she even gives them pale faces and goes on to portray a mulatto girl as if she were really only a white girl who is fascinated by folk Negroes, gin, awkward language in general, and foul-mouthed repetitiousness in particular. Eunice, the unlikely heroine, has all the earmarks of an overromantic unhip ofay beatnik who is hooked on folk music as a form of "escape." Everything she does betrays her identity to the reader if not to the other characters in the book, who after all are as unlikely as she is. She says, does, and is interested in all the wrong things for the wrong reasons.

The story line of *Mojo Hand*, although not easy to follow, is as simple as it is unconvincing. Eunice hears a folk blues record by a guitar player named Blacksnake, falls in love with him and Art and "real" life, leaves her cotillion-oriented (wow!) middle class mulatto parents in California, sets out for Louisiana with guitar on her knee looking for Blacksnake. She finds him and the blues, the blues as defined in ofay jazz mags—that is, she talks nasty, does low down, gets pregnant, and so becomes a "real person" among "real people" instead of being a paleface imitation of life. Which gets pretty close to condemning Constance Baker Motley as a phony because she finished law school instead of going on the road with, say, T-Bone Walker. But then, look at all the confusion caused by white people who mistake Congressman Adam Clayton Powell for good old Cab Calloway of the Cotton Club days. One loud Hi-de Hi-de Hi-de-ho and most of Powell's troubles with "the white world" would probably vanish overnight.

Neither *Five Smooth Stones* nor *Mojo Hand* should be confused with literature. As for *Mojo Hand*, it is a fiasco from the very outset and can be dismissed and forgotten as if it never happened. That its young author would rather be a novelist than a social science expert is somehow clear enough; but as yet her conception of the art of fiction is as aboriginal as that of certain widely patronized Negro literary figures who have yet to realize that banal sayings, slang anecdotes, dirty remarks, and bad song lyrics do not become literature simply because they are published in book form.

As for *Five Smooth Stones*, it seldom rises above the comfortable sentiments of the middle brow ladies' magazines and the TV serials. As fictional journalism, however, it is a fascinating and insightful behind-the-scenes account of some of the personal tribulations interwoven with the public political struggles of the civil rights movement. But even so, except where her key characters are involved, the author, like most other writers, shows little understanding and appreciation of what the Southern Negro's extremely complicated resistance to provocation really means. Thus, she not only oversimplifies and misrepresents it as fear, but also in the process she in effect deemphasizes white insecurity-become-hysterical by treating it as if it were only high-handed callous brutality.

Whether or not *Five Smooth Stones* becomes the best-seller its publishers are hoping for, it seems definitely headed for most social science reading lists. And the author is not very likely to object in either case. It is obvious that she set out to write a popular star-crossed civil rights romance, a plea for good citizenship and a Black Primer for White Folks, all in one. What she seems to have forgotten, however, is the fact that, for those who do not already agree with you, fiction is most compelling as propaganda not when it is used primarily as an aspic for the ideas behind the writer's commitment to a cause but when the narration is compelling.

WARREN MILLER AND HIS BLACK FACE VAUDEVILLE*

Warren Miller is much too slick and much too superficial for his work to be mistaken as serious fiction. But you never know for sure. What with book promotion being what it is these days and what with his subject matter being life in Harlem, his very slapdash slickness may actually be the means by which he may yet slide into some highly

*This essay was written in 1964, before Warren Miller's death. It is printed here without changes.

important position as a very special expert on Negro Matters. All too often it happens.

One of his books, *The Cool World*, has already been made into a deadly serious avant garde propaganda film, which has been generally dismissed as Art but praised as realistic documentation. It is no more realistic than the book itself, which was much more concerned about being cute about everything than about being accurate about anything. But so it goes, and it should surprise no one in Harlem if the mass media elect Warren Miller number one U.S. white Negro. So it went back in the days of the king of jazz and the king of swing and so it could go again. As a matter of fact, James Baldwin—who, by the way, knows much more about the goings on in Greenwich Village, Saint-Germain-des-Prés, and even Saint-Tropez than he is ever likely to know about Harlem, who certainly knows infinitely more about the guerrilla warfare of New York intellectuals than he has ever actually known about uptown street gangs, and whose scintillating prose style is much closer to Oscar Wilde than to the vernacular of Harlem—has called *The Cool World*, "One of the finest novels about Harlem that has ever come my way." Stuff.

The Cool World is not only not fine, it is hardly a novel at all. Whatever his literary potential may be otherwise, when Warren Miller writes about Negroes and Harlem, he immediately becomes a second-rate blackface comedian, an opportunistic clown cutting topical capers for the entertainment of, as they say in Amagansett, the "white world" (*shitman get hot man stay cool man shitman soul man shitman*). Many white Americans have always gone for this kind of old razzmatazz, and they still pay well for it. And, of course, there are also those ever so smooth Negro con artists who operate in the sad, fuzzy world of the white U.S. liberal, and who will allow themselves to be sprayed with this kind of you-know-what just to prove how tolerant Negroes are, or how superior they are to it. One well-known NAACP bigwig, for instance, used to have one of those Aunt Jemima memo boards hanging in his kitchen during open house just to prove

how sophisticated he was! He ain't. He something else. He white folks
number one Negro mispronounced as Baldwin does it when referring
to himself on TV.

Those who insist on working their way through the everlasting coy-
ness of the language that screens *The Cool World* will not find themselves in a landscape created by an imaginative novelist. They will
find a series of patently contrived situations hastily derived from the
currently fashionable generalizations of the so-called social sciences.
They will find themselves in the prefabricated world of the up to date
social worker, a newspaper stage-set with crudely carved ebony and
mahogany puppets moving their lips in a snazzy jazzy tempo while an
inept ventriloquist mouths overworked Marxist and psychiatric clichés disguised as the untutored wisdom of the curbstones:

> Hurst live in a cellar an dont know whut the world all about. He dont
> know the world run by crooks pushers and hood from top to bottom.
> In the white houses an in the vegetable stores on the corners all of them
> got big hands in the pie. Its no world to be nice in . . .
> Harrison slam his book shut. It go Thuck. He stand up and go to the
> window an look out. He say to the window. "They make us live like
> animals. Is it any wonder then that some of us act like animals an some
> of us become animals. The fantastic thing is how few of us succum to
> their idea of us." An he went on like that standing there at the window
> not looking at us lookin out at Harlem.

And so on.

This kind of language is supposed to project the sensibility of fourteen year old Duke Custis, the first-person narrator protagonist,
whose great ambition is to keep a pistol and become the absolute ruler
of his gang. This boy's existence is represented as being so circumscribed that he has no significant awareness of the rich diversity of life
about him in Harlem, to say nothing of life in New York at large. Nor
does his sensibility reflect any meaningful contact with the contents
of radio programs, movies, TV, magazines, or even comic books. His
conception of space travel is that of an idiot. But Luann, the gang's

teenage prostitute, takes the cake. She doesn't even know about the subway! What ever happened to the good old A train, so long familiar to every Negro cotton picker arriving from Alabama?

Now if a writer cannot, will not, or at any rate doesn't identify with his characters, he is not likely to write truly about life as he actually knows it. Certainly he cannot condescend to his characters and at the same time expect his readers to believe in them. The fact is, Warren Miller simply cannot imagine himself as Duke Custis. Much has been made of the fact that Miller is a white man who lived in Harlem for five years. This is all very well, but as a writer he seems unable to imagine himself living in Harlem as a Negro for five minutes.

The Harlem described by Warren Miller could never produce a James Baldwin. Thus Baldwin's endorsement of *The Cool World* would seem exaggerated to say the least. (But there is a curious consistency operating here. For the Harlem described by James Baldwin himself could not possibly produce a James Baldwin either.)

II

The Cool World was a slapdash job. It was also slapstick, but one is not certain how much of the clowning was really intentional. *The Siege of Harlem* (McGraw-Hill, 1964) is also slapdash, and here the slapstick is all too intentional. It is a minstrel show in which the writer comes pumping on stage doing a saggy bottomed, tangle footed buck and wing in the guise of Joel Chandler Harris, which he ain't; and he ain't no Octavus Roy Cohen either. Neither is he any Roark Bradford, however he may yearn for them good old green fried chicken pastures.

Here you find Uncle Remus uptown telling bedtime Amos and Andy war stories to a group of children who have such side splitting musical comedy names as M'boya, Jomo, N'Krumah, Ahmad, Shabad, and such like. Harlem has become a nation within New York City, has nationalized the numbers racket, and there are such hilarious vaudeville landmarks as Station WEB Du Bois, checkpoint Frederick Douglass, the Black House, and so on. No need to catalogue the cornballisms. Not even the best comedians at the Apollo Theatre can bring stuff this thin to life. Not even the great Pigmeat Markham can make this stuff stack. (Not that you can't still make yourself a fortune by putting on a costume and conning the media into advertising you as a politicalized Father Divine. After all, media people, who are nothing if not "committed" regard that as being far more "relevant" than such "razzmatazz" as "Stompin' at the Savoy.")

So much for *The Siege of Harlem*, unless somebody turns it into a TV spectacular. In color yet. But whenever you complain about how some white writer misrepresents Negro life, somebody always wants to know if you think it is possible for any white person to write accurately about any Negroes. The question almost always has racist implications, but the real issue is not racial but cultural. Of course it is possible. Why shouldn't it be possible? If Ernest Hemingway could write good stories about Italy, France, Spain, and Cuba, and if numerous other writers can produce outstanding books about people who lived not only in distant lands but in distant times, why the hell shouldn't a white writer be able to do an excellent book about contemporary Harlem?

The same question comes up when you complain about the inauthenticity of most white jazz musicians. Can a white man really play Negro music? Of course he can. If he is a good enough musician and respects the medium as he would any other art form. If he develops the same familiarity with its idiomatic nuances, the same love of it, and humility before it as the good Negro musician does. Why not? But certainly not if he is really ambivalent about it. Not if he hangs around with it for a while and then withdraws and allows himself to become a "white hope." Not if he allows his publicity to convince him that he is superior to the masters he knows damn well he is still plagiarizing.

Of course white writers can write well about Negroes. Some of William Faulkner's very finest characters are Negroes. And of course white writers are just as free to have as much fun with Negro characters as with any other. Most of Faulkner's Negroes in *The Reivers* are very funny indeed. But Warren Miller's feeble attempts at ridicule only expose his own provincialism, which he sadly mistakes for a superior sophistication. Routine Negro comics do a better job of spoofing the civil rights movement every night.

For one thing, Miller just doesn't seem to be able to resist the all-American temptation to put Negroes in their place by reducing them to stereotypes. Joel Chandler Harris was certainly no great shakes as a writer, but doggone my cats if his talking animals aren't infinitely more human than any character in either *The Cool World* or *The Siege of Harlem*.

Nevertheless, Negroes would do well to keep an eye cocked on Warren Miller, slapdash, slapstick, and all. With your white Negro anything is possible. Say if the sequel to *The Siege of Harlem* is another mirthful matinee piece called *Porgy and Bess Stomping at the Savoy and the Walls Come Tumbling Down*, and then this very same Warren Miller grows a beard or something, goes serious and slaps together still another one about how once upon a time a boy in Boston heard a record nightmare by Artie Shaw and became an expert on jazz and the jazz life and had a cotton field romance with a Negro girl and became an expert on Negro sex life as it really is and then was befriended one night by a Negro hipster and became an expert on the narcotic life as it really is and went on to spout a steady stream of magazine articles explaining the civil rights movement as it really is, this very same Warren Miller could very easily be mistaken as a very genuine and understanding friend of Negroes. The trouble is that the Indians used to have friends like that. And look what happened to the Indians. They now live in ghettos. Or is it Casbahs? As Jelly Roll Morton or somebody said: *If you see dear Mrs. Equitone tell her I bring the horoscope myself: one must be so careful these days.*

WILLIAM STYRON AND HIS TROUBLESOME PROPERTY

The most fundamental shortcoming of almost all fiction written by white Americans about their black fellow countrymen is also almost always the most obvious. It is, given the deepseated racism of most Americans, also the most predictable. In almost every instance, the white American writer starts out either unable or unwilling to bring himself to make a truly intimate and profoundly personal identification with the black protagonist whose heroism he himself has chosen to delineate and whose sense of life he has elected to impersonate, if not emulate.

In fact, there are times when the emotional distance between the white writer and his black subject matter becomes so great that it seems like an act of deliberation or even calculation—as if what really matters most were not the fabulous self-extensions and enhancements inherent in the storyteller's magic of make believe but rather the writer's own petty provincialisms and preoccupations with social status. Such writers often behave as if the slightest notion of a black compatriot as a storybook hero compels them to equate the strongest Negroes with the most helpless. Or so it seems.

William Styron remarked several years ago that even so great a novelist as William Faulkner created Negro characters who, although marvelously drawn, were *observed* rather than *lived*. Even Faulkner, wrote Styron in "This Quiet Dust," an article for *Harper's* magazine (April 1965), "hesitated to think Negro." Styron was also moved to point out that not even Dilsey, who, as he concedes, comes so richly alive in *The Sound and the Fury*, is created from what he calls a sense of withinness. At the last moment, he insists, "Faulkner draws back, and it is no mere happenstance that Dilsey alone among the four central figures from whose points of view the story is told is seen from the outside rather than from that intensely inner vantage point, the interior monologue."

It was also William Styron, the author of *Lie Down in Darkness*,

The Long March, and *Set This House on Fire*, and hence a writer to be reckoned with, who contended, not without some deeply felt passion, that it had become the moral imperative of every white Southerner to break down the old law (which requires the denial of the most obvious of all Southern entanglements) and come to know Negroes. Nor was the fact that Styron himself comes from a lower middle class Tidewater Virginia background likely to strike most Negroes as being either surprising or even curious. On the contrary, many Negroes have long since come to feel that more forthright involvement can almost always be expected from reconstructed or even partially reconstructed Southerners than from any other white people in the United States.

Whatever degree of liberal fellowship the reconstructed Southerner has been able to attain—according to a number of Negroes who are anything but naive or sentimental about such matters—is thoroughgoing and dependable precisely because it is something achieved rather than received. The Northern liberal may or may not back up his protestations with action. But the Southerner's first liberal *remark* is likely to be a bridge burning action in itself. Thus, his statements are often a reliable index to the actual extent of his commitment. Or so many Negroes would have it, and there is the best of Robert Penn Warren, C. Vann Woodward, Ramsey Clark, and yes, Lyndon Johnson to bear them out.

In *The Confessions of Nat Turner* (Random House, 1967), however, Negroes will find very little evidence of the reconstruction many may have felt they had reason to anticipate. The very news that a writer of Styron's talent and determination had undertaken a novel about a Negro whose greatness is a matter of historical record (no matter how smudged) was itself cause enough for high hopes. But even better was the fact that a white Southerner had felt a moral imperative to go all the way and tell the story as his own. Those Negro intellectuals who keep check on such things were downright enthusiastic in their endorsement. Even the black nationalists who place race above literature were at least willing to wait and see. After all, Negritude, as the mulatto exponents of Afro-Americanisimus are wont to say, is only a state of mind, and of course there's that old saying about "room for many more." And besides, as black barber shop politicians were quick to acknowledge, it is infinitely more useful to The Cause for a William Styron to become Nat Turner than for Benny Goodman to become Jimmie Noone or for Stan Getz to become a paleface Lester Young, or numerous others to become Miles Davis and Charlie Parker.

But what Negroes will find in Styron's "confessions" is much the same old failure of sensibility that plagues most other fiction about black people. They will find a Nat Turner, that is to say, that many white people may accept at a safe distance but hardly one with whom Negroes will easily identify. The Nat Turner whom Southern Negro school children celebrate (or used to) in pageants during Negro History Week was a magnificent forefather enshrined in the national pantheon beside the greatest heroes of the Republic. There is an old song which goes:

> Well you can be milk-white and just as rich as cream
> And buy a solid gold carriage with a four-horse team
> But you caint keep the world from movering round
> Or stop old Nat Turner from gaining ground

These folk lyrics are about a dedicated man who did far more than declaim great phrases (later to become national clichés) about taxation without representation, liberty or death, and the times that try men's souls. He was, like all epic heroes, a special breed of man who had given his last full measure of devotion to liberation and dignity.

What Southern Negroes will find in Styron's version, alas, is not the black man's homeric Negro but a white man's Negro (specifically, Mister Stanley M. Elkins') Sambo—a Nat Turner, that is to say, who has been emasculated and reduced to fit all too snugly into a personality structure based on highly questionable and essentially irrelevant conjectures about servility (to which Styron has added a neo-Reichean hypothesis about the correlation between sex repression and revolutionary leadership). Instead of the man of meditation who fasted and prayed to become the Moses of his people, the good shepherd who left a legacy of activism to American ministers which was never more operative than at present, both black and white men of the gospel will find here a black man who really wants to marry somebody's white sister—a man with a sex hangup who goes out into the wilderness to meditate only to get a simple thing like freedom all but hopelessly confused with masturbation while having fantasies about white women.

Ironically, in spite of Styron's expressed intention to get deeper inside his Negro hero than Faulkner did, he seems somehow to have begun by overlooking the fact that the *Negro* conception of Nat Turner was already geared to the dynamics of ritual and myth and hence to literature. In any event, his own seems to have been restricted to such assumptions as underlie sociopolitical science and hence the melodramatic success story. Thus, the Nat Turner who nourished the hopes of Negroes is a tragic hero who symbolizes the human spirit victorious in defeat. Whereas Styron has been able to concede him only "a kind of triumph"—a sort of social science B-plus for effort— for almost succeeding. As if the definition of success were suddenly limited to the consummation of a revolution (which would have annihilated all of Styron's great grandparents) and thus as if heroism were being measured only in terms of its concrete military contribution to the class struggle. (To concede a "kind of triumph" to Robert E. Lee is readily understandable and appropriate. Lee fought on the wrong side and became the biggest loser in the nation's history. But he also became one of the nation's greatest symbols of dignity in defeat.)

But then "This Quiet Dust" shows Styron, who ordinarily is anything but a dialectical materialist, falling into the trap of establishing a Marxist context at the very outset, misled perhaps by too many one-sided historians. Styron *disagrees* with Marxist historian Herbert Aptheker. But he does not reject Aptheker's frame of reference. Aptheker seems to be seeking revolutionary potential. Styron is talking about a failed potential of the same kind. Anyway, he seems to have begun by accepting the old pro-slavery image of white brutality and black docility recently resurrected by historian Elkins, the father of Samboism, in the interest of his own Marx-Freud or psychopolitical theory of black castration. Negro students are likely to find it absolutely incredible that a would-be soul brother could so fail to appreciate what "troublesome property" their ancestors were as to write, as Styron does, that for two hundred and fifty years slavery was "singularly free of organized uprisings, plots and rebellions." Compare this with the non-Marxist view of U. B. Phillips (in *Life and Labor in the Old South*): "The advertising columns of the newspapers bustled with notices of runaways; and no plantation record which has come to my hand is without mention of them."

Styron's failure of sensibility, because of which the best he has been able to do by his own choice of a darling protagonist is to make him a somewhat queer exception to black emasculation, is due at least in part to an overexposure to untenable historical information. After all, Elkins, perhaps too impressed by Nazi cold bloodedness, oversells the psychological damage of oppression on Negroes while making next to nothing of what the never relaxed preoccupation with black codes, fugitive slave laws, patrol systems, and disciplinary cruelty did to white people. The slave owners and drivers like many present-day police were not simply high-handed and callous, they were mostly always on the edge of hysteria from the fear of black uprisings.

Perhaps what on balance is almost certain to strike many Negroes as the pathetic rather than the heroic quality of the action in *The Confessions* also comes from not relying on Negro folk heritage. To Styron the story of Turner's insurrection is not an exemplary endeavor (ending with Nat in jail, echoing, say, Prometheus bound) but only a historical irony, "a decisive factor in the ultimate triumph of the pro-slavery forces."

It so happens, however, that the Nat Turner of Negro folklore is not only a figure ready-made for bards, gleemen, and dramatists but is also one that stands up well under careful documentation. He is, for example, also the Nat Turner of so scholarly a historian as Kenneth Stampp, for whom Turner's forty-eight-hour feat was "an event which produced in the South something resembling a mass trauma, from which the whites had not recovered three decades later. The danger that other Nat Turners might emerge, that even more serious insurrections might someday occur, became an enduring concern as long as the peculiar institution survived. Pro-slavery writers boldly asserted that Southerners did not fear their slaves—but fear of rebellion, sometimes vague, sometimes acute, was with them always."

Now, reviewers who have seized upon white post-insurrection atrocities as a precedent for an inevitable and overwhelming defeat of black militants by the white backlash have not only allowed their need for historical reassurance to becloud the actual historical significance of valid literary implications, but could only have done so by neglecting their homework in U.S. history in the process. "The shock of Nat Turner caused Southerners to take preventive measures," Stampp reports, "but these," he adds, "never eliminated their apprehension *or the actual danger.* [Italics added.] Hardly a year passed without some kind of alarming disturbance somewhere in the South. When no real conspiracy existed, wild rumors often agitated the whites and at times came close to creating an insurrection panic."

The fact is, slavery survived for only thirty-two years more. Emancipation was proclaimed in 1863. Moreover, almost every major figure of the Civil War was already alive at the time of Nat Turner's rebellion. Lincoln himself was twenty-two years old and a flatboatman about to enter politics. Grant was nine. Sherman was eleven. Jefferson Davis, twenty-three, and Robert E. Lee, twenty-four, were both officers already out of West Point. Frederick Douglass was fourteen. Harriet Tubman was eight. William Lloyd Garrison was twenty-six, and Harriet Beecher Stowe was twenty!

As for such a statement as, "Ask any Negro if he is prepared to kill a white man and if he says yes, you may be sure that he is indulging in the sheerest brag," which Styron puts into the mouth of Nat Turner, it would have been regarded as the sheerest nonsense by precisely those Confederate soldiers who defeated the Union's black regiment (the Massachusetts 54th), led by the splendid young white colonel, Robert Shaw, Harvard '60, in the Battle of Fort Wagner. But speaking of ironies, for a scene that at best has only a questionable basis in fact Styron has invented a white Major who, while counter-attacking Turner with integrated forces, says, "That's the spirit boys . . . fire away lads." Which should remind Negroes of nothing so much as Colonel Shaw's dying exhortation to his Negro troops, "Onward boys."

That William Styron is a novelist who is capable of extraordinary self-extension is obvious to anyone who is familiar with the effects he achieved with the interior monologue of Peyton, the central female character of *Lie Down in Darkness*. Nevertheless, he may have done better to use another or perhaps even several different points of view for *The Confessions of Nat Turner*. The withinness of the first-person narration, after all, is not necessarily the best way to tell a story. As the in-character speculations of white Southern types, some of Styron's misconceptions may have come off as brilliant, creative details. As the thoughts of Nat Turner they will probably strike most Negroes as ridiculous. It is hard to believe that either the author of Uncle Remus or William Faulkner could ever have written, "The life of a little nigger child is dull beyond recounting," to say nothing of presenting it as the conception of a Negro, certainly not one who has reached page 138 of a highly poetic 428 page confession.

The moral imperative to know Negroes does not necessarily require other people to "think Negro." But storytellers who would do so must in effect be able to sing the spirituals and/or swing the blues (as, for example, Stephen Vincent Benét did in his story "Freedom's a Hard-Bought Thing"). A narrator who is properly tuned in on what underlies the spirituals would hardly allow the kind of vile language in the presence of a man of God like Nat Turner that a Harlem poolroom hoodlum would not tolerate in the presence of any known minister.

As for swinging the blues, the affirmative beat of which is always geared to the rugged facts of life, if you run Schillinger exercises instead of riffing down-home, you only *think* you're swinging. Which, of course, also applies to any Negro writer who assumes that "black consciousness" is only a matter of *saying* you're black while writing about black experience.

JAMES BALDWIN, PROTEST FICTION, AND THE BLUES TRADITION

Not so very long ago, as these things are reckoned in the annals of human letters, James Baldwin, then a promising young Greenwich Village intellectual from Harlem, wrote an article for *Partisan Review* (June 1949) about *Uncle Tom's Cabin*. It was called "Everybody's Protest Novel," and what made it especially significant was the fact that in it Baldwin, a Negro whose personal commitment to militant social and political action was unquestionable, seemed to be firmly and completely, if somewhat hastily, rejecting social protest in fiction as bad art, a mirror of confusion, dishonesty, and panic, as sentimental fantasy connecting nowhere with reality.

He stated that the avowed aim of such fiction was to bring greater freedom to the oppressed. But he was unenthusiastic about this lofty purpose in itself, nor did he share the then current optimism about the effectiveness of books produced by those committed to it. In fact, he was convinced that "novels of oppression written by Negroes . . . actually reinforce . . . . the principles which activate the oppression they decry."

Baldwin overstated his case, of course, but many serious students of American literature were very much impressed by what they thought all of this implied about his own ambitions as a writer. They assumed that more than anything else he was stating his own personal objections to the narrowness of propaganda fiction as such. They assumed that whatever else was intended, his statements about Harriet Beecher Stowe represented his own esthetic orientation. It is easy to see why. "She was," he wrote, "not so much a novelist as an impassioned pamphleteer; her book was not intended to do anything more than prove that slavery was wrong; was, in fact, perfectly horrible. This makes material for a pamphlet but it is hardly enough for a novel. . . ."

At this time Baldwin seemed very much concerned about the fact that he was living in an over-mechanized civilization which overlooked, denied, and evaded man's complexity, treated him as a time-saving invention, a deplorable conundrum to be explained by science. Protest fiction, he felt, was a part of all this, a formula created "to find a lie more palatable than the truth." But as for himself, he was seeking himself and the power to free himself not in the mechanical formulas and in causes, but within what he called a "web of ambiguity, paradox, hunger, danger, and darkness." It was the power of revelation, he declared, that was "the business of the novelist, this journey toward a more vast reality which must take precedence over all other claims."

He then went on to indict *Uncle Tom's Cabin* for, among other things, its self-righteous sentimentality and its senseless and unmotivated brutality, including a theological terror of blackness and damnation. He also called it the prototype of the American protest novel, and in the process he described the hero of Richard Wright's *Native Son*, the most celebrated protest novel of the day, as Uncle Tom's descendant, an exactly opposite portrait perhaps but flesh of Tom's flesh. But then Wright himself had called the people of his previous book by its title, *Uncle Tom's Children*. There was no argument on that score. There was, however, or so it seemed at the time, a more fundamental conflict. Richard Wright seemed to represent the very qualities in fiction that James Baldwin deplored most heatedly.

In fact, the very attempt of fiction such as Wright's to improve the conditions of life was regarded by Baldwin at that time as a betrayal of life. The tragedy of the hero of *Native Son*, he wrote, was not that he was cold, hungry, black or American but that he has accepted a theology that denies him life, "that he admits the possibility of his being subhuman and feels constrained therefore to battle for his humanity." Baldwin then concluded his article as follows: "The failure of the protest novel lies in its rejection of life, the human being, the denial of his beauty, dread, power, in its insistence that it is his categorization alone which is real and which cannot be transcended."

Some two years later, Baldwin, then a very special young U.S. expatriate from Greenwich Village and the streets of Harlem living in Paris among other U.S. expatriates from Greenwich Village, the Ivy League, the Big Ten, and even the genteel South, and among Africans mostly from the French colonies, and not far from the French existentialists, continued his by then much admired remarks about protest fiction. In another article, "Many Thousands Gone," also for *Partisan Review* (November–December 1951), he took *Native Son* to task again. A necessary dimension had been cut away, he said at one point, because the other Negroes in the story are seen only from Bigger Thomas' limited point of view, "this dimension being the relationship that Negroes bear to one another, that depth of involvement and unspoken recognition of shared experience which creates a way of life."

He also characterized the climate of *Native Son* as one of anarchy and unmotivated and unapprehended disaster; "and it is this climate common to most Negro protest novels," he went on, "which has led us all to believe that in Negro life there exists no tradition, no field of manners, no possibility of ritual intercourse, such as may, for example, sustain the Jew even after he has left his father's house." And then came the following highly suggestive statement: "But the fact is not that the Negro has no tradition, but that there has as yet arrived no sensibility sufficiently profound and tough to make this tradition articulate."

At the time the implications seemed unmistakable. It was assumed by almost everybody concerned about such matters, that all this was still another indication that here was a young writer-in-progress whose single passion was to give his own fiction greater human depth and richer historical reverberation than he had found in any of the novels he mentioned.

Overlooked in all of the enthusiasm, however, was the astonishing fact that in addition to *Uncle Tom's Cabin* and *Native Son*, Baldwin had mentioned only *Gentleman's Agreement, The Postman Always Rings Twice, Kingsblood Royal* and *If He Hollers Let Him Go* (!), and had alluded to *The Sound and the Fury*, one of the outstanding achievements of modern fiction, only to protest an alleged racial discrimination. But perhaps this was deliberately overlooked. After all it was the assumed promise that really mattered. The means of fulfillment could always be evolved in the process. At any rate, it is not erudition as such that counts in a novelist.

Or isn't it? At least for something? As a matter of fact the very same paragraph in which Baldwin declared the existence of an as yet unrealistically articulated Negro tradition, contains a significant clue to his subsequent difficulties and confusions as a serious writer and the clue concerns a matter of erudition. "For a tradition," he continued, "expresses, after all, *nothing more* than the long and painful experience of a people; it comes out of the battle waged to maintain their integrity or, to put it more simply, out of their struggle to survive." (Italics added.) And then in the next sentence he added the following observation: ". . . when we speak of the Jewish tradition, we are speaking of centuries of exile and persecution, of the strength which endured and the sensibility which discovered in it the high possibility of the moral victory."

All of which is utterly confusing. Baldwin doesn't mention a single Jewish novel that would justify such a statement. And no wonder. Whatever else the great Jewish tradition in literature represents, it not only represents protest, it is *characterized* by a great deal of protest as such. But then perhaps Baldwin had built-in his confusion at the very outset. A tradition involves *much* more than the long and painful experiences of a people. The modern Jewish tradition, which someone has referred to as an instantly erectable wailing wall, may well represent centuries of exile and persecution, but it also represents much more. As did the ancient Greek and Roman traditions. As do the modern French and English traditions.

As for the tradition of U.S. Negroes, Baldwin may or may not realize that he is making a fundamental statement about it when he says that it is only in music that the Negro in America has been able to tell his story. Actually this story is also told in folktales and lore, sayings, jokes, and various other forms. Nonetheless, music does contain the most comprehensive rendering of the complexities of the American Negro experience. Whatever the reason, very few U.S. Negro writers (or painters, for example) rank in range and achievement beside musicians like Louis Armstrong, Scott Joplin, or even Charlie Parker, not to mention the great Kansas City stylists and Duke Ellington.

But it should be clear that what U.S. Negro musicians express represents far more than the fact that American black folks been 'buked and been scorned and nobody know de trouble dey seen. Distinctive as it is, U.S. Negro music, like U.S. Negro life, is, after all, or rather first of all, also inseparable from life in the United States at large. Thus, as an art form it is a direct product of the U.S. Negro sensibility, but it is a by-product, so to speak, of all the cultural elements that brought that sensibility into being in the first place. The spirituals, for example, always expressed more than a proletarian reaction to poor pay and bad working conditions. They did reflect life on the plantation and the effects of political bondage; but they were also a profound and universally moving expression of Protestant Christianity, interwoven with New England Puritanism, and frontier elements, American aspirations in general and many other things, including an active physical existence and a rich, robust, and highly imaginative conception of life itself.

As for the blues, they affirm not only U.S. Negro life in all of its arbitrary complexities and not only life in America in all of its infinite confusions, they affirm life and humanity itself in the very process of confronting failures and existentialistic absurdities. The spirit of the blues moves in the opposite direction from ashes and sackcloth, self-pity, self-hatred, and suicide. As a matter of fact the dirtiest, meanest, and most low-down blues are not only not depressing, they function like an instantaneous aphrodisiac! And there are also significant implications of affirmation inherent in the basic fact that U.S. Negro music has always been a part of a great tradition of dance and physical labor.

All of which (and more) would seem to be of immediate and fundamental interest to any serious student of American culture, to say nothing of a serious writer of American fiction. And yet James Baldwin, for all his understandable dissatisfaction with the thinness of Richard Wright's characters and situations, and for all his fine, youthful arrogance about a sensibility sufficiently profound and tough to make the Negro tradition articulate, has never written in terms of any of the sustaining actualities of that tradition in any of his own stories.

Instead, he has relied more and more on the abstract categories of social research and less and less on the poetic insights of the creative artist. So much so that the very characteristics of protest fiction which he once deplored in the work of Harriet Beecher Stowe and Richard Wright now seem to be his stock in trade; they are in any case the things he is now world famous for. His best-selling novel *Another Country*, for instance, reflects very little of the rich, complex, and ambivalent sensibility of the novelist, very little indeed, no more than does the polemical essay *The Fire Next Time*. What it actually reflects in this connection, is the author's involvement with oversimplified library and laboratory theories and conjectures about the negative effects of racial oppression.

And like *Native Son*, it does so for a very good reason. It was designed to serve a very worthy cause, the cause of greater political, social, and economic freedom and opportunity for Negroes in the United States. And the current civil rights movement has profited from his recent books and his position as a public figure in many very tangible ways. In fact, he has become one of the best known heroes of the Negro revolution, a citizen spokesman, as eloquent in his own way as was citizen polemicist Tom Paine in the Revolution of '76, a major achievement in itself.

Polemics, however, are not likely to be epics. They are likely to be pamphlets, even when they are disguised as stories and plays. Thus, ironically enough, Baldwin's historical role in the civil rights struggle has also been all but indistinguishable from the one played by Harriet Beecher Stowe in the Civil War. And with some of the same exasperating confusion. For in spite of what he once declared about near paranoiac novels of oppression actually reinforcing the principles that activate the conditions they decry, he himself has found it expedient in his work to degrade U.S. Negro life to the level of the sub-human in the very process of pleading the Negro's humanity—something he once said one had only to accept!

Baldwin writes about Harlem, for example, with an evangelical sense of moral outrage, and his declarations on this subject are said to have stirred the conscience of the nation. But he never really accounts for the tradition that supports Harlem's hard headed faith in democracy, its muscular Christianity, its cultural flexibility, nor does he account for its universally celebrated commitment to elegance in motion, to colorful speech idioms, to high style, not only in personal deportment but even in the handling of mechanical devices. Intentionally or not, much of what he says implicitly denies the very existence of Harlem's fantastically knowing satire, its profound awareness and rejection of so much that is essentially ridiculous in downtown doings. Sometimes he writes as if he had never heard the comedians at the Apollo Theatre. Life in Harlem is the very stuff of romance and fiction, even as was life in Chaucer's England, Cervantes' Spain, Rabelais' France.

But what Baldwin writes about is not really life in Harlem. He writes about the economic and social conditions in Harlem, the material *plight* of Harlem. But far from writing in terms of a U.S. Negro tradition, he confuses everything with Jewish tradition and writes about life in a black ghetto! In point of fact, James Baldwin, like most native-born U.S. Negroes, is probably a part-white Anglo-Saxon Protestant of Southern derivation. Sometimes he likes to say that he comes from a long line of field hands (and maybe a Texas sheriff or so, too), but he often writes as if he were really a black, brown, or beige New York Jewish intellectual of immigrant parents. On these occasions, there is very little to indicate that the spellbinding power of much of his polemical eloquence really comes out of his background as a boy-preacher in a Harlem storefront church.

A serious novelist, like all other good citizens, should, needless to say, support worthy political causes; but that he should distort his work to do so is another matter altogether. In "Everybody's Protest Novel," Baldwin strongly implied that protest and distortion were inseparable, that protest fiction insists on false categories, rejects life, decries the beauty and power of human beings. But are these generalizations necessarily so? One has to think only of the basic and very clear-cut element of protest in all of the fiction of James Joyce. And among other outstanding novels of the twentieth century alone, what of *The Sun Also Rises*, *Light in August*, *The Magic Mountain*, *The Castle*, or, for that matter, *The Great Gatsby*? (The element of social protest as such underlies as much of the action in the upper middle class world of *The Great Gatsby* as it does in the revolutionary proletarian milieu of André Malraux's *Man's Fate*.)

Nor is the element of propaganda in itself necessarily detrimental. The advertisement of alleged values is a fundamental aspect of all literature, as is the damnation of all that would jeopardize or destroy what is held to be of value. In this sense, Henry James, of all people, produced some of the best propaganda ever written. There is no doubt in anybody's mind that the author of *The Ambassadors* and *The Turn of the Screw* was for goodness and against evil, and he made a convincing case for his position; but he did not oversimplify the virtues of his heroes, the vices of his villains, the complexity of their situation, or the ambiguity of their motives.

But perhaps Baldwin had in mind political propaganda as such, which of its very nature almost always tends to gear itself to expedient means and immediate action. Perhaps this does create very special problems for the artist. Perhaps it leads him in spite of himself to oversimplify all situations in terms of the remedial program to which he is committed, and of course this could easily involve him in the kind of writing that produces election campaign slogans and advertising copy for cure-all medicines. But in these terms, political propaganda contains no *unique* dangers. Propaganda that oversimplifies life in terms of faith, hope, charity or romantic love produces a distortion of reality which is every bit as misleading.

Nevertheless, there are many reasons why it is all but impossible for a serious writer of fiction to engage his craft as such in a political cause, no matter how worthy, without violating his very special integrity as an artist in some serious way. All of these reasons are complicated and some may seem downright questionable, but perhaps none is more important than the fact that, as well-meaning as he may be, the truly serious novelist has what almost amounts to an ambivalence toward the human predicament. Alarming as such ambivalence may seem, it is really fundamental to his open-minded search for the essential truth of human experience.

There is first of all the serious novelist's complex awareness of the burdensome but sobering fact that there is some goodness in bad people however bad they are, and some badness or at least some flaw or weakness in good people however dear. In fact, sometimes the artist comes pretty close to being politically suspect; because on the one hand he is always proclaiming his love for mankind and on the other he is forever giving the devil his due!

And then there is a crucial ambivalence in his eternal and even infernal involvement with the ironies of *antagonistic cooperation!* He is all for achieving the good society, the salubrious situation, the excellent environment. But at the same time he insists that the beautiful community does not automatically produce either beautiful people who stay good or sweetness and light that lasts forever afterwards. Not only this, but he actually seems to be more excited about the fact that sorry situations, ugly communities, trying circumstances, and impossible environments, along with whatever else they do, *of their very nature* produce not only good people but incomparable *heroes* who come from the awful darkness but bring sweetness and light.

Perhaps it is in the nature of things that activists, whether young or middle-aged, will have little patience with such intellectual checks and balances. Nevertheless, the serious apprentice to the art of fiction can never afford to dispense with them.

II

For several years before Baldwin's articles, Richard Wright was a famous U.S. Negro expatriate living in Paris among the most famous French existentialists, who then were having a field day protesting against U.S. can goods, refrigerators, automobiles, and most of all U.S. dollars in the hands of U.S. citizens. Wright, who seemed to regard himself as, so to speak, U.S. Negro-in-residence, gave them additional U.S. absurdities and atrocities to protest about. He also liked to function as American political pundit for the African colonials along the boulevards and around the old Latin Quarter.

He was by way of becoming something of an existentialist himself, but he was still given to ripping red hot pages of accusations from his outraged and smoldering typewriter and angrily flinging them all the way back across the Atlantic and into the guilt ridden lap of America. During this time, he also flung one such book at the guilt ridden face of pagan Spain and two or three at the guilt ridden face of white folks everywhere.

It was bad enough that the fiction Wright began to turn out during this time was even worse than that of Jean-Paul Sartre (which was really going some, by the way); much more important is the fact that for all the down-home signifying and uptown sassiness he put Sartre and Simone de Beauvoir hip to, or maybe precisely because of it, he was unable to keep the ever square but news prone Mister Sartre, the world's fastest academic hip-shooter, from being sucked in on the politically benevolent racist notions of *negritude*, an all but hopelessly confused theory or doctrine of international Negroism—or is it black nationalist internationalism?

At any rate, negritude, notion or doctrine, not only tends to mistake tradition (or cultural inheritance) for racial inheritance (or racial mysticism), it also encourages the kind of esthetic nonsense that has involved an alarming and increasing number of young and not so young U.S. Negroes in programs, movements, and organizations that can only make it even more difficult for them to realize the infinite potential of the black dimensions of the *American* tradition.

Most of the programs for the promotion of what sometimes is called the "black arts" are more political than anything else, and naively political at that. Many so-called Black Artists identify themselves not with the United States but with Africa, which is political naiveté coupled with an incredible disregard for the dynamics of socio-cultural evolution. Politically naive also is their amusing disregard for the national boundaries on the continent of Africa. Americans that they are, they seem to be forever confusing the countries of Africa with the states of the United States. And if this is pan-Africanism, then how naive can you get?

Some of the black arts affiliates are anti-American, anti-American white folks, that is. At least they pretend to be, some belligerently so. But so far, what they intend to accomplish either in government or the arts is not very clear. So far it has only added up to a whole lot of black anarchy, which of course is considered to be a legitimate enough objective by some ideologies, and not for such pseudo-sanguinary/pseudo-nasty esthetic reasons as may be bragged about during some obscene intellectual seance in some Greenwich Village night club where the speakers say another four-letter word when they really mean spit and confuse blood with strawberry Kool-Aid.

Whatever their objectives and however political, every last one of the so-called black arts movements seems to be commercially oriented toward white American audiences above all others; and curiously enough not one is seriously considered to be subversive. Far from it. As a matter of fact, most of the promotions, encouragement, and financial underwriting which is not smuggled in from abroad comes from devoted white patrons. But that is a very special story in itself, as is the fact that for his own perverse reasons both personal and political, the U.S. white who involves himself in these activities seems to regard the whole thing as some new fashionable outrageous but very safe game in which he is not so much rejected as envied and not so much ignored as wooed! Roughly perhaps, but he seems to like it like that.

In some ways, it all seems like one of those boring acts from one of those third rate but ever clever clown shows by the grand old off-Broadway darling of the beatniks and Susan Sontag's campfire girls, Jean Genet, the French scatologist whom J.-P. Sartre calls a modern saint! Indeed, for all its homemade overtones of Uncle Tom's chillun scandalizing Miss Ann and Mister Charley in front of company, most of the pretentiously aggressive racism in the black arts movement in New York, seems to come from the Genet play that has been translated as *The Blacks*. (Incidentally, the French title of this play is not *Les Noirs* but rather *Les Nègres*, which to U.S. Negroes usually means something else altogether!)

In other ways, however, one is also reminded of some of the less political but by no means less naive capers that characterized so much of the so-called Negro renaissance back in the nineteen twenties. This New Negro movement, as it was sometimes called, was also a black arts movement encouraged and supported by white people. The positive role played by the renaissance in the development of black artist self-consciousness is not simply to be conceded but celebrated. *The New Negro*, Alain Locke's anthology of the movement, is still an outstanding landmark in the history of black American expression. But to the extent that the renaissance was influenced by decadent white esthetes who confused black U.S. peasants with jungle aborigines, it also encouraged and subsidized more primitive abandon between the Hudson and Harlem rivers in uptown Manhattan than ever existed near the Congo. In fact, actual primitive life is nothing if not formal. Primitive behavior is the very opposite of wild abandon. It conforms to taboos. Abandon, like bad manners and crime, is not inherent in the restrictions of primitive discipline by any means. It is rather one of those natural products of the freedom and individuality that comes with what is called civilization. It is the super-civilized avant garde bohemian, not the superstition-ridden savage, who is forever and ever in wild eyed, hot-collar, soap-box, street-marching or window-breaking rebellion against all sorts of restrictions—some of them purely imaginary.

The current black arts movement, like the one before it, is nothing if not avant garde, ersatz tiger noises underneath the bamboo tree boom boom and all. But the avant garde sort of thing is not exclusive to the cognoscenti these days. It also makes sensational news copy for the New York dailies, *Time*, *Life*, *Look*, *Newsweek*, NBC-TV, CBS, and ABC. Some of it gets staged through the angelic efforts of New York theatrical matrons, some of them female. Some of it gets printed by the big, fat publishing firms; and some of it comes out on Columbia and RCA Victor records.

Meanwhile, one can only hope that in spite of the popularity of negritude in some circles at the moment, there are also U.S. Negro writers whose literary insights will enable them to do much more than turn out shrill, defensive, and predictable counter-propaganda against the doctrine of white supremacy, as important as this propaganda is. Their literary insights should also enable these writers to realize that they have as much responsibility for representing the mainstream of U.S. life as anybody else. It is always open season on the truth, and there never was a time when one had to be white to take a shot at it.

Indeed, if there is one thing that all U.S. Negroes think they know about American literature it is that white writers seldom deal with the realities of American experience. Negroes think they know far too much about the everyday doings of the white people around them to be taken in by the phony bedtime stories in most of the books and magazines, in spite of the fact that most white people seem to allow themselves to be taken in by them. Black people think they know quite a bit about how this and much more happens. One can only hope they learn how to get into fiction some of what they really know and how they truly feel, rather than what somebody tells them they are supposed to know and how somebody tells them they're supposed to feel.

Many white writers go on year after year turning out book after solipsistic book in which they pretend that the world is white. In this they go hand in hand with most U.S. journalists, photographers, and motion picture producers. But any U.S. Negro sharecropper surrounded by a field of snow white cotton knows better than that. And he knows that the world is not black either. He knows that the only color the world has is the color of infinity. Whatever that color may be. This particular sort of U.S. Negro knows very well that the white man, for all his relative political and economic power, is not free. Perhaps not many Negroes have read *The Waste Land*, but this particular one has heard the blues, and some of them really are about Miss Ann and Mr. Charley. But he is not cheered by the fix they're in; he is sobered by it—as his great great grandfather was sobered by the spirituals that sometimes whispered *nobody knows the trouble I seen when I seen what was really happening in the* BIG HOUSE. No wonder great great grandpa took religious salvation so seriously.

And yet your negritude promoter, for all his bamboo boom boom jive, often gives the impression that he is out to paint the world black only because he believes it's white and that white is really all right but he's going to change it out of spite! But who knows? Perhaps this is only a part of the political fakery involved in this kind of confidence game. How *could* one know? Your negritude promoter sometimes also identifies himself with the most militant integrationists!

Thus does the American species of negritude bring itself by a commodious vicus of recirculation back to protest fiction and Marxist environs. Whereupon enter the old effeterati, now become the politerati, doing an ofay version of the one-butt shuffle to the fading but still audible strains of the old nineteen thirties dialectical boogie woogie.

These white friends of the Negro, that is to say, friends and friends-in-print of Negro Causes (or is it the Negro Cause?), are very sincere in many ways, and they have done much good in some ways. But they have also done and continue to do untold harm in a number of perhaps unrecognized but very fundamental ways. They encourage inferior standards and values by accepting or pretending to accept shoddy and immature workmanship. They sanction inadequate education by going along with what they know, if they know anything, is intellectual rubbish and esthetic nonsense. And furthermore, only the most snobbish and most self-indulgent condescension would permit them to tolerate so much arrogant stupidity and subversive irresponsibility.

It is about time U.S. Negro writers realized that whether or not these particular white friends themselves have any literary taste and maturity (and one wonders), they do not assume that Negro writers have any. Nor do they assume that Negro writers have any major literary ambitions. They seem to assume that for Negroes literature is simply incidental to protest. And it is about time Negro writers began to wonder why. It is about time they started asking themselves why these people are happiest when Negroes are moaning and groaning about black troubles and miseries. It is undeniable that these friends also tolerate and seem to enjoy being insulted, accused, bullied or baldwinized from time to time, but that is another one of those stories about choosing one's own punishment.

And it should also be remembered that these people never show real enthusiasm for the affirmative elements in U.S. Negro life. Quite the contrary. These are the self-same people who insist on explaining away qualities such as tough-minded forbearance and faith, compassion, musical expressiveness, and even physical coordination as being marks of oppression or even embarrassing evidence of racial inferiority.

U.S. writers and would-be writers who have any valid literary ambitions whatsoever obviously cannot afford to allow themselves to be overimpressed by the alleged superiority of the academic or professional background of their white-friends-in-print. Only people who have learned nothing at all from literary biography and have no fundamental understanding of the ironies involved in the creative process itself would hold, as these people so often do, that Negroes will be able to write first rate novels *only after* all oppression is removed, *only after* such time as Negroes no longer feel alienated from the mainstream of U.S. life.

What could be more misleading? Writers have always thrived on oppression, poverty, alienation, and the like. Feodor Dostoevski, for example, was very poor, much oppressed, and in addition to all sorts of other personal problems, he was epileptic. He was certainly alienated. He was imprisoned; and one time he came within minutes of being officially lynched. But he wrote good books. Because he liked good books. Because his mind and imagination functioned in terms of good books. Even in jail. A writer who is oriented toward good books will at least try to write good books. But the sad fact is that there is very little to show that very many U.S. Negro writers have ever actually tried to write major novels.

There is certainly justification for some doubts and even suspicions about the *literary* value of the white-friends-of-the-Negro-Cause. One can only doubt that they know how art comes into being—or suspect that they know only too well. But be that as it may. They *could provide* a literary atmosphere in which Negroes would become oriented toward major works of art. But they do not. They do something else altogether. They actually discourage interest in art by overemphasizing and oversubsidizing the social sciences and by insinuating that Negroes who are interested in great art are not really interested in the everyday problems and realities of life. They accuse them of trying to escape the rigors of oppression by fleeing to the Ivory Tower, as if to say great art is for later, when and if you get to be as human as white folks. Right now your "thing" is to tell it like it is, which means show your ass!

None of this is intended as any excuse for U.S. Negroes themselves. Many things may be segregated, but great books and great ideas are not. Not really. Not even the Ku Klux Klan has shown any great concern because a Negro was sitting somewhere in a quiet corner reading Goethe or Thomas Mann. (They are much too busy seeing to it that the white pupils get the trade schools first!) No, the argument here is only to indicate the literary quality of the Negro's white well wishers. But to make a long story short, all you have to do is compare the kind of encouragement given by the typical white literary patron with the aspirations of the managers and promoters of Negro prizefighters. Financial double dealing aside, the backers of Negro boxers are out to produce champions of the world.

It is about time all U.S. Negroes took a closer look at all their friends-of-the-cause. To be conned by such self-styled good will as is usual with so many of these cheap-note aristocrats is not only to invite contempt and not only to encourage it, but also to deserve it.

III

Ralph Ellison wrote an article about Richard Wright which was published in the *Antioch Review* in the summer of 1945. This was four years before James Baldwin came to write "Everybody's Protest Novel" and some six before he was to do "Many Thousands Gone." Baldwin, as has been seen, was sharply critical of Wright, who incidentally was an old personal friend and onetime benefactor. Ellison, also an old personal friend, was generous almost to a fault.

So much so that when Wright encountered him shortly afterwards all Wright could do was shake his head in pleased bewilderment, somewhat, one imagines, as the tunesmith of *Body and Soul* must have done upon meeting Coleman Hawkins; and all he could say was almost exactly what one imagines the tunesmith would have said: "Man, you went much further than the book. Much further." (He himself was not to go even as far again.)

All Ellison, a former trumpet player and student of music composition, could do was shake his head in turn and smile reassuringly and reply, "Well, what you wrote made it possible for me to say what I said about it. All I was trying to do was use what you put there. All I was trying to do was play a few riffs on your tune. It was your tune. I just hope I didn't embarrass you. I just hope I did it justice." He did it more than justice.

Ellison's article was a commentary on *Black Boy*. This autobiographical record of Wright's childhood and youth employed all the techniques of fiction and was obviously intended to be a literary work of art as well as a personal document. Ellison called it "Richard Wright's Blues," and his remarks did go far beyond the book itself. They included what the book itself stated, and as in all really perceptive literary criticism, they suggested what was also represented, symbolized, ritualized.

Richard Wright, in spite of the shifts in his formal political affiliations, was always essentially a Marxist thinker. It is true that he maintained, and no doubt believed, that Marxism was only a starting point for Negro writers; and he himself was certainly the kind of intellectual who realized that Negro folklore had important literary significance. He also had a very extensive knowledge of world history and cultures, of ideas as such, and of contemporary world literature. But although his wide intellectual interests, so much broader than those of most other U.S. Negro writers, were a very active part of his everyday writing equipment, he remained primarily a Marxist. He read Eliot, Stein, Joyce, Proust, Hemingway, Gorky, Nexø, and most of the others, and he used much of what he learned, but he was almost always restricted by the provincial limitations of dialectical materialism. He used Freud, for example, primarily to score Marxian points; and even his later involvement with existentialism seemed to have political revolution as its basic motive.

Ellison was very much aware of the comprehensive range of Wright's intellectual and literary background, and in passing he suggested parallels between *Black Boy* and Nehru's *Toward Freedom*, Joyce's *Portrait of the Artist as a Young Man*, Dostoevski's *House of the Dead*, Rousseau's *Confessions*, and Yeats' *Autobiography*. But what impressed him most was that, knowingly or not, Wright had written a book that was in essence a literary equivalent to the blues.

The blues [Ellison wrote] is an impulse to keep the painful details and episodes of a brutal experience alive in one's aching consciousness, to finger its jagged grain, and to transcend it, not by the consolation of philosophy but by squeezing from it a near-tragic, near-comic lyricism. As a form, the blues is an autobiographical chronicle of personal catastrophe expressed lyrically. And certainly Wright's early childhood was crammed with catastrophic incidents. In a few short years his father deserted his mother, he knew intense hunger, he became a drunkard begging drinks from black stevedores in Memphis saloons; he had to flee Arkansas, where an uncle was lynched; he was forced to live with a fanatically religious grandmother in an atmosphere of constant bickering; he was lodged in an orphan asylum; he observed the suffering of his mother, who became a permanent invalid, while fighting off the blows of the poverty-stricken relatives with whom he had to live; he was cheated, beaten and kicked off jobs by white employees who disliked his eagerness to learn a trade; and to these objective circumstances must be added the subjective fact that Wright, with his sensitivity, extreme shyness and intelligence, was a problem child who rejected his family and was by them rejected.

Thus along with the themes, equivalent descriptions of milieu and the perspectives to be found in Joyce, Nehru, Dostoevski, George Moore and Rousseau, *Black Boy* is filled with blues-tempered echoes

of railroad trains, the names of Southern towns and cities, estrange-
ments, fights and flights, deaths and disappointments, charged with
physical and spiritual hungers and pain. And like a blues sung by such
an artist as Bessie Smith, its lyrical prose evokes the paradoxical, almost surreal image of a black boy singing lustily as he probes his own
grievous wound.

"Their attraction" he added, referring again to the blues near the
end of the article, "lies in this, that they at once express both the agony
of life and the possibility of conquering it through sheer toughness of
spirit. They fall short of tragedy only in that they provide no solution,
offer no scapegoat but the self."

Baldwin, who made no mention of *Black Boy* or of Ellison's commentary when he wrote about the Negro tradition and the Negro sensibility in "Many Thousands Gone," once stated in an address at the
New School in New York that as a writer he had modeled himself on
none of the white American writers, not even Hemingway or Faulkner, but on black musicians, black dancers, and so on, even on black
whores (or did one hear right?), and of all most assuredly on the blues
singers. He then spoke lovingly about Billie Holiday and lamented the
current personal and legal difficulties of Ray Charles.

But Baldwin's Broadway play, *Blues for Mister Charlie* (1964), had
very little if anything to do with the blues. It fills the stage with a
highly stylized group of energetic and militant self-righteous Negroes
hollering and screaming and cussing and accusing and talking out of
school and under other folks' clothes, and threatening to raise hell
and all that, but generally feeling as sorry for themselves as if they
had all just come from reading *An American Dilemma*, *The Mark of
Oppression*, and most of the "liberal" magazines. There is an up tempo
beat which *could* go with a classic Kansas City shout, but what comes
out sounds more like the reds than the blues.

Baldwin's criticism of *Native Son* was essentially valid. The people,
the situations, and the motivation in that quasi-realistic novel were
more than oversimplified. They were exaggerated by an overemphasis

on protest as such and by a very specific kind of political protest at that. Oversimplification in these terms does lead almost inevitably to false positions based on false assumptions about human nature itself. Every story whatever its immediate purpose is a story about being man on earth. This is the basis of its universality, the fundamental interest and sense of identification it generates in other people.

If you ignore this and reduce man's whole story to a series of sensational but superficial news items and editorial complaints and accusations, blaming all the bad things that happen to your characters on racial bigotry, you imply that people are primarily concerned with only certain political and social absolutes. You imply that these absolutes are the sine qua non of all human fulfillment. And you also imply that there are people who possess these political and social absolutes, and that these people are on better terms with the world as such and are consequently better people. In other words, no matter how noble your mission, when you oversimplify the reasons why a poor or an oppressed man lies, cheats, steals, betrays, hates, murders, or becomes an alcoholic or addict, you imply that well-to-do, rich, and powerful people don't do these things. *But they do.*

Baldwin in his essays on Wright seemed sensitive to this sort of embarrassment. He accused Wright of trying "to redeem a symbolical monster in social terms," and he spoke of the truth as implying "a devotion to the human being, his freedom and fulfillment; freedom which cannot be legislated, fulfillment which cannot be charted." He also seemed firmly convinced that categories were not real and that man "was not, after all, merely a member of a society or a group"—but "something *resolutely indefinable, unpredictable.*" (Italics added.)

These seemed like the assumptions of a writer who is interested in literature. Assumptions like these underlie all of the world's great stories. The unpredictable is the very stuff of storytelling. It is the very stuff of dramatic power, suspense, thrills, escapades, resolutions; the very stuff of fears, hopes, quests, achievements. It is the very stuff of the human condition.

That a sophisticated intellectual like Richard Wright knew all of this goes without question. But he chose to operate within the framework of his basic political commitment. This was an unfortunate choice. But in spite of his arbitrarily circumscribed point of view, he wrote a number of things that were politically useful, and there were also times, especially in certain parts of *Uncle Tom's Children* and *Black Boy*, when the universal literary values of his work automatically went beyond the material objectives of political ideology.

Now, Baldwin in effect began his literary career by rejecting Wright's achievements as being inadequate and also dangerous. The grounds for his rejection generally seemed solid enough. And he seemed to promise not only something different but something more.

So far he has not fulfilled that promise. The only thing really different about Baldwin's work to date has been his special interest in themes related to the so-called sexual revolution. And this is different only from Wright; it is not at all different from a lot of other writers these days, all of them white. Otherwise, Richard Wright is the author that James Baldwin the novelist, playwright, and spokesman resembles more than any other, including Harriet Beecher Stowe.

Baldwin once complained about the climate of anarchy and unmotivated and unapprehended disaster in *Native Son*. But in his own recent novel, *Another Country*, he seems to think this sort of climate has some profound, absurd, existentialist significance. It does not. Wright's existentialism, such as it was, had led to the same mistake in *The Outsider*, which Baldwin had already spotted in *Native Son*.

Both Baldwin and Wright seem to have overlooked the rich possibilities available to them in the blues tradition. Both profess great pride in Negroes, but in practice seem to rate the theories and abstract formulations of French existentialism over the infinitely richer wisdom of the blues. Both, like most other intellectuals (and/or most of the social scientists), seem to have missed what should be one of the most obvious implications of the blues tradition: *It is the product of the most complicated culture, and therefore the most complicated sensibility in the modern world.*

The United States has all of the complexities of all the other nations in the world, and also many of its own which most other nations are either not yet advanced enough or powerful enough to have. And in all these areas of U.S. life one finds Negroes. They are always reacting to what is happening and their reactions become elements in the blues tradition. Racial snobbishness and U.S. provincialism and deference to things European keep many Americans from realizing it, but the most old-fashioned elements in the blues tradition are often avant garde by the artistic standards of most other countries in the world. Europeans seem to appreciate this better than most Americans.

Somehow or other James Baldwin and Richard Wright seem to have missed the literary possibilities suggested by this. Ralph Ellison has not. He went beyond Richard Wright in the very process of commenting on *Black Boy*, and he went beyond every other American writer of his generation when he wrote his first novel. The possibilities he had talked about in "Richard Wright's Blues" were demonstrated most convincingly when he published *Invisible Man*, probably the most mature first novel, American or whatever, since *Buddenbrooks*. (It was certainly more mature both in craftsmanship and in vision than *This Side of Paradise*. And, of course, Hemingway's first was not *The Sun Also Rises* but *Torrents of Spring*, and Faulkner's was *Soldiers' Pay*!)

Invisible Man was *par excellence* the literary extension of the blues. It was as if Ellison had taken an everyday twelve bar blues tune (by a man from down South sitting in a manhole up North in New York singing and signifying about how he got there) and scored it for full orchestra. This was indeed something different and something more than run of the mill U.S. fiction. It had new dimensions of rhetorical resonance (based on lying and signifying). It employed a startlingly effective fusion of narrative realism and surrealism; and it achieved a unique but compelling combination of the naturalistic, the ridiculous, and the downright hallucinatory.

It was a first rate novel, a blues odyssey, a tall tale about the fantastic misadventures of one American Negro, and at the same time a prototypical story about being not only a twentieth century American but also a twentieth century man, the Negro's obvious predicament symbolizing everybody's essential predicament. And like the blues, and echoing the irrepressibility of America itself, it ended on a note of promise, ironic and ambiguous perhaps, but a note of promise still. The blues with no aid from existentialism have always known that there were no clear-cut solutions for the human situation.

Invisible Man was mainstream American writing in the same sense that U.S. Negro music is mainstream. In spite of his status as an entertainer, or sometimes perhaps as a direct result of it, the Negro jazz musician, representing the very spirit of American life itself, has, it seems, always been oriented to something different and something more. And there is much that all U.S. writers can learn from him about working with American experience in esthetic forms that are vernacular and sophisticated at the same time, particularly and peculiarly American and universally contemporary at the same time.

In terms of cultural assimilation, the blues idiom at its best is Omni-American precisely because it sounds as if it knows the truth about all the other music in the world and is looking for something better. Perhaps someday one will be able to say the same thing about American fiction. Black writers can do much to bring about that day, and there is every reason why they should. They will not do so as long as they mistake the illusions of social science for actuality.

PART III

Getting It Together

IDENTITY, DIVERSITY, AND THE MAINSTREAM

A SHORT HISTORY OF BLACK SELF-CONSCIOUSNESS

The preoccupation with symbols and rituals of black consciousness currently so noticeable among so many civil rights activists and passivists alike is frequently misrepresented as an entirely new development. Some of the slogans and gestures may be new; and it well may be that never before have any Americans insisted in giving such revolutionary significance to a new fashion in *hair texture*. (Once and for all, how much culture and identity can you get from hair texture?) But in most other respects, the present wave of interest in self-definition and self-determination is not an innovation but a resurgence of the exuberant self-delight that characterized the so-called Harlem Renaissance or New Negro movement no longer ago than the nineteen twenties.

The New Negro movement was very specifically concerned with black identity and black heritage. Nor was it unresponsive to social and political matters. But its most significant achievements were in literature and the arts rather than in the area of social revolution. Its outstanding writers included James Weldon Johnson, Alain Locke, Walter White, Claude McKay, Countee Cullen, Rudolph Fisher, Langston Hughes, Jean Toomer, and Arna Bontemps. The artists included Aaron Douglas, Palmer Hayden, Richmond Barthé, and Augusta Savage, and there were "black conscious" performers and entertainers beyond number.

And how can even the most casual student of black culture in the United States not take note of the fact that the decade of the nineteen twenties is still known as the Jazz Age? It was from the Negro musician, not from a white writer named F. Scott Fitzgerald, that this title was derived. The nineteen twenties was the first great hey-day of the jazz- or blues-idiom musician. The music of King Oliver, Bessie Smith, W. C. Handy, Louis Armstrong, Jelly Roll Morton, James P. Johnson, and hundreds of others was impressing an affirmative consciousness of blackness not only upon other Negroes and upon white Americans, but upon the world at large as never before.

Perhaps the most magnificent synthesis, historical continuity and esthetic extension of all of the best elements of the New Negro period are to be found in the music of the Duke Ellington orchestra. No other institution in the United States represents a more deliberate and more persistent effort to come to terms with black heritage as it relates to the ever shifting complexities of contemporary life. Nor has Ellington simply clung to traditional folk forms. Culture hero that he is, he has not only confronted every esthetic challenge of his times, but has grown ever greater in the process. (Someday, Ellington may well come to be regarded as the Frederick Douglass of most black artists. He is already regarded as such by most musicians.)

During the depression of the nineteen thirties, the cultural emphasis generated by the New Negro movement gave way to a direct and very urgent concern with abstract economic theory and a general politicalization of all issues. In consequence (in part at least) black consciousness as such seems to have been de-emphasized in the interests of the polemics of class struggle dialectics, and black culture was redefined in accordance with the integration-oriented policies of friendly but paternalistic white liberals, left wing intellectuals, Communist party organizers, and other do-gooders and supporters of black causes of that period. Blackness as a cultural identity was all but replaced by blackness as an economic and political identity—or condition, plight, and blight. U.S. Negroes, that is to say, were in effect, no longer regarded as black people. They were now the Black Proletariat, the poor, the oppressed, the downtrodden minority. Sometimes, as a matter of fact, it was as if white left wing intellectuals had deliberately confused cultural issues with questions of race. In any case, there came a time (which is not yet passed) when it was not at all unusual for paternalistic white friends of black sufferers to condemn any manifestations of interest in black culture as a medium for identity as racism and separatism. By this time, many white friends even refused to concede that the blues was unique to U.S. Negro life style. Suddenly, music was just music and just as suddenly, non-Negro Benny Goodman, not Louis Armstrong, Fletcher Henderson, Count Basie, or Duke Ellington, was King of Swing, and Gene Krupa, not Chick Webb or Jo Jones, was their dyed-in-the-blue rhythm man. Moreover, they knighted Benny Goodman himself as a big fat liberal because he was nice enough to permit Negroes like Teddy Wilson, Lionel Hampton, and Charlie Christian to perform on the same stage with white "jazz musicians."

Perhaps the most comprehensive example of the post–New Negro attitude toward black experience is found—some current ideologists of blackness will be surprised to learn—in the fiction of Richard Wright, precisely because of its deficiencies. At times, as has been seen, it was as if Wright, who had every reason to know better, regarded Negroes not as acquaintances and relatives to be identified against a very complex cultural background, but rather as human problems struggling to become people. Sometimes Wright also gave the impression that he felt that the writer's basic function was to politicalize everything. Time and again he depersonalized the personalities as well as the motives and even the environment of his characters—in the interest (so far as one can tell) of revolutionary political theory. Few will deny that the social objectives behind Wright's theories were of the very highest order. But neither can it be denied that such theories contributed very little to the promotion of black identity in the sense in which it is being approached by the young people of today. Such theories, in fact, are most likely to lead to an oversimplification of the whole question of identity by their overemphasis on class as if it were the main clue to motives and manners. This, in any case, is where the theories led Wright. In *Black Power*, he seems to have found it easier to identify with Africa as a land of class brothers than as the homeland of some of his most important cultural antecedents.

In the fiction of Richard Wright, many of the same elements of black experience that were so fascinating to Negro writers of the renaissance period, and which the great Negro musicians have never ceased to celebrate (or to be inspired by), are subordinated to political conjecture. Some evidence of Wright's negative regard for the "black consciousness" of the nineteen twenties may be found in his essay "Blue Print for Negro Writing." He wrote there: "Today the question is: Shall Negro writing be for the masses, moulding the lives and consciousness of those masses towards new goals, *or shall it continue begging the question of the Negro's humanity.*" (Italics added.) Then several paragraphs later: "There is a Negro church, a Negro press, a Negro social world, a Negro sporting world, a Negro business world, a Negro school system, Negro professions; in short, a Negro way of life in America. The Negro people did not ask for this, and deep down, though they express themselves through their institutions and adhere to this special way of life, *they do not want it now. This special existence was forced upon them from without by lynch ropes, bayonet and mob rule.* They accepted these negative conditions with the inevitability of a tree which must live or perish in whatever soil it finds itself." (Italics added.)

Perhaps this attitude, which is very much the same as that of self-inflated white welfare workers, accounts at least in part for the fact that the identity of Bigger Thomas, the protagonist of *Native Son*, is more political than black. In any case, as Wright depicts him, such soul brother characteristics as Bigger possesses have much less to do with a total complex life style than with Wright's rather academic conception of the similarity of black violence to the behavior of rats in a maze. Bigger, as Wright makes clear enough in "How 'Bigger' Was Born," an article published in *The Saturday Review of Literature*, is a political symbol, really a parable figure in a political sermon about the revolutionary implications of the oppression of black Americans.

Thus, those who are seriously interested in the actual texture of life in the Chicago of Bigger Thomas (how it felt to be among Negroes, to walk along a South Side street, to sit in a bar, to be in love, etc.) would do well to supplement reading *Native Son* with a dozen or so recordings of Earl Hines' great Grand Terrace orchestra. Indeed, students of black heritage will find it highly rewarding to compare the images that Richard Wright felt were representative of black experience in the nineteen thirties and forties with the music to which black style was literally geared. Despite the fact that the musician has long occupied the position of supreme artist for U.S. Negroes, Wright almost always wrote as if he were totally unrelated to what Count Basie, Jimmie Lunceford, Fats Waller, Lionel Hampton, Louis Jordan, and others were saying about black experience during his day. At a time when Wright was making such statements as, "I thought of the essential bleakness of black life in America . . ." and ". . . I brooded on the cultural barrenness of black life . . ." Duke Ellington, whose audiences were larger than ever and whose orchestra had greater range than ever, was creating "Concerto for Cootie," "Cotton Tail," "Jack the Bear," "Portrait of the Lion," "Bojangles," "Jump for Joy," "In a Mellow Tone," "Sepia Panorama," "Harlem Airshaft," "Ko-Ko"; and for his first concert at Carnegie Hall, that citadel of white European identity, was attempting to make a comprehensive, affirmative statement about black heritage and identity in "Black, Brown, and Beige."

What with all the high pressure propaganda about the brotherhood of man and all the promises of one world (as opposed to the traditional self-aggrandizing nationalistic, or tribalistic, states), the trend away from any special positive emphasis on black consciousness per se continued during World War II and the first years of the United Nations.

Negroes were no less concerned about their rights as American citizens during all this time, to be sure. They made the double "V" sign and worked for victory over fascism abroad and victory over segregation and second class citizenship at home. In point of historical fact, it is the wartime generation that is most responsible for the accelerated activism that has come to be known as the Civil Rights Movement or the Negro Revolution. Nevertheless, that generation, whose leaders by and large were derived directly from the same intellectual environment that had produced Richard Wright, placed little emphasis on black consciousness and black culture. Perhaps the universal prominence of Ellington, Basie, Dizzy Gillespie, and Charlie Parker meant that the crucial role of black consciousness was simply being taken for granted. But the point is that spokesmen did not articulate issues in terms of it.

Given the differences between Ralph Ellison and Richard Wright on the blues idiom, it is not surprising that Ellison's novel, *Invisible Man*, published in 1952, addressed itself in an entirely different manner to the problem of black identity, black heritage, and black consciousness. The protagonist of *Invisible Man*, who becomes politically involved (much the same as Richard Wright or Angelo Herndon did), is a metaphorical ghost in spite of the fact that he has the most obvious physical features. White people see him not as an individual person, but as a problem. In a sense, he is even more invisible to himself. As Ellison once said, "The major flaw in the hero's character is his unquestioning willingness to do what is required of him by others as a way to success, and this was the specific form of his 'innocence.' He goes where he is told to go; he does what he is told to do; he does not even choose his Brotherhood name. It is chosen for him and he accepts it."

The climax of *Invisible Man* is, in itself, a highly significant statement about self-definition. The hero, as if to foreshadow the somewhat more flamboyant gestures of some of the young activists of the nineteen sixties, disengages himself from the ever so integrated but never quite desegregated Brotherhood and goes underground to hibernate and meditate on the relationship of identity to reality.

In view of the troubles of the invisible man, there is no wonder that some older students of black identity have a number of misgivings about Eldridge Cleaver. At first they thought (or hoped) that he was the Invisible Kid coming back up out of his hole and making the scene as a cool stalking Black Panther, using the Constitution like a Mississippi gambler with a deck of cards. So they edged forward waiting for him to start riffing on all the stuff he had learned from Rinehart and Ras the Exhorter, and had been down there getting "together." And then they discovered that not only was he a member of the *Ramparts* magazine brotherhood, but had chosen to define himself largely in terms of the pseudo-existential esthetique du nastiness of Norman Mailer, who confuses militant characteristics with bad niggeristics precisely because he wouldn't know a real bad Negro until one happened to him. That such a promising, young intellectual as Eldridge Cleaver would allow himself to be faked out one inch by the essentially frivolous notions of a jive-time fayboy playboy—to whom the essence of black experience seems to be the Saturday night spree, and to whom jazz is the music of orgasm—instead of utilizing the immensely superior insightfulness of the blues, is enough to scandalize any chicken-shack piano player who ever read a book by Mickey Spillane.

The point of course is not that there is anything inherently wrong about being influenced by white writers. What black writer isn't? The point is that bad taste in white intellectuals is something that black leaders and spokesmen can least afford. Whether white people, including the philanthropic foundations, can afford their customary taste for black hype artists remains to be seen. The fact that Cleaver rejects counter-racism is commendable. But who the hell needs a brown-skinned Norman Mailer?

The current campaign to stimulate greater academic interest in black studies represents a resurgence of appreciation for the black components of American culture. Such campaigns have been a long time coming. Some completely sincere but misinformed campaigners, however, are not nearly as constructive as they so obviously intend to be. They wish to establish a historical context of black achievement. But they often proceed as if respectable traditions of black heroism exist only outside the United States. Yet few glories that they may find to identify with in ancestral Africa are likely to be more directly significant or more immediately applicable than the legacy of courage and devotion to human dignity and freedom that they leave so largely unclaimed at home.

Not that the African past is unimportant. On the contrary, it represents a heritage that merits the most careful and enthusiastic study. But certainly not primarily in the interest of *race* pride, as those who have been overconditioned by the psycho-political folklore of white supremacy insist. And the danger exists that even the slightest emphasis on race pride leads all too easily to what Arthur Schomburg quite accurately labeled "puerile controversy and petty braggadocio."

Schomburg, for whom the famous Schomburg Collection of Negro Literature and History in Harlem is named, placed the fundamental relevance of African culture in clear perspective back in 1925. The following statement from "The Negro Digs Up His Past," which Schomburg contributed to Alain Locke's *The New Negro*, is as applicable to the black studies programs of today as to the Negro renaissance of the nineteen twenties. "Of course," he goes on to say, after having rejected the excesses of black counter-racism, "the racial motive remains legitimately compatible with scientific method and aim. The work our race students now regard as important, they undertake very naturally to overcome, in part, certain handicaps of disparagement and omission too well known to particularize. But they do so *not merely that we may not wrongfully be deprived of the spiritual nourishment of our cultural past, but also that the full story of human collaboration and interdependence may be told and realized.*" (Italics added.) Nor was Schomburg alone in this view. Such major U.S. Negro historians and scholars as Carter G. Woodson, Benjamin Brawley, Charles Wesley, W. E. B. Du Bois, James Weldon Johnson, Benjamin Quarles, and John Hope Franklin, have always regarded a knowledge of Africa as being basic to an adequate understanding of America—so that "the full story of human collaboration and interdependence may be told and realized."

THE ROLE OF THE PRE-AMERICAN PAST

Many Americans of African (and part-African) ancestry who are forever complaining, mostly in the vaguest of generalities, and almost always with more emotion than intellectual conviction, that their black captive forefathers were stripped of their native culture by white Americans often seem to have a conception of culture that is more abstract, romantic, and in truth, pretentious than functional. Neither African nor American culture seems ever to have been, as most polemicists perhaps unwittingly assume, a static system of racial conventions and ornaments. Culture of its very essence is a dynamic, ever accommodating, ever accumulating, ever assimilating environmental phenomenon, whose components (technologies, rituals, and artifacts) are emphasized, de-emphasized, or discarded primarily in accordance with pragmatic environmental requirements, which of course are both physical and intellectual or spiritual.

There is, to be sure, such a thing as the destruction of specific cultural configurations by barbarians and vandals. But even so, time and again history reveals examples of barbarian conquerors becoming modified and sometimes even dominated by key elements of the culture of the very same people they have suppressed politically and economically. In other words, cultural continuity seems to be a matter of competition and endurance in which the fittest elements survive regardless of the social status of those who evolved them. Those rituals and technologies that tend to survive population transplantation seem to do so because they are essentially compatible to and fundamentally useful in changed circumstances. So, for example, the traditional African disposition to refine all movement into dance-like elegance survived in the United States as work rhythms (and playful syncopation) in spite of the fact that African rituals were prohibited and the ceremonial drums were taken away. On the other hand, the medicine man was forcibly replaced by the minister and the doctor— and he has met or is meeting the same fate in Africa!

As for those white American immigrants who faced no slave system and so presumably were not stripped of their "culture," in point of fact they were still stripped by the necessities of pioneer readjustment. Needless to say, they were not stripped altogether—but neither were the black chattel bondsmen. If the African in America was unable to remain an African to the extent that he may have chosen to do so, neither were very many Europeans able to remain Europeans even though they were able to construct exact duplicates of European architecture in Virginia and Maryland—and to the extent that they did remain Europeans, they often were out of practical touch with life around them. Nothing can be more obvious than the fact that for most practical everyday intents and purposes almost all non-English-speaking immigrants were stripped of their native tongue. Nor are French, German, Spanish, and Italian taught in American schools in interest of ethnic identity and pride. They are taught primarily as tools for research. In any case, that the black man was the victim of brutal treatment goes without saying, but how much of his African culture he would have or could have kept intact had he come over as a free settler is a question that should be discussed against the fact that the pressure on "free white Americans" to conform is (as non-Protestants, for example, know very well) greater than is generally admitted. The

question of African survival should also be discussed in full awareness of the fact that the dynamics of American culture are such that
the average American citizen is a cultural pluralist.

II

Many black New Yorkers seem to be insisting on their loss of African culture not so much because they actually feel deprived of it but
because they have somehow allowed themselves to be theorized into
imitating and competing with white and somewhat white immigrants
whose circumstances are not really analogous. There is, for instance,
much theorizing by the Jewish friends, sweethearts, spouses, and colleagues of black New Yorkers about the importance of a Jewish ancestral homeland—but no one has as yet demonstrated that U.S. Jews
are in any practical sense better off since the establishment of the vest
pocket state of Israel, as marvelous as that little nation has turned out
to be—nor has it been shown that the fall of Lumumba, Tshombe, or
Nkrumah added to the problems of black Americans.

It is not Jewish culture as such that accounts for the noteworthy
academic performance of Jewish pupils—which performance seems
to impress black New Yorkers no end. Rather it is much more likely
to be the traditional Jewish cultural *orientation* to the written word
as the basis of formalized and routinized education. Indeed, so far as
specific cultural details are concerned, a significant number of outstanding American Jewish intellectuals appear to represent Germany
to a far greater extent than they represent the Middle East.

The definitive academic conditioning or intellectual "occupational
psychosis" or mental orientation of the American Jewish intellectual,
scientist, technician, and even journalist seems to have been derived
largely from the tradition of the Talmudic scholar, that inimitable
master of research and midrash. In any case, it is the Talmudic scholar's traditional orientation to painstaking documentation which appears to be most functional. What sustains the fine Jewish student,

that is to say, is neither Hebrew nor Yiddish, nor specific precepts from the synagogue, but rather his overall conditioning to (or attitude toward) written communication and linguistic discipline, plus a respect for prescribed procedures.

The Afro-American tradition, on the other hand, is largely oral rather than written. Even its music is likely to be transmitted largely through auditory means rather than by notation even when both pupil and teacher are musically literate. The great Jewish conductors, concert-masters, and virtuosi, by contrast, proceed very much as if they were Talmudic scholars with scores and instruments. Indeed, Euro-Americans in general are Talmudic scholars in the sense that they tend to read and talk about such musical qualities as, say, dissonance, cacophony, atonality, and so on perhaps nearly as much as they listen to or perform music that contains these characteristics. Afro-American performers and listeners alike tend to proceed directly in terms of onomatopoeia.

In his very perceptive books, *Made in America* and *A Beer Can by the Highway*, John A. Kouwenhoven, whose observations on the nature of America belong beside those of Constance Rourke, states that contemporary American culture is the result of the conflict or interaction of two traditions in the United States over the years. He called one the learned or academic and the other the vernacular, or folk or native. This distinction is a particularly useful one in the present context. The learned or documentary orientation to experience is of its very nature essentially conservative and even antiquarian. In traditions that are essentially learned, even revolutionary action is likely to be based almost as much on the documentation and analysis of past revolutions as upon the urgencies of a current predicament. Literacy, that is to say, is always indispensable to such a cultural orientation or life style.

Americans from Africa, however, are not derived from a life style that has been, or indeed has even needed to be, as concerned with preserving and transmitting the past per se as Europeans have been.

Not that the past was considered entirely forgettable. Far from it. But the African concept of time and continuity (or of permanence and change) seems to have been different, and certainly the concept of history, heritage, and documentation was different. (Afro-Americans, of course, came neither from Egypt nor from the famous Lost Cities.) It is hardly surprising if African conceptions of education were also different.

In all events, it is not only possible but highly probable that the "cultural dislocation trauma" suffered by Africans transported to frontier America was considerably less than European-oriented polemicists imagine, precisely because the African's native orientation to culture was less static or structured than they assume, precisely, that is to say, because the African may have been geared to improvisation rather than piety, for all the taboos he had lived in terms of. The fact that these taboos were not codified in writing may have contributed to a sense of freedom, once he was beyond the "pale."

But perhaps most important of all, it should never be forgotten that nothing is more important to man's survival as a human being than is his flexibility, his adaptability, his talent for accommodating himself to adverse circumstances. Perhaps it is a one-dimensional and essentially snobbish conception of culture which prevents some black- and white-oriented polemicists from realizing that there is probably more to be said for the riff-style life style that Negroes have developed in response to the adverse circumstances of their lives in the United States, than can be said for the culture they were so brutally stripped of. And, besides, look at what actually happened to the Africans who remained at home with their culture intact. Some "African bag" polemicists cop out at this point. But contemporary African leaders, spokesmen, and intellectuals do not. They are the first to explain that they were invaded and colonized by *Europeans*—and by European technology, upon which they are now more dependent than they ever were before. Nor do African officials hesitate to send as many students as possible to Europe and to segregationist America. Not to become white, but to enable the students to extend themselves in terms of the culture of the world at large.

Perhaps it is also pretentiousness that prevents some psycho-political theorists from realizing that just as "Talmudic scholarship" applied to technology may account for the ability of Jewish and other literate peoples to survive and thrive in alien cultures all over the world, including South Africa, so may riff-style flexibility and an open disposition towards the vernacular underlie the incomparable endurance of black soulfulness or humanity.

There is, nevertheless, as much to be said for the vernacular tradition as for the learned tradition—and as Kouwenhoven's investigations suggest, even more to be said for the interaction of the two. At the advent of the phonograph, to take an example from recent cultural history, the typical U.S. Negro musician, not unlike his African ancestors, was clearly more interested in playing and enjoying music than in *recording* it for posterity. As a matter of fact, many Afro-Americans in general still tend to regard phonograph recordings more as current duplications (soon to be discarded as out of date) which enable them to reach more people simultaneously than as permanent documents. Euro-Americans, on the other hand, started record collections and archives, which eventually came to include the music of black Americans. Thus, it is the Euro-American whose tradition of scholarship and research has provided at least the rudiments of a source of musicological data that black historians and students in quest of musical heritage may someday make the most of.

Similarly, it is African creativity that has produced in African art one of the most marvelous achievements of the human imagination. But, as every art dealer knows, it is the Europeans who have been most interested in preserving it, and its fantastic value on the world art market is geared not to the valuation made by Africans but to the valuation of galleries and museums in Europe and America. Further, such are the practical realities that African scholars, artists, and art dealers seem far more interested in what white European and

American art dealers and museum directors think about African culture than what Harlem polemicists think.

When outraged Afro-Americans indict those whose bigotry is the cause of the omissions, distortions, the wholesale falsification and outright suppression of information about black people of the United States, the merits of their case are beyond question. Indeed, the deliberate debasement of the black image has been so viciously systematic and often times so exasperatingly casual that the scope of white malevolence is hard to exaggerate.

The absence of readily available documentary materials in Africa on the history and culture of the peoples of that continent, however, can hardly be blamed on the vandalism of slave traders and certainly not entirely upon the ruthless disregard by European colonials for African culture. Though some missionaries were Huns of a sort, the British Museum, the Musée de l'Homme, and the American Museum of Natural History contain impressive evidence that not all Europeans were set on obliterating African history or denying the significance of its culture. The fact of the matter is that white archaeologists and anthropologists have been instrumental in stimulating contemporary Africans to develop a European-type concern with the documentation and glorification of the past—and glorification of the present for posterity.

It is quite true that conventional European histories of the world have largely ignored African achievements. But what of histories of the world written by Africans down through the years? Were all of these destroyed by European barbarians, or did they never exist? The chances are that those African peoples for whom there is little or no "autobiographical" record conceived of time, reckoned time, and dealt with the passage of time in ways that, as suggested earlier, belonged to an orientation that was essentially different from that of most of the peoples of Europe. It is not impossible that some African cultures were as profoundly conditioned by the vanity of vanities as was the preacher in Ecclesiastes—or as the traveler in Shelley's "Ozymandias."

That U.S. Negroes should enjoy the privilege of introducing additional African elements, including new fashion accents, ornaments, and trinkets, into the pluralistic culture of the United States not only goes without saying but, as the ads in *Ebony, Jet,* and the black weeklies suggest, give as big a boost to black business as to black vanity. Nevertheless, those who are so deeply and fervently concerned about the status of black culture and the prestige of black studies are likely to be motivated by forces and precedents that are not nearly so African as European or Euro-Talmudic, as it were. Thus, it is all too true that the "Americanization" process that captive Africans were forced to undergo stripped them of many of the native accoutrements that they held most dear and wished to retain. But it was also a process of Americanization that has now equipped and *disposed* them not only to reclaim and update the heritage of black Africa but also to utilize the multicolored heritage of all mankind of all the ages.

BLACK PRIDE IN MOBILE, ALABAMA

More often than not—or so it seems—when black New Yorkers get going on television about black identity, black pride, black heritage, and the need for what many now call black studies, they speak as if the Schomburg Collection (which many white students of Negro culture know is located in the very heart of Harlem) were either nonexistent or off-limits to black people. They make sweeping statements that suggest that they are really only shucking for the networks (and the foundations, to be sure) or are completely unaware of the pioneering, even if sometimes somewhat less than comprehensive, work of historians like Carter G. Woodson and Benjamin Brawley. They sound as if they never heard of the Association for the Study of Negro Life and History, which has been publishing the *Journal of Negro History* since 1916 and the *Negro History Bulletin* since 1937.

Some black polemicists are forever complaining that white historians have been omitting and deliberately suppressing important facts about Negro achievement, and justification for their outrage is overwhelming. But for some reason they themselves seldom if ever make even the slightest mention of the work of Negro historians like Rayford Logan, John Hope Franklin, and Benjamin Quarles, three contemporary scholars of the highest professional standing who have devoted long careers to correcting the historical perspectives on U.S.

Negro life. Some may make vague references to Du Bois (or even to E. Franklin Frazier whose sociopolitical view of Negro heritage was emphatically negative!). Otherwise, those most likely to be mentioned or even quoted are Malcolm X and Marcus Garvey, both of whom were spokesmen of high purpose who aspired to be activists rather than historians, research specialists, and survey technicians. Both inspired black pride in thousands of their followers, but neither had either the time or the means to engage in primary research on U.S. Negroes, to say nothing of archaeological, anthropological, or philological research on the infinitely varied black peoples and civilizations of Africa.

But then so many of the most militant black polemicists appear to have swallowed the assumptions and conclusions of precisely those writers who, like Frazier, describe the black American experience as adding up to little more than a legacy of degradation and despair—writers whose concern for the welfare of black people may be beyond reproach but whose opinion or esteem for them is often so low that it moves beyond condescension to contempt! As a result you often hear some of the most scandalous statements about black people repeated by the same black militants who complain loudest about the negative regard in which black people are held. This, in any case, too often tends to be the story in New York.

It is not quite the same down-home. For example, Mobile, Alabama.

II

In conversation and particularly in meetings and open forums, your Southern Negro civil rights spokesmen and activists are likely to make liberal use of many of the slogans and generalities about black identity, black pride, and black heritage heard everywhere in the North these days. So much so, as a matter of fact, that an inattentive outside observer could easily forget where he is. Indeed, unless he remains alert, a native-born Southerner who has been away a number of years

might also do the same thing; for when the subject turns to black consciousness, even the traditional barber shop bull session, which used
to be anything but academic, has begun to sound somewhat like a
Northern campus caucus of television-oriented black power panelists
doing their thing for the six o'clock report.

So much so that after a while you realize that you are the TV, and
they're talking not with you and to you but at you and into you and
seeing themselves zooming close as the titles breeze upward. So much
so that you almost expect them to pause, not for your reply or the next
question, but for the commercial.

When they finally get down to the specifics of programing, however, black Mobilians (who are really mostly various shades of brown
and beige) are likely to formulate social, economic, political, and educational objectives that are significantly different from those that have
recently been turned into such sensational news copy elsewhere.

When they get down to specifics they forget about television for a
while and see you as yourself again or whoever they remember you as
having been or whomever it pleases them to think you have become.
Then they talk to you man to man, Negro to fellow-man, homefolks
to our boy back down home from up the country and homefolks to
homefolks about other folks elsewhere—but not without doing a little
chicken butt signifying in the process either: "Now of course you folks
up North, you folks up in New York, y'all in Yuyorick . . ." That is an
indispensable part of the ritual. Establishes perspective. Adds proper
(and anticipated) dimension of down-home ambivalence.

Then old home week can begin: *"Well, I'm for the brother everywhere because we all members in this mess together, you know what
I mean. But man, some of these new Northern kiddies ain't nothing
but new style white folks you-know-what. You dig? And don't know it.
That's the killing part about it. All that big mouth talk about whities and
honkies and that. Man, most of the time that ain't nothing but exactly
what the man want to hear so he can have an excuse to do anything
he want to. O.K. Remember them cattle prods? They didn't really hurt*

nobody, right? But they got Bull Connor and Al Lingo into all kinds of trouble because everybody all over the country was talking about what an outrageous thing that was, remember? So the man goes and finds him somebody to go on TV and start bragging about Negroes getting up rifle clubs. But who you reckon manufactured all the rifles in the goddam world and who know the serial number on every rifle in the USA. Look, we were finally getting white folks so even them poor sap suckers from back up in the hills were getting careful about how they were saying Neegrow. No more of that Nigra stuff, know what I mean? So they find somebody to get up there and say Negro is ugly because it's white talk and black is beautiful because they just found out. So now white folks up North out talking about blacks like the old slave traders, talking about blacks, coloreds, and whites like down in South Africa . . . Johnny Come Blackly, you know what I mean? Johnny come blacker than thou. But I will say this much. They finally found a way to make some of these high yallers want to give up blow-hair for clinker tops. Man, I saw a peola down here from Harlem or Philly or somewhere wearing a reverse conk. Now that's a switch. At least for a while. Man, they got some of them yaller cats up there on TV carrying on like they blacker than everybody else. You seen that stuff? Hell, they got them so you got to be looking dead at a cat to tell what color he is these days. You hear some Northern-talking cat coming on like he the ace of spades and you look up and he as white as a Scandinavian snowbird. You know what Malcolm X's nickname was? Red, Deetroit Red. Of course, me I'm just a dark-skinned Frenchman with some African ways and some African in the right places myself."

Currently the most newsworthy of the civil rights groups in Mobile is NOW (Neighborhood Organized Workers), and Christmas 1968 it organized a Black Christmas boycott. Whatever the boycott's merits and shortcomings, its objectives were not secession but desegregation. Those who organized it were far more concerned with getting greater black participation in all of the economic and political affairs of their city than with black symbolism, nationalistic or otherwise.

There are overtones of black nationalism, of course, and some black retailers always profit during such times. But as for what some New Yorkers now call "black community control" and "black community development," when black Mobilians talk about where it's at, they are referring to city hall, the city fathers, the industrial/commercial complex, and the like. According to members of NOW, unless you exercise significant influence over municipal funds and policies (they may or may not say the "establishment" or the "white power structure"), black power slogans just help to create black communities that will be far more like colonies than the metaphysical ghettos Northern spokesmen complain about.

Specifics cited by a key member of NOW are typical of those black Mobilians most actively involved in desegregation: "*For one thing we intend to get more of our people on the city payroll. We are due a share of all that. Take for example two guys going around reading water meters and things like that. You don't need much education and training for that. No reason in the world why one of them can't be black, and there are thousands of jobs like that. You see that fine new Municipal Auditorium and Arena? Well, they have some black maintenance and security people in there, but you see we think we ought to have black folks in the box office and on the staff, some committeemen and on the board of directors too. We're not boycotting that place to get a black branch, that's crazy, look how long it took them to get this one, and they've been controlling all the money like you know, since forever. That doesn't make any sense at all. That's the one and we don't need but one, and it's supposed to be as much ours as anybody else's.*"

In general when you talk to militants down South about defense, they are less given to making ill-tempered threats about burning down everything in sight than to expressing a level-headed determination to use counterforce against certain traditional white methods of intimidation used by terrorist elements in the Ku Klux Klan and other white supremacy groups.

As for having a movie-style "shoot out with the lawmen," not many black Mobilians seem particularly impressed with what has been reported about the performance record of black Northerners during such showdowns over the past few years. Most were impressed with the so-called riots in Watts, Newark, and Detroit, but not with the fire power of the black communities involved and certainly not with the accuracy of the sniper fire. They are convinced that the riots did a lot of good and moved the struggle into another phase and onto another level. But much of the talk in the North about "violent confrontation" makes them somewhat uneasy because references to Che Guevara and quotations from Mao and the speculations of Frantz Fanon strike them as being more bookish than relevant and in any case they doubt the tactical wisdom of provoking an enemy who is not only armed to the teeth but is also already on the edge of hysteria. Some admit that an old Southern superstition about people who go around making the loudest threats do not follow up big talk with action also makes them uneasy. "Look," said more than one, "if you really getting ready to do something to somebody, it just don't make sense to tip them off, man." But that is only down-home superstition, of course.

Nevertheless, most black Mobilians seem to feel that the most practical way of striking back at police brutality is through NOW-style policies. Meanwhile should a gundown situation arise, it is the typical black Southerner, more than a few Mobilians insisted, not the typical Harlemite, whose traditional intimate personal experience with weapons is most likely to pay off in terms of dependable marksmanship. "Because you see harassment is all right for pinning down police for a while. You can do that with firecrackers; but before long they going to start checking and find you ain't hurting nobody. But, man, all this is crazy anyhow. All that wolfing and now y'all got gun control worse than ever."

As for the impact of local chapters of violence-oriented militants, said one peppery Mobilian, an old poker player, who used to be a baseball umpire: "*OK, so I'm impressed with what some of them might do to somebody like me and you if they catch us in the dark or something, but hell ain't nothing new about that. You can always do something dirty to another one of your people that you don't like and get away with it because the law don't care and white people don't care. But I bet you they don't jump no cat that's really in cahoots with the white folks. Take like up there in Harlem. OK, y'all always talking about cleaning up the black community, but I bet a fat man the last ones you start messing with is them very cats that's pushing junk for the white mob, you see my point? Because that's the white mob's nigger, you see what I mean? Well, just take around here. They jump up and bomb a black man's business like that cat's liquor store the other night, but I ain't heard a thing about them hitting on none of them cracker stores downtown."* (Who bombed the store at issue is actually not clear. White Mobilians on TV tried their best to make that particular bombing look like the work of NOW, while many Negroes including some members of NOW were not so sure that the whole thing hadn't been planned and executed by white people.)

III

In general, black Mobilians are considerably less polemical than New Yorkers on the subject of black heritage. But after all, black teachers in Mobile, like perhaps most others throughout most of the South, have been observing Negro History Week (the week in February that includes Lincoln's and Frederick Douglass's birthdays) for decades. It must be said that Alabama teachers have been incredibly apathetic about the ridiculous materials on black people in the textbook on Alabama history. But on the other hand their libraries have always tried to promote and spread interest in black publications of all kinds, and everybody is quick to point out that books like Woodson's *The Negro in Our History*, Brawley's *Negro Builders and Heroes*, and John Hope Franklin's *From Slavery to Freedom* have been used as standard references in Negro schools and colleges throughout the South all along.

Actually there never was a time when Southern Negro colleges were not aspiring to be the so-called Black University serving the special needs of black American youth. Thirty-odd years ago, for instance, when the generation of parents and grandparents now in their fifties were college age, almost every campus had teachers, scholars, or historic figures in residence who were widely known and honored for the role they played in matters relating to black heritage. At Howard, for example, there were Kelly Miller, Alain Locke, and Sterling Brown; at Tuskegee there was Monroe N. Work heading a Department of Records and Research and editing the *Negro Year Book*; at Atlanta University there were Du Bois and later Ira De A. Reid; at Fisk there were James Weldon Johnson and Charles S. Johnson, and so on.

Anyway, when involved Mobilians get down to specifics about black heritage they are likely to begin not with self-rejection but rather by saying that the special displays and programs of Negro History Week were never enough to remedy the omissions and distortions in the books used in regular courses in history and social studies. Then, in response to inquiries about offerings presently under consideration at the local school board, they summarize as follows: They do not want black heritage courses to be either extracurricular or elective. They not only want them required but required of all pupils. They do not want them restricted to "black" schools or to black pupils in "white" schools because they are convinced that white pupils need such studies even more urgently than Negroes—who in truth already absorb at least a smattering of black heritage from *Ebony*, *Jet*, and other national Negro publications. As some of them see it, the problem of improving the Black Image has as much to do with teaching white school children to honor Denmark Vesey and Nat Turner as with anything else.

Then, because they are thinking and talking like teachers and supervisors and not like TV spokesmen, they begin speculating about what will really happen when the actual classwork begins and there is not so much publicity. So they start remembering how students respond to assignments and, being teachers, they also know how precious student enthusiasm always is, but, being experienced teachers and in some instances parents to boot, they know enough about it not to exaggerate its significance. Nor do they confuse the emotional response to statements about black pride at political rallies with the academic motivation that comes from genuine historical curiosity. So they come back to specifics for school board policy. Perhaps the current emphasis will generate greater historical curiosity among larger numbers of black students (and white ones too), but meanwhile now is the time to add missing black dimensions to existing courses. Now is the time to revise and update existing text materials, no little job in itself.

As for race pride as such, there are those who think it is a good thing which has nothing to do with racism. But some others are not so sure. Some flatly reject it as a highly questionable educational objective. Others see it as representing a regression toward social provincialism and political chauvinism, of which they feel the U.S. has far too much already. Still others point out that the most urgent problems facing U.S. Negroes just simply do not have very much to do with any demonstrated lack of black pride. To them all the television talk about blackness is mostly a misuse of valuable time and mostly adds up to a misdirection of valuable energies; and they frankly doubt whether those who are doing it have any practical standards by which to calculate what degree of black pride must be developed (and by what means and through what measurable stages) before Negroes can get the hell on with the business of employment, housing, and equal protection under the law.

Nor do many of the so-called brothers on the street, on the block, and in the barber shop disagree: "*Now look, you know good and well color ain't what Rockefeller is proud of. Hell, the only time you ever hear real big white folks bragging about the color of their skin is when they got a good deep tan. You know what Rockefeller is proud of? All that money and power. And you know what Wallace and all the rest of them proud of? The same thing. Hell, anybody get up there on TV talking about Negroes don't have no pride ain't talking about no Negroes*

I know. Because you see, sometimes I think the whole trouble is we got too much pride. And I say we don't need to be getting no louder and prouder because what I want to see is more of our young folks getting smarter and when you got that you don't have to be up there bragging about it. Because as soon as you start carrying on like that I got to start worrying about how come you so loud because if you really proud you supposed to be cooling it. You see what I mean? Because then I got to start asking myself if you really believe it. And now I'm going to tell you something else. Black is beautifuler than ever, but them A&P specials are kinda pretty too, and ain't no flies on Sears Roebuck. Goddam it, everywhere you turn somebody talking about black, black, black. Hell, me I want to talk about the goddam stock market report, I want to talk about all them calculating machines and stuff. Black my behind. Hell, I'm old fashioned. Any joker come calling me black better make damn sure he blacker than me."

And after all, the Indians never had any shortage of red pride. Their red identity was unmistakable and their sense of red heritage had long since become a part of their religion. But they needed more than a legacy of bow and arrow confidence and barebacked courage. They had every right to be proud of their hair as well as their feathers and buckskin and so on, but they did not have any factories and merchant fleets to be proud of. In other words, redskin pride was never any problem. The war drums took care of that business very well. Perhaps even too well, because they hopped up a number of young braves to the point where they were only too willing to risk dying for the cause without understanding the complexity of the issues. The redskin troops were magnificent. But the combat plans were out of date. *Nobody in the councils of war knew enough about world history, world geography, and demography.* The failure to understand the connection between the paleface invaders and the people on the other side of the Atlantic was disastrous. Nor was paleface pride a decisive factor since the terrified white colonists were able to offset their insecurity and lack of dignity with, among other things, superior technology.

But when qualified Negro or so-called black teachers and supervisors in New York get closer to the specifics of curriculum construction, they do not often confuse the stimulation of black pride with the refinement and extension of historical insight either. Nor do they mistake themselves as television spokesmen simply because the news media might choose to create the impression that anybody making statements about black studies is a fully qualified expert in the field of education. Most seem to go along with the black consciousness campaign as an activist tactic; and more often than not they also approve of black militancy despite the fact that some of it violates their sense of scholarly integrity (philosophically shrugging off gross oversimplification and wild exaggeration as the dues you pay for long overdue revolutionary change). But even so they also know how easy it is for self-pride to degenerate into self-inflation, empty arrogance, and chauvinism; so they want good news that meets the highest tests of reliability. They want courses in history and culture that will improve everybody's perspective on the universality of human experience and will enrich everybody's sense of context and identity.

The main difficulty, however, is the fact that black teachers in New York have less authority in such matters than do their colleagues in the South. In Mobile, those from the so-called black community who exercise most influence on school board policies relating to black heritage or the "black dimension" of American culture are likely to be teachers and principals, not all-purpose spokesmen and overnight experts. Perhaps in time the same will be true in New York. But as of now, black professionals in education in New York seem to enjoy less scholarly prestige among top school officials and other powerful white-friends-of-black-causes than the very same black students who otherwise are considered to be suffering from the gravest academic deficiencies and who paradoxically are complaining precisely because they are inadequately trained. Indeed, it is not at all unusual for white New Yorkers to allow themselves to be instructed in language usage, history, anthropology, economics, and even clinical psychology by students that they themselves rate substandard, and then presume to instruct their black professional equals and betters on the whys, wherefores, and needs of black experience.

That legendary Southern Negro refugee who used to brag that he'd rather be a lamp post in Harlem than the mayor of Mobile was probably not a school teacher—or maybe the lamp post was where the action was in those days. Anyway, as any black Mobilian old enough to remember will readily confirm, educators down-home would have regarded such empty-headed arrogance with contempt at least as far back as thirty or forty years ago. As brutal as conditions in Alabama were back during the depression of the nineteen thirties, nobody could have conceived of white Mobilians ignoring the advice of a dedicated professional like Benjamin F. Baker, then the principal of Mobile County Training School, or of Ella Grant of the Prichard School, for that of semi-literate bull session experts and para-literate adolescent intellectuals. And black parents did not accuse teachers like B. F. Baker or Miss Ella of being Uncle Toms or white folks' Negroes either —for the simple reason that they were not.

BLACK STUDIES AND THE AIMS OF EDUCATION

As little as it has been noted by the experts, the petitions for courses in black history and culture now being pushed by Negro students across the nation may actually be as much a repudiation of the content and point of view of existing offerings in the social sciences as they are a protest against anything else. In fact, such petitions, which frequently sound like ultimatums, may even be the direct and natural, if not the inevitable, result of the all but exclusive emphasis that so many schools and most of the media have been placing on the so-called findings of the socio-economic research technicians. In any case, the slogans now being chanted by the insistent young petitioners represent an unmistakable refutation of the most popular academic and generally social scientific assumptions about the nature of black experience—all that misery and ugliness—in the United States.

What student activists are now proclaiming is that black is beautiful and that it is beautiful to be black but that bigoted white historians and vicious white image makers in general have been distorting the beauties and denying the glories of blackness all these years. In other words, what the students are demanding are not more courses in the origin, development, and extent of black wretchedness. On the contrary, they first of all expect to find in the courses they are demanding historical clues to the pathological condition of white Americans. Their frequent references to the sickness, insecurity, and brutality of white Americans make that clear. Further, all the catch phrases about black identity, black power, and black pride make it even clearer that they expect the history they are demanding to reveal a magnificent, hither-to sneakily obscured tradition of black heroism and mis-attributed achievement.

Such a basic and comprehensive student rejection of social science–oriented interpretations of black culture as being mostly an accumulated legacy of shame and sorrow is, however, far more implicit than deliberate. It has much more to do with the inevitable, or at least the probable, consequences of the petitions than with any premeditation or calculation, much less any speculation based on specific investigation, documentation, and insight. It may actually even be more incidental than intuitive. But the result is likely to entail a significant shift in academic emphasis nevertheless, and such a shift will not necessarily be less valid or less revolutionary for not having been derived from a more precise intellectual formulation.

But perhaps there would be less confusion if it were. There is, after all, quite a lot to be said for knowing as much as possible about what you are involved in and what it is likely to encompass sooner or later. Certainly the basic intentions of black students are for the most part beyond reproach. Yet it may be that because they are unable to spot the intellectual shortcomings inherent in current social science formulations of crucial issues, they frequently become lost in a maze of terminological nonsense. They also often seem totally unaware of the possibility that at best the academic categories may not only be an inadequate source of information (not to mention wisdom), but at worst, so far as U.S. Negroes are concerned, may be downright vicious in effect, if not by design.

For example, it is hard to say whether psycho-political theoreticians who define what is obviously and quite specifically *political* behavior based on political awareness (developing among U.S. Negroes as a result of the civil rights movement) as if it were the development of black *manhood*, are being vicious or just plain stupid. To mistake new-found *insight* and *technique* for new-found *courage* is to misunderstand the very nature of human motivation. Surely there is a significant difference between cautious hesitation (because you don't know what you're doing) and cowardice (because you jest nat'l born scared).

At any rate, many so-called black militants often seem to be overresponding to white norm/black deviation survey data-oriented conjectures and doubletalk precisely because they are unprepared to identify it as the pseudo-scientific folklore of white supremacy it so frequently is. And by doing so they are likely to be reinforcing the very same condescending and contemptuous white attitudes toward black experience to which they are so vociferously opposed. Perhaps even worse, they encumber themselves with those irrelevant theoretical and sometimes completely phony issues and highly questionable abstractions such as race pride, black identity, black consciousness, black art, black beauty, and the like, instead of striking directly at more concrete problems.

If U.S. Negroes don't already have self-pride and didn't know black, brown, beige, and freckles, and sometimes even m'riny is beautiful, why do they always sound so good, so warm, and even cuss better than everybody else? Why do they dress so jivy and look so foxy, standing like you better know it in spite of yourself? If black people haven't always known how beautiful black is, why have they always been walking, prancing like they'd rather be dancing, and dancing like everybody else is a wall-flower or something? If Louis Armstrong doesn't know he has black beauty to spare how come he can create more beauty while clowning than them other people can giving all they got? How come a hardboiled cat like Johnny Hodges got so much tenderness and elegance left over? And what's Coleman Hawkins doing turning the blues into such finespun glass, and what were Dizzy Gillespie and Yardbird Parker doing all them acrobatic curlicue lyrics about? How come Count Basie and

Lionel Hampton think they can make a hillbilly jump, stomp, and rock —and almost do it? Why does everybody take it for granted that Duke Ellington can wipe out anybody anywhere, anytime he wants to?

And if black people have such low self-regard, why the hell are they forever laughing at everybody else? How come as soon as they get something desegregated so many of them feel so at home that they subject to try to take it over by sheer bullshit (which they would never try in an all-black situation)? How come they're forever talking as if superstars like Willie Mays, Jim Brown, Oscar Robertson, and even Leontyne Price come a dime a dozen in the black community? And if they really feel so stupid, how come a third-rate Harlem hipster is always so certain he got him a square as soon as he spots an Ivy League white boy in a nonacademic situation?

Rhetoric of black militancy aside, what Negroes are obviously concerned, resentful, angry, and increasingly violent about is not too little identity or beauty or pride but too much exclusion from the power mechanisms and resources of the nation at large, including the publicity mechanisms which should acknowledge and advertise black as being beautiful and as American as blackberry jam. Most Negroes know very well that their main problem is exclusion from equal protection under the law, exclusion from equal job opportunities, exclusion from adequate housing and public services, and exclusion from the technical training required not for subsistence on a black reservation but for affluence in an automated space age society.

There is good reason to believe that it is precisely because they are all but hopelessly overimpressed by the folklore of white supremacy and the fakelore of black pathology that so many young (and not so young) Negroes are now becoming so ensnarled in ill-digested and conflicting ideologies of blackness, blackmanship, and blackman spokesmanship. And the result is that some are beginning to embrace concepts of black communities, black states, and even black nations, concepts that are not only much closer to the racism of past centuries than to cultural nationalism but that are also based on notions about economics that are so utterly outmoded it would be generous to call them tribal.

, Any number of black spokesmen who should know better have become so exhilarated with visions of a black millennium that they seemingly completely forget that secession has been tried and found unfeasible. Save your confederate money boys—the antique rates gonna rise again. White suburbanites are only moving to the outskirts of town, they're not seceding from the stock exchange, or even A&P. Nor do many rhetorical separatists seem to have investigated, or even to have heard anything at all about, life on the Indian reservations. But then neither do many seem to bother themselves in the least about such establishment-oriented nuisances as monetary stability, balance of payments, public utilities, public health facilities, social security, food and drug regulations, not to mention heavy industry, tariff, tax assessment and collection; not even a whisper about automobile tags and drivers licenses. The corporate structure of contemporary life in the United States is just simply not something you can ignore or verbalize out of existence because black is beautiful. But there are those who are talking as if they just might overthrow the whole power structure any day now and begin all over black, though as yet they have not knocked off a single bigoted labor union—just so the establishment will get the message.

When the courses in "black heritage" actually get under way (and the current emphasis on white norm/black deviate folklore is placed in proper perspective) and black students really begin to zero in on black civilizations, black kingdoms and heroes, the chances are that they are also going to find out something else: most revolutions, liberation movements, and slave rebellions, like most attempts at prison breaks, fail—not because each was betrayed by "Uncle Toms" (incidentally, Miss Harriet Beecher Stowe's Uncle Tom was not a traitor to the cause), but mostly because they were inadequately planned and inadequately timed. Attentive students of black history will also find that many of the most celebrated black rulers were able to maintain themselves in power precisely because they knew how to fake would-be rebels out of position, and into a rhetorical bag. In other words, power structures, whether white or black, do not just curl up and die because the rebel cause is impeccable. You'd better believe that many times when they seem to be giving in they are really sucking you in. Some forms of permissiveness are devastating.

The quasi-scientific rhetoric of liberation goes over very big at rallies, nonviolent demonstrations, folk festivals, and on TV, and of course these things are very much a part, and a very useful part, of every contemporary freedom movement. Nevertheless, a man who is actually involved in a prison break can ill afford to risk precious time on purely theoretical barriers when there are so many real and unmistakable ones to overcome. Thus, when black militants at Ivy League colleges begin agitating for separate areas and exclusive courses and facilities, perhaps their parents may be pardoned for questioning whether they are spearheading a drive to freedom or misdefining and hence misdirecting themselves and their efforts back into the warden's stronghold.

Certainly U.S. Negro parents have earned some right to be skeptical about any gesture that suggests separatism, no matter how you rationalize it. Especially when those making it begin by admitting that they do not know very much about what has gone on before. One of the duties of black parents and elders who respect the obligations that *they* inherited from *their* parents is to see to it that nobody comes along and either loud-talks or fancy-talks black people into the worst trap of all: self-constriction, and even self-enslavement, through self-hypnotic verbalism. That's the bag white Southerners have been trying to put black folks in ever since emancipation. The black studies department of the University of Alabama, for example, has had black facilities and black instructors for years—located in Montgomery, 100 comfortable miles away from Tuscaloosa. In other words, people like Miss Autherine Lucy (who is now a parent) have had something to say about separate tables—but who remembers that kind of historical detail? (Yes, and what will the five year olds of today think of dashikis fifteen years from now?)

As for what Africans have been thinking of them all along, here's what Tom Mboya, Kenya's late Minister of Economic Development and Planning, writing in the *New York Times Magazine*, had to say: "[Some black Americans] think that to identify with Africa one should wear a shaggy beard or a piece of cloth on one's head or a cheap garment on one's body. I find here a complete misunderstanding of what African culture really means. An African walks barefoot or wears sandals made of old tires not because it is his culture but because he lives in poverty. We live in mud and wattle huts and buy cheap Hong Kong fabrics not because it is part of our culture, but because these are conditions imposed on us today by poverty and by limitations in technical, educational, and other resources."

II

The lack of intellectual coherence on the part of young people from whose ranks the black intellectuals, technicians, spokesmen, and leaders are expected is cause for some uneasiness and at times even some exasperation but not for alarm. For the very fact that black students are petitioning for courses in history is significant evidence that they feel the need for a larger and more consistent view of things. Historical research is in itself a quest for a basis for consistency, a benchmark for further explorations.

But the atmosphere of crisis that has been generated by the confusion among some of the white Americans who control the "education establishment" *is* cause not only for alarm but for red alert and hot pursuit. For, as with so many of the white people who encourage and subsidize so much bad art among black writers, they either do not know what education is, or they know only too well.

After all, since when did students ever love existing courses of study? Since when were they not on the lookout for snap courses, preferably ungraded ones. Since when didn't they doubt the practical relevance of classroom procedures—particularly when the assignments involve hard work. Haven't students always wondered what the comma splice and quadratic equations have to do with English, Irish, German—or especially American identity? Since when didn't students ridicule teachers as being out of touch with what was really happening in the streets? And since when were students not right at least some of the time? As somebody in Harlem said not long ago, "Hell, even a stopped clock has correct time twice a day." Since when didn't students overstate their case? Why not see how far you can push things? Especially when all you need is a few black enameled clichés because you know the authorities are only going to try to match you with their own, and then give up and call in the police and then feel rotten about it. Why not?

A petition for courses in black heritage is essentially only a request for a more comprehensive approach to the American heritage. There is no reason in the world why an appeal for more comprehensive instruction should be cause for administration hysteria, or why the prospect of new historical dimensions should trigger pandemonium in the community of scholars. Ordinarily, scholars welcome opportunities for new research. Ordinarily, intellectuals would be only too eager to establish new perspectives on some area of the American experience. And needless to say, whatever in the African past is valid for black Americans is of immediate and fundamental significance to other Americans. Cultural values have universal relevance, as witness the benefits Europeans derived through Picasso, Braque, Klee, et al., from African sculpture alone.

It is the responsibility of school administrators and course of study technicians to separate the sense from the nonsense in all requests and proposals no matter what color the source. Curriculum experts who cannot make practical distinctions between vague opportunistic generalities and insightful observations about the basic educational values of newly suggested subject matter have no business formulating course objectives and projecting student outcomes in the first place. When a petition demands, for example, that courses be made more relevant to the black community, school officials must be able to make certain that such courses are no less relevant to computer and space age technology. It is also their responsibility to remind certain petitioners that for people who maintain excellent surveillance of secret nuclear explosions in the remote areas of the Soviet Union and can evaluate the heartbeat of astronauts orbiting the moon, it is a very simple matter indeed to monitor and control black enclaves on the other side of the dining hall, the other side of the campus, or the other side of town. (Certain kinds of privacy are a thing of the past.)

Technical specialization aside, the fundamental objective of American education must be to produce, as it were, fifty-dimensional citizens—people whose open dispositions are compatible with contemporary innovations in communication and transportation and who are therefore able to live in terms of the resources of each one of the fifty United States.

Negro parents, for their part, have every right to expect and even require white instructors to be open minded enough about black students, so that when confronted by one sporting an Afro-natch hairdo (which might really be more Polynesian than African) and/or a dashiki (often of cloth made in Holland for the Dutch East Indies and the African trade), the white instructor will neither condescend to the black student nor cop-out before him, but will check him out (as the lynx-eyed old Dr. W. E. B. Du Bois or the late great Charles Houston, mentor of Justice Marshall, might have done) to determine if he is for real or just shucking on the latest kick. A black or honey-brown student with his head buried in a book by Frantz Fanon, Che Guevara, Malcolm X, or Eldridge Cleaver may be searching for intellectual equipment for modern living, or then again he may only be gathering quotations against the day when at last his call comes to go on David Susskind's vaudeville hour. It is the educator's job to be able to relate current books to many other books.

After all, good instructors had been capitalizing on student interests long before John Dewey put teacher training colleges hep to progressive education or the pupil-centered classroom. Thus, student requests for courses in black heritage, including African history, should be met because such courses also provide instructors additional opportunities to develop a richer perspective on the world-at-large for all students. But instructors should also be alert and knowledgeable enough to realize that some of the answers that black students in Northern cities are seeking may also be in the history of white immigration. And to know that not a few of the problems of the contemporary South are the direct outgrowth of unresolved issues of the Reconstruction era. In other words, the practical extensions are a matter of imaginative classroom procedure. Dewey never promised that the permissiveness of progressive education would make the instructor's work any easier. He claimed only that it could make learning easier, and more effective. Pupil-interest exploitation instruction is no snap; it is rather an unending challenge to the teacher's ingenuity. And though teaching may employ scientific method, it is not a science. It is an art, a fine art.

III

Some school authorities seem not to understand that continuity through change is precisely what tradition and therefore education (the continuous restructuring of experience) is all about. Instead, they are inclined to view the question of black studies primarily as another instance of generation conflict. But they miss a point that the nation has every right to assume its intellectuals and educators would be the first to understand: Students asking for courses in history, literature, and art may be quite obviously, even if not specifically, at issue with existing academic categories, but they are hardly rejecting their elders, at least not all of them. On the contrary, they are returning to older and even ancient generations for ancestral guidance, that background and point of departure, that equipment for flexible living that the social science–oriented *present* has failed to provide.

In any case, school authorities should be able to see the so-called generation gap for the pop media concoction that it is. In the first place, the notion of a generation gap as now used implies that there are only two generations. But since grandfather and mother are still very much around (indeed, and still running things) that makes three, and baby brother and sister make at least four! Certainly school officials whose daily involvements include the federal government as well as the nursery school cannot proceed as if there were only two generations on the scene at one time. Furthermore, wherever a gap does exist, it is not the older people but the younger ones who must be most concerned with closing it. After all, it is not the youngsters who are engineering the space age but their elders, and they are moving on. The youngsters have to get with it because they are the ones who are going to be stuck with it. When the older man tells the young man in the film *The Graduate* to check into plastics, he really is trying to put him hip to something. You cannot ignore plastics just because black is beautiful and wants to be powerful, and white being powerful is eager to be beautiful. When the older woman seduces the young man, she may well be a witch, of a sexy sort. But she is hardly a square, and she may also be initiating him into the complexity and ambiguity of contemporary actuality. In spite of the soap opera ending of *The Graduate*, present-day young people really do not have the option to go back to the days when Mickey Rooney was good old clean cut Andy Hardy.

Perhaps it would not be a bad idea for a few generation-oriented school authorities to reconsider some of the implications of *Goodbye, Mr. Chips*, the novel or the (old) movie. Mister Chips lived to see too many generations come and go to hang himself up worrying about the gaps between them. Yes, yes. Of course he was somewhat out of touch with the latest slang (and stuff), but he made up for it with charm and by doing his own thing. So he did manage to put students in touch with some of the wisdom of the ages. And he fully understood that young men always have to find their own way by trial and error.

On the other hand, activist instructors whose support for black

student struggles goes beyond the old-fashioned white liberal senti-
mentalism about "helping those poor kids" must realize that it is not
enough to say: "Those black militants are trying to tell us something."
Instructors should be able to tell students something. Historians can
do much to teach young revolutionaries what the dynamics of revolution actually involve. Competent historians will not permit students
to be misled by bombastic platitudes about the masses and "the real
people" or the "average" black man, but will point out that the student's own responsibility lies precisely in the fact that he is trying to be
better than average, and that revolutions are not really made by angry
mobs thrashing about in all directions but by enlightened charismatic
leaders, and that rebellions succeed when such leaders are technically
proficient enough to select the most vulnerable targets and apply the
most practical tactics and weapons. Who else is supposed to clarify
such things if not teachers and intellectuals? By the same token, nobody was ever the agent of more black confusion than those white
instructors who are always so eager to help black drop-outs, addicts,
and criminals, but who (perhaps for some extremely peculiar reason) seem compelled to regard the very students who wish to educate
themselves about the world at large as being black people no longer!
As if those who presume to speak for black people and certainly those
who opt to lead them did not owe it to their followers to know as
much as possible about the world in all its ramifications.

As long as black students are allowed to ignore those fundamental
intellectual disciplines and those broad sources of information that
will enable them to question and evaluate the basic assumptions underlying all of the policies and programs being formulated for black
communities (whether by black leaders or others) they are very likely
to continue to entangle themselves in conflicting clichés. And as
things now stand these clichés are likely to be inseparable from the
pseudo-scientific folklore of white supremacy, no matter how revolutionary those using them think themselves to be.

Regardless of intentions and of degrees of urgency, the physical no less than the verbal responses of people who are insufficiently historical in orientation are likely to turn out to be more hysterical and irrelevant than truly purposeful, truly pragmatic, accurate, appropriate, and either immediately or ultimately effective. A gamble or calculated risk, it should be remembered, is a matter not of impulse but of the most comprehensive deliberation possible in the circumstances.

Finally, as for the so-called generation gap, the eternal as well as the most immediate problem underlying the formulation of the aims of education and the establishment of specific courses of study and subject matter credits, whether for nations or tribes, is the problem of continuity: not whether elders can adjust to the changes being wrought by younger people but whether the young people can acquire the information and insight necessary to survival. Indeed not the least among the actualities that all young revolutionaries must come to terms with is the very real possibility that theirs may be that foolheaded generation that might blow the whole shebang, kit and keboodle, and be that terminal generation that, as history shows, all nations and cultures great and small decay into. Anyway, the question of endurance comes before that of surpassing. The old saying that begins, youth must be served, should end, but so alas must the fullness of time.

EPILOGUE
SITUATION NORMAL: ALL FOULED UP

I *n the fall of 1966, the editors of* Partisan Review *invited a number of writers, including the author, to participate in a symposium called "What's Happening to America." SNAFU was accepted, processed as far as the corrected galley proofs, and was then not printed for lack of space. Since the author never got around to pasting it up as a piece of Harlem storefront graffiti (and couldn't in any case decide which store-front had the greatest* Partisan Review *readership), it is printed here as an epilogue which picks up a number of themes in this book and as a not quite outdated uptown memo which includes something more than the usual platitudes about conditions inside the Eight Ball.*

There never was a time when the United States was not deeply en-snarled in a moral and political crisis. Warren G. Harding felt that the nation did not need heroics but healing during his administra-tion: "not nostrums but normalcy; not revolution but restoration; not surgery but serenity." But Harding's understanding of the essential nature of U.S. life was easily as questionable as his vocabulary—or perhaps he was an ex-radical suffering battle fatigue. At any rate, there was no "normalcy" before the Revolutionary War, and what with the War of 1812, the question of slavery, and westward expansion, there was none before the Civil War. Unsettled Reconstruction problems have only increased in complexity, and the normal state of the nation since the Spanish-American War has been that of one critical situation overlapping another. Thousands have escaped oppression and extermination elsewhere and found relative security here, but many basic constitutional issues have never been settled. Crucial constitutional amendments have yet to be forcefully applied. Nevertheless, the specific questions about which *PR* expresses anxiety are urgent and require comment.

1. Presidential elections seem as valid as ever. Whether Elijah Muhammad, Norman Mailer, George-Lurleen Wallace, William Buckley Jr., or Martin Luther King is in the White House makes all the difference in the world. JFK was a man of much broader scope and nobler sentiment than most people expected, but only after the assassination did the landslide majority begin to like him like Ike. The system didn't force Ike to do very much and couldn't force JFK to do more than Congress allowed. As for LBJ and the quest for consensus, he is accused on all sides: of going too far in Vietnam, too fast on civil rights; of being too good at compromise, and too arrogant in his use of power.

2. The problem of inflation is very serious indeed, and, so far as one can tell, probably grows out of seemingly irreconcilable conflicts between agricultural interests and those of labor and industry. There is also the role that advertising now plays in production, not to mention the coming of automation. But the intellectual, whether literary or all-purpose, seldom knows any more about inflation than about foreign policy, military strategy, fall-out, air pollution or water fluoridation. Such things concern him, to be sure, and he is bound to have personal opinions about them. His picket slogans, however, should be consistent with the limitations of his information.

*

3. Not everyone agrees that there is a split between the administration and U.S. intellectuals. Nor is there general concurrence as to who is and who is not an intellectual. Perhaps as good a guideline as any is a remark by the narrator of *The Walnut Trees of Altenburg*. "I know now," he says, "that an intellectual is not only a man to whom books are necessary, he is also any man whose reasoning, however elementary it may be, affects and directs his life." Definitive or not, it is a viable conception, and it is also comprehensive enough to include McGeorge Bundy, Nicholas Katzenbach, Maxwell Taylor, and John K. Jessup, as well as George F. Kennan, Hans Morgenthau, and Irving Howe. Moreover, it excludes those who, for all their involvement with books and ideas, are essentially sentimental, and among these of course, there are liberals and radicals along with conservatives and reactionaries.

A split between any U.S. administration and some liberals and most radicals is not only predictable, it is healthy. Much of the current dissent, however, seems to be degenerating into petulance. This is self-defeating, for as criticism becomes more hostile than reasonable, the administration is only likely to harden itself against it—or ignore it.

4. Most white Americans are obviously and often all too unconsciously committed to White Anglo-Saxon Protestant supremacy. The narcissism implied by such widely used terms as *non-white* and *assimilation* (not to be confused with desegregation or integration) is as unmistakable as it is casual. The findings and categories of social science are as irrelevant to the civil rights of native-born U.S. Negroes as to those of ignorant hillbillies and newly arrived immigrants. But somehow most white Americans seem to feel that white-oriented statistical surveys indicate whether or not Negroes are eligible for things that the Constitution already guarantees. The Department of Labor, for instance, issues the highly questionable Moynihan Report which explains the problem of Negro status in terms of the abnormal structure of Negro family life at a time when Negroes themselves are

conducting nationwide demonstrations and riots against *segregation* in education and housing, *discrimination* in employment, and police *racism*!

On principle, white liberals and radicals give or "grant" sympathetic assistance to the civil rights movement, to be sure; but few Negroes are convinced that this indicates a comprehensive commitment to equality or even represents a truly intimate intellectual involvement with the fundamental issues of citizenship in an open, pluralistic society. Indeed the most serious as well as the most universal Negro indictment against the so-called liberal and radical writers is that at bottom they are as white-oriented as the mass media journalists. Even some U.S. Jewish intellectuals seem to regard Wasps as the chosen people. It is not at all unusual for second generation Jewish writers to refer to native-born multi-generation U.S. Negroes (most of whom it so happens, are part-white) as a non-white, *unassimilable* minority. Unassimilable with whom? Is Norman Podhoretz more assimilated than Count Basie?

What U.S. Negroes themselves want, it should be easy enough to see, is their share of the material benefits of U.S. life—*and they intend to upset enough smugness to get it.* For the rest, they are far more ambivalent about the so-called white world than white people seem able to realize. Nor is this simply a matter of sociopolitical action. What Louis Armstrong has been doing to popular songs all these years is an infinitely more accurate index to fundamental U.S. Negro attitudes towards "white culture" than are some of the embarrassingly superficial and contradictory gestures of alienation currently so popular among some black nationalists and "Afro-Zionists."

5. Perhaps current foreign policies will enable the U.S. to muddle through as Britain used to do, and perhaps not. Meanwhile the drift and confusion seem likely to continue not so much because the administration is so obstinate but because no one has come forth with any truly compelling and practicable alternatives. Few people are

more obviously opposed to current policies than Senator William Fulbright, for instance, who not only has expressed solemn doubts and made pointed insinuations but has also conducted televised Senate hearings to air the nation's motives and has certainly been receptive to ideas critical of the present course of affairs. Neither the administration, Congress, nor the public, however, seem convinced that there is a workable Fulbright Alternative. Former Ambassador George F. Kennan suggests that the nation can disengage itself from some of its foreign involvements, and even allow some of its "allies" to go communist, without doing any serious damage to its power or moral prestige; and there is every evidence that he is as competent and responsible as he is bold. But Kennan's general guidelines for deescalation in Vietnam are not geared to evacuation but to defense perimeters. And there is no Kennan Alternative either.

Those who suggest that U.S. foreign policy is becoming an adjunct to military power seem to imply that military power exists as an end in itself. It does not. It is an instrument of national interest. And as materialistic as national interests always are, those of the U.S. are largely modified by moral considerations. Indeed, administration involvement with the moral clichés of internationalism (derived from liberal and radical ideas of the nineteen thirties) is probably as great a source of current confusion as anything else. At any rate, the nation's moral stance is not necessarily hypocritical simply because the President must always be less than candid about American material interest in "good" and "bad" wars alike.

6. At the present time not even the most open of institutions adequately represent the magnificent diversity that U.S. communication and transportation facilities make accessible to the average citizen. It is entirely possible, however, for artists and intellectuals to synthesize images and concepts that will be revolutionary enough to destroy existing restrictions (which are often mistaken for sophistication). When that happens U.S. education will fulfill its unique potential and

produce The Truly Representative Contemporary Man. Perhaps every serious writer proceeds on the assumption that a sufficiently vernacular and revolutionary image can be created to initiate a millennium during his generation.

7. The impression of young people that one gets from the mass media is not at all promising, but mass media reports are not geared to accuracy or responsibility but to sensationalism. Perhaps some young people are as frivolous as ads encourage them to be; but most, as ever, are no doubt primarily concerned with growing up. Far too many college students now seem to substitute social science methodology for the discipline of the humanities, but most young Americans show very fine prospects nonetheless, and the current crisis is probably good for them. The civil rights movement, for instance, reveals thousands of young U.S. Negroes (to whom fouled-up situations have always been normal) who display an open disposition to new ideas and experiences and a sense of responsible adventure which if not yet properly celebrated is already being emulated.

CHRONOLOGY

1916   Born on May 12 in Nokomis, Alabama, to sixteen-year-old Sudie Graham, at the home of one of her relatives. Graham (b. circa 1900), a Nokomis-area native living in Tuskegee, Alabama, will in the fall enter the teacher training program at Tuskegee Institute. Father, John Lee Young (b. circa 1895), is one of a middle-class black family in Tuskegee; he had met Graham the year before, when she worked as an assistant in his aunt's real estate firm. To protect her educational prospects and the Young family name, Graham gives the infant to Hugh and Mattie Murray (b. circa 1868 and 1882, respectively), a childless couple of her family's acquaintance, who legally adopt him as Albert Lee Murray. Hugh Murray, who appears Caucasian in a photograph and will be remembered by his adopted son as resembling William Faulkner, is identified as black ("B") on the U.S. Census. He is illiterate and works in a lumberyard. Mattie Murray, who is black and literate, is a homemaker. By year's end the family will move to Magazine Point, Alabama, a suburb three miles north of Mobile and about forty-five miles southwest of Nokomis. Murray will remember Magazine Point as a rough, poor black neighborhood alive with music and "rife with juke joints." Adjacent African Hill or Africatown is home to the survivors (and descendants of survivors) of the schooner *Clotilda*, the last U.S. ship to import slaves from Africa, in 1860. (Scooter, the protagonist-narrator of Murray's semi-autobiographical novel *Train Whistle Guitar*, recalls the rivalry between the neighborhoods as follows: "When somebody from up there used to call us them old sawmill quarters niggers, section gang niggers and foggy bottom niggers who didn't come from anywhere but from looking up a mule's ass back on the old plantations back in slavery times, all I thought was that they were trying to get even because we were also not only closer to all the best places for hunting both land game and water game, but we also had a baseball team that was in the same class as those from Chickasaw and Whistler and Maysville and Bayou La Batre and Biloxi.") The hulk of the *Clotilda*, which was scuttled then burned by her legally embattled owner, can still be seen at the mouth of Chickasaw (Chickasawbogue) Creek throughout Murray's childhood. Murray's neighborhood was rezoned for industrial use and razed in midcentury, but nearby neighborhoods retain the look and winding streets of the area, as well as the sort of shotgun-style house in which Murray grew up.

1920   Appears in U.S. Census of 1920 as the son (not adopted) of Hugh and Mattie Murray. By this time the Murrays are also raising three other children, aged ten to eighteen (and all with the last name Leatherwood), whom they list as "adopted."

1927   Works intermittently as a gofer during construction of the Cochrane Bridge, spanning the Mobile River. (Will later recall twice meeting Zora Neale Hurston, once while she was collecting folklore from workmen during the construction of the bridge, and again while she was interviewing community elder Cudjo Lewis, one of the last survivors of the *Clotilda*. In Murray's first novel, *Train Whistle Guitar*, Lewis is the model for Unka Jo Jo.) Adoptive father Hugh Murray manages semipro baseball teams, some featuring Mobile native Satchel Paige (a model for Gator Gus in *Train Whistle Guitar*). Murray closely follows the 1927 New York Yankees via newspapers; recalls it as a watershed moment in personal literacy, a realization that he is able to read more than what he is assigned in elementary school. In fall begins fifth grade at Mobile County Training School, which he will attend through 1935.

1930   Sudie Graham, who had moved to Mobile years earlier to be near Murray and whom he calls his auntie (Miss Tee in *Train Whistle Guitar*), marries and has a son, Murray's half-brother James Burke. (Burke, who will have a career in the military, writes to Murray in 2002, "I remember the auntie bit, but she *always* told me you were my *brother*.")

1931–35   As student in high school program of Mobile County Training School, participates in theatrical productions, playing Aubrey Piper in *The Show-Off*, a comedy by George Kelly, and Thea Dugger in *Bad Man*, a Harlem Renaissance "folk play" by Randolph Edmonds. Appears in Negro History Week pageants, one time performing a juba dance to "Juba," from R. Nathaniel Dett's piano suite *In the Bottoms* (1913). Excels in French and Latin. Paints. Plays baseball and basketball. In sophomore year is voted best all-around student by the faculty.

1935   In January travels to Tuskegee Institute for a regional high school
        basketball tournament. There, through arrangements made by
        Sudie Graham Burke, meets for the first time his biological father,
        John Young. (Young is now a foreman at the institute's power
        plant, where he has worked since returning from World War I,
        and the father of Murray's eleven-year-old half-sister, Rowena
        Young.) Graduates from Mobile County Training School and is
        granted full-tuition scholarship to Tuskegee. Picks cotton for a
        week ("It seemed heroic to me") to earn the bus fare to Tuskegee,
        205 miles from Magazine Point. Matriculates at Tuskegee, where
        he lives with Young and his family.

1935–39 Studies education at Tuskegee. Takes four years of ROTC train-
        ing. Studies military science and tactics under Benjamin O.
        Davis, Sr. (the first black general in the U.S. Army), during his
        freshman year, and under Benjamin O. Davis, Jr., during his se-
        nior year. Joins Alpha Phi Alpha fraternity. Becomes president of
        Tuskegee chapter of Alpha Kappa Mu honor society. Works in the
        power plant with John Young during the summers. Also works as
        a cook in the veterans' hospital in Tuskegee. Mentored in modern
        literature by English department chairman Morteza Drexel
        ("Mort") Sprague, a charismatic teacher still only in his twenties.
        Reads James Joyce, T. S. Eliot, Hemingway, Faulkner, Edna St.
        Vincent Millay, E. E. Cummings, Wallace Stevens, W. H. Auden,
        William Saroyan, Charles and Mary Beard, Sigrid Undset, Ro-
        main Rolland, Kenneth Burke, and many others. Notices that
        many of the books he has been borrowing from the library have
        also been checked out by upperclassman Ralph Ellison, a clerk at
        the library's circulation desk and a fellow protégé of Sprague.
        (Ellison and Murray have a few brief conversations in the library
        but will not become friends until the 1940s in New York City.) In
        junior year writes one-act play, *Odds and Ends*, which is staged by
        Tuskegee's Little Theater on the evening of April 28, 1938. The
        setting is a shoe store in Mobile and the play has seven characters,
        none played by Murray. (Only a program survives.) Pays close
        attention to contemporary theater through periodicals and an-
        thologies. After reading Thomas Mann's essay "The Coming Hu-
        manism" in *The Nation* (December 10, 1938), seeks out the
        author's *The Coming Victory of Democracy* and *Joseph* novels.

1939   Graduates from Tuskegee with BS in education. Reads Joyce's
        Finnegans Wake when it is published in the spring. Takes job as
        principal of Damascus Junior High School in Damascus, Georgia
        (population 477). When he misses a bus connection en route to
        Damascus and is stranded at night in Columbus, Georgia, a fel-
        low black traveler points him to Ma Rainey's house. Rainey lets

him sleep on her couch. (He will write about this episode, and of Rainey's kindness, in *South to a Very Old Place*.) Reading includes Kierkegaard, Sir James George Frazer, Virginia Woolf, and John Dewey.

1940   Position in Damascus proves disappointing. In the 1940 Census is listed as again living in Mobile with Hugh and Mattie Murray. In summer begins graduate coursework in education at the University of Michigan, likely his first trip outside the South. Reading includes Marx and Nietzsche. Studies Thomas Mann's work in depth. Returns to Tuskegee in the fall to teach in the night school and direct the Little Theater company.

1941   On May 31 marries Mozelle Menefee (b. 1920), who grew up in Tuskegee and has just completed her sophomore year at the Institute. Postpones honeymoon, and spends summer doing graduate coursework on theories of reading instruction at the University of Chicago and at Northwestern University. Returns to Tuskegee in the fall. Begins to develop two signatures, one for official documents, with a circular A, the other for writing his name in books, with a stylized, pointy A. Will maintain this system, with few exceptions, for the rest of his life.

1942   Teaches English at Tuskegee and directs the Little Theater company. In summer takes honeymoon trip to New York with Mozelle; they stay at Hotel Theresa in Harlem, then the hotel of choice for black show business and sports figures. Renews acquaintance with Ralph Ellison.

1943   On January 5 enlists in U.S. Army, and reports for duty one week later. Sent to Utah for basic training. Attends Army Administration School at Atlanta University from March through May. Mozelle graduates from Tuskegee in the spring. Murray attends Officers Candidate School in Miami Beach, Florida, from September through January 1944. Commissioned second lieutenant. Daughter, Michele Alberita Murray, born on October 3.

1944   Transferred in January to Tuskegee Army Air Field and soon becomes assistant training coordinator for the Tuskegee Airmen. Studies War Department Pamphlet 20-6, *Command of Negro Troops*, published in February. Reading includes Kafka, Arthur Koestler, Anaïs Nin, and the autobiography of Giambattista Vico. Enjoys discussing Faulkner's work with Colonel Noel F. Parrish, commander of Tuskegee Army Air Field.

1945   In April takes training-instructor course in San Antonio, Texas. Promoted to training coordinator at Tuskegee Army Air Field on

June 25. On August 2 is transferred to Army Air Forces Camou-
flage School in Buckley, Colorado. (He will later say that this
transfer had something to do with plans for an Allied invasion of
Japan, and that he had expected to end up in the Pacific theater.)
Promoted to first lieutenant on August 8. Japan surrenders on
August 14. Camouflage School ends on August 18. Returns to
Tuskegee Army Air Field. Mozelle begins teaching career in Ala-
bama public schools.

1946   On January 4, through arrangements made by an Army buddy
related to Ellington band member Harry Carney, has backstage
meeting with Duke Ellington after Ellington's fourth annual concert at Carnegie Hall. In October applies to remain on active duty
during demobilization of the U.S. armed forces then under way.
Application is denied. On November 13 the Army determines
Murray's position to be redundant. Instructed to use sixty days of
accrued leave time before being demobilized.

1947   Officially placed on reserve duty on January 14. Returns to Tuskegee Institute as instructor of freshman and sophomore English.
In the fall enters the master of arts program in English at New
York University. Lives at 147 Bainbridge Street in Bedford-
Stuyvesant, Brooklyn, with Mozelle and Michele. Takes courses
with Margaret Schlauch (Chaucer) and Oscar Cargill (American
literature). Pursues active social life in Greenwich Village. Forms
friendships with Maya Deren, Joseph Campbell, Seymour Krim,
and Anaïs Nin. Spends his days studying, writing, and research-
ing at the Forty-second Street branch of the New York Public Library. Frequently meets Ellison for lunch. (Ellison is working on
Invisible Man in an office on loan from Francis Steegmuller at
Forty-ninth and Fifth Avenue.) After classes at NYU, Murray
goes sometimes to the Fifty-second Street nightclubs to hear
Charlie Parker, Dizzy Gillespie, and other jazz musicians, and
sometimes to Ellison's Harlem apartment to listen to him read
from *Invisible Man*. Attends New Year's Eve party at Ellison's.
Reading includes Constance Rourke and art historian Heinrich
Zimmer.

1948   Writes master's thesis, "*The Waste Land* and *The Sun Also Rises*: A
Comparative Study." Returns to Tuskegee in the fall and begins
two-year stint of teaching. Master's thesis approved in October.

1949   Works on a semi-autobiographical novel concerning the childhood and adolescence of Scooter, a poor Alabama-born "jack
rabbit raised in the briarpatch" who, in the extant version, with
the help of several larger-than-life mentors, passes all the tests of

life to become, successively, an accomplished student, a jazz musician, and a writer.

1950   Begins ten-year correspondence with Ralph Ellison (which he will coedit, annotate, and in the year 2000 publish as *Trading Twelves: The Selected Letters of Ralph Ellison and Albert Murray*). Ellison reports on the progress of *Invisible Man*—"the goddamnedest experience of my life"—and encourages Murray to complete his *Bildungsroman*. In late spring sails to Paris to study French at the Sorbonne courtesy of the GI Bill. Receives $300 grant for the trip from Tuskegee, equivalent to five weeks' salary before taxes. Stops first in Lisbon, Genoa, and Venice. Arrives in Paris in mid-June and stays at the Hotel Londres. Meets and forms friendships with James Baldwin, Jean Hélion and Pegeen Guggenheim, René Liebowitz, and H. J. "Kappy" Kaplan, a diplomatic attaché and Paris correspondent for *Partisan Review*, whose apartment is a social and cultural center. Meets Sidney Bechet. Meets painter Romare Bearden, who will become a close friend and intellectual comrade. Reconnects with Duke Ellington. Meets Ollie Stewart, foreign correspondent of the *Baltimore Afro-American*, who will devote half of his July 1 "Report from Europe" column to Murray's presence in Paris and work on a novel. Worries about being recalled to active duty when Korean War begins on June 25. Writes to Mozelle for news of war preparation at Tuskegee. Kaplan takes his family to the United States for the summer in late June or early July, and Murray moves into his apartment at 132 boulevard du Montparnasse, one floor above Henri Matisse. (Murray will recall that it was possible to catch glimpses of Matisse at work from the open elevator.) In August visits Antibes with Baldwin, whom he teaches how to swim. Leaves Paris on August 29. Returns to Tuskegee via Montreal and New York.

1951   Recalled to active duty in U.S. Air Force on June 6. Assigned to Tuskegee Institute as assistant professor of air science and tactics and teaches courses in geopolitics as well. Takes course at Air University at Maxwell Air Force Base in Montgomery, Alabama. Buys lot number three on Hudson Street at the intersection of Bibb Street in Tuskegee. Hires architect Bill Mann, an old friend from Tuskegee, to design a house. Completes first draft of semi-autobiographical narrative, provisionally titled "Jack the Bear," that will eventually yield the novels *Train Whistle Guitar* (1974) and *The Spyglass Tree* (1991). Sends manuscript to Ellison late in the year. Interviews Duke Ellington on local radio show.

1952   Ellison provides detailed feedback on manuscript in February letter. Murray follows reviews of *Invisible Man* closely when Random House publishes novel in the spring. Receives mixed criticism of "Jack the Bear" from Ellison's editor, Albert Erskine, who feels that Murray is under the spell of Faulkner. Reads André Malraux on art.

1953   Takes course for Air Force instructors at Ohio State University. Visits Cuba and returns home with conga and bongo drums, which he takes up playing. Submits novel, now retitled "The Briarpatch," to Arabel J. Porter, editor of *New World Writing*, a recently launched "paperback magazine" published by New American Library. Porter excerpts a section of "The Briarpatch" as a short story, "The Luzana Cholly Kick," and, in October, publishes it in issue number four. In a biographical note preceding the story, Murray writes: "We all learn from Mann, Joyce, Hemingway, Eliot, and the rest, but I'm also trying to learn to write in terms of the tradition I grew up in, the Negro tradition of blues, stomps, ragtime, jumps, and swing. After all, very few writers have done as much with American experience as Jelly Roll Morton, Count Basie, and Duke Ellington." Writes to Porter that being included in the anthology (which also includes Jorge Luis Borges, Gore Vidal, Nadine Gordimer, Shelby Foote, Robert Motherwell, and others) was like being "in the World Series in your first season in organized baseball" and "just about the best thing that could happen to an apprentice."

1954   Promoted to captain in the U.S. Air Force on March 11. Helps arrange for Ellison to speak at Tuskegee.

1955   Construction of house in Tuskegee begins in April. The Murrays will never live in it. In August Murray is transferred to Nouasseur Air Base, just outside Casablanca, Morocco. Lives first in Casablanca and then on the base. Buys Leica M3 camera for $244 in the fall. Begins discussing photography with Ellison, who had worked as a professional photographer in the late 1940s.

1956   Serves as chief of military training at Nouasseur. Tuskegee house completed in March and rented out. Rent covers mortgage and yields a small profit (rent collection overseen by local bank). At the request of the U.S. Information Service, begins lecturing (in French) on jazz at various Moroccan venues, including the Maison d'Amérique in Casablanca and the U.S. embassy in Rabat. Receives commendations from American diplomats and superior officers. Visits Greece in May. In the summer drives with Mozelle and Michele from Spain to Italy. They then travel through Europe with Ellison (then in residence at the American Academy in Rome) and his wife Fanny.

1957   Vice President Richard Nixon visits Nouasseur in March. Murray writes to Ellison about the surprisingly large number of blacks in Nixon's entourage. Murray writes memo to Air Force superiors in April: "I am particularly interested in working in a position involving international relations, perhaps in conjunction with an Attaché, Mission, or Advisory Group type assignment." Suffers mild heart attack on May 18. Recuperates at base hospital. Visits West Germany in June and the Netherlands in October. Returns to duty on November 20.

1958   Visits West Germany in January. In April is transferred to Air Reserve Flying Center at Long Beach (California) Municipal Airport and is placed in charge of personnel. In July buys home at 1515 West 166th Street, Compton, for $13,500.

1959   In the spring is reassigned by Air Force from position as personnel specialist to that of supply officer. Writes ardent letter to superiors protesting his new assignment as beneath his level of training, established skill set, and previous achievements. Also argues that reassignment violates established protocol, as he was not briefed ahead of time. Letter is either ignored or not acted upon. Takes three-month supply management course for Air Force officers in Amarillo, Texas. Becomes officer accountable for air base property in Long Beach.

1960   On June 20 photographs Duke Ellington's recording sessions at the famed Radio Recorders studio in West Hollywood. Travels in summer throughout California.

1961   In January, as base accountable officer, signs documents closing the Air Reserve Flying Center in Long Beach. Begins new assignment at Headquarters Air Base Wing, Air Force Systems Command, at Hanscom Field in Bedford, Massachusetts, twenty miles northwest of Boston. Placed in charge of Materiel Control Office, becoming responsible for sixty-four aircraft, some experimental. Lives in base officers' quarters while Mozelle and Michele stay in Compton so that Michele can finish high school there. Promoted to major "as a Reserve of the Air Force" on March 11. Quickly becomes a friend of Charlie Davidson, proprietor of the Andover Shop in Cambridge and a tailor, jazz buff, reader, and raconteur. (The Murrays and the Davidsons will become lifelong friends, attending the Newport Jazz Festival and sometimes vacationing together.) Begins attending Alpha Phi Alpha gatherings around Boston. In June sells home in Compton for $15,525. Moves with Mozelle and Michele to 54 High Road in Bedford following Michele's graduation. Becomes chief of logistic branch at Hanscom on September 16. Michele enters Juilliard in the fall to study dance and lives with Ralph and Fanny Ellison in New York City.

1962   Sells house in Tuskegee on March 19 for $9,500. (Cost of lot and construction was $11,500, but probably realizes a small profit after seven years of rent collections and tax deductions.) Approaching fifth anniversary of heart attack, receives extensive physical examination at Hanscom from May 1 to 4. On May 15 a panel of Air Force physicians at Andrews Air Force Base, in Washington, D.C., determines that he be assigned early retirement due to arteriosclerotic heart disease. Glowing report of physician at Hanscom emphasizes Murray's otherwise excellent health, and notes that Murray has never been prescribed cardiovascular drugs, perhaps to leave the door open for an appeal. The doctor writes, toward the end of a long report, "Patient is a well-developed, well-nourished, middle-aged man who appears neither acutely nor chronically ill and who is in no acute distress. . . . At the present time I do not think he has any symptoms due to heart disease." Yet Murray accepts early retirement. Retires on June 29, with the permanent grade of major. Will live another fifty-one years and never suffer further heart problems. Stands five foot eight and weighs 168 pounds. Letter of appreciation from his commanding officer states that Murray is "the prototype of the military man whose leadership qualities, devoted service, military bearing, and desirable personal qualities motivate our younger personnel to emulation." Moves to New York and rents apartment 8P at 45 West 132nd Street in the Lenox Terrace Apartments complex in Harlem, a middle- and upper-middle-class residential development whose residents have included many distinguished Harlem professionals and politicians, such as Congressman Charles Rangel, New York governor David Patterson, and Manhattan borough president Percy Sutton. The enclave of six large buildings between Lenox Avenue and Fifth Avenue is less than a decade old when the Murrays move in. Their eighth-floor corner apartment has two bedrooms, one and a half bathrooms, a balcony, and spectacular views of Harlem and midtown. The Murrays will live here for the rest of their lives. Renews friendship with Romare Bearden in Manhattan. (The view from Murray's balcony of the west side of Lenox Avenue between 132nd and 133rd Streets will be Bearden's vantage point for his giant collage *The Block* [1971], which will be acquired by the Metropolitan Museum of Art in 1978. Two photographs by Murray of that portion of Lenox Avenue, taken from his balcony circa 1971, are also part of the Metropolitan Museum of Art's permanent collection.) Tries to revive prospects of "The Briarpatch," unsuccessfully submitting it to editor Peter Davison at Atlantic Monthly Press.

1963   Works assiduously on an essay, begun years before, on what he calls the "blues idiom," a special character of expression born of a determination to achieve "elegance in the face of adversity." The essay, called "The Hero and the Blues," will soon grow into a book-length manuscript. Mozelle begins teaching in New York City preschools.

1964   On January 20 enjoys stint as on-camera theater critic, reviewing three plays in an arts segment of *The World at Ten* on WNDT, New York. Publishes first work of nonfiction in July 3 issue of *Life*, an omnibus review of what the editors bill as "seven new works on the racial crisis." At Ellison's suggestion, begins reviewing books for *The New Leader*, a biweekly magazine of politics and opinion edited in New York by Myron Kolatch. Michele begins work as a professional dancer at the World's Fair in Queens.

1965   Ellison brings Murray on board as a credited consultant for three documentaries for educational television (WNET, New York). (Ellison, through his work with the Carnegie Commission, had been lobbying for the creation of a public television network.) Two are on jazz (*Jazz Goes Intellectual: Bop!*, featuring Dizzy Gillespie, and *Jazz: The Experimenters*, featuring Charles Mingus and Cecil Taylor) and the other is on Ellison himself (*Ralph Ellison: Work in Progress*). Murray serves as "technical consultant" and may have done some script work as well. Michele begins dancing with the Alvin Ailey Company. (She will work with other companies as well, including the Lar Lubovitch Company, before becoming a featured dancer with Ailey circa 1968.) Around this time begins tradition of throwing downhome-style New Year's Day parties—pigs' feet, black-eyed peas, collard greens, cornbread, bourbon—which will continue for several decades.

1966   During the New York City transit strike in January, Murray chauffeurs Michele and her dancer-colleagues from Harlem to the Clark Center in midtown for Ailey Company rehearsals. (He will abandon car ownership within the next few years.) In February is invited by editor Kirkpatrick Sale of *The New York Times Magazine* to write an essay on current and historical relationships between blacks and Jews. (Essay is rejected, with apologies from Sale.) In April speaks at the Peace Corps Training Center in Arecibo, Puerto Rico. Mozelle begins teaching in New York City public schools. "The Luzana Cholly Kick" (1953) is reprinted, under revised title "Train Whistle Guitar," in John Henrik Clarke's landmark anthology *American Negro Short Stories*, published by Hill and Wang. Murray's essay on James Baldwin is a frequently cited highlight of *Anger, and Beyond: The Negro Writer in the United States*, a wide-ranging anthology of previously unpublished writings edited by Herbert Hill and published by Harper & Row. Mort Sprague dies, at age fifty-seven, at the end of the year. Sprague, to whom Ellison dedicated his essay collection *Shadow and Act* (1964), had been paying close attention to Murray's magazine work and writing to him about it.

1967   In April, begins two-year involvement with New York's Center for Urban Education (CUE), a public-education policy institute funded from 1964 to 1973 by the U.S. Office of Education. Contributes essays to CUE periodicals (*The Urban Review*, a bi-monthly journal, and *The Center Forum*, a monthly newsletter) and works as researcher and consultant on several of CUE's multimedia educational initiatives. Writes draft of essay that will become Part I of his collection *The Omni-Americans*. Publishes negative review of William Styron's novel *The Confessions of Nat Turner* in December 4 issue of *The New Leader*.

1968   For the Smithsonian Institution's Archives of American Art Oral History program, interviews painters Charles Alston (Bearden's older cousin), Emma Amos, Merton Simpson, and Hale Woodruff. Teaches course at Columbia University School of Journalism. "Train Whistle Guitar" is revised for inclusion in Theodore L. Gross and James A. Emanuel's anthology *Dark Symphony: Negro Literature in America*, published by Free Press. Editor Angus Cameron at Knopf, responding to a proposal from Murray, says that he is interested in publishing a collection of his essays and reviews but disagrees with him on a few points. Meanwhile, two of CUE's top editors, David E. Outerbridge and Harris Dienstfrey, leave the institute to establish their own book-publishing firm. They admire Murray's work, and invite him to contribute to their list.

1969   Second excerpt from "The Briarpatch" is published in February issue of *Harper's* as "Stonewall Jackson's Waterloo." The magazine's editor, Willie Morris, then sends Murray on an assignment to assess the South, especially his native Alabama, in the wake of desegregation. This long nonfiction piece, part personal memoir, part interview-based journalism, will be Murray's chief project over the next two years. (Murray's interview subjects include Robert Penn Warren, C. Vann Woodward, Walker Percy, and many southern newspaper editors and reporters.) On March 3, Outerbridge and Dienstfrey make a formal offer to publish Murray's collection of essays *The Omni-Americans*. Murray, his discussions with Knopf having reached an impasse, accepts. In October acquires James Oliver Brown as literary agent.

1970   *The Omni-Americans* is published by Outerbridge and Dienstfrey in March. A Book-of-the-Month Club alternate selection, the collection is widely and enthusiastically reviewed. (Robert Coles, in *The New Yorker*, writes that Murray "speaks for himself [and] as a man who is proud of his people and their considerable achievements. . . . His purpose [here] is to set forth those achievements and to warn against America's 'experts,' especially what he calls 'social survey technicians,' [who] do not see the richness, the complexity of the black man's experience in America; they merely contribute to the caricatures that so many of us cannot get out of our heads.") Takes two-week vacation with Mozelle to Sag Harbor, Long Island, in July. In August delivers first post–*Omni-Americans* lecture, "Beyond Separatism," to Brandeis University's Summer Adult Institute. Serves as O'Connor Professor of Literature at Colgate University in the fall. Duke Ellington, then in residency in Los Angeles, interviews Murray for job as co-author of his autobiography. (In the end Ellington will write *Music Is My Mistress* [1973] with longtime confidant Stanley Dance.)

1971   Brown sells book rights to *Harper's* article to Joyce Johnson, an editor at McGraw-Hill and an acquaintance of Murray since 1969. In March Willie Morris is fired from *Harper's* and magazine publication of the article, scheduled for the fall, is canceled. Murray serves as visiting professor of literature at the University of Massachusetts–Boston. "Train Whistle Guitar" is reprinted in his friend Toni Cade Bambara's anthology *Tales and Stories for Black Folks* and is admiringly quoted at length by Toni Morrison in *The New York Times*. Michele tours Soviet Union with Alvin Ailey company. In November *South to a Very Old Place* is published by McGraw-Hill to excellent reviews. (Robert R. Gross, in *Saturday Review*, writes that Murray, by intermingling "reminiscences of youth with engaging conversation, cultural criticism, and comments on his folk heritage," has created "a disciplined work of art: a reflective and elegant rendering of one man's coming to terms with his roots.") *The Omni-Americans* is reprinted in paperback by Avon Books.

1972 In January Ruth Ellington (Duke's sister and music publishing manager) throws book party for *South to a Very Old Place* at 333 Riverside Drive (which is also Duke's mailing address). In February accepts invitation from the University of Missouri–Columbia to deliver the Paul Anthony Brick Lectures for fall 1972. Revisits "The Hero and the Blues," his essay on the blues idiom, and begins adapting the material for a series of three hour-long lectures. *South to a Very Old Place* named a finalist for the National Book Award in the Arts and Letters category. Jack Valenti, formerly a top aide to President Johnson, writes to Murray regarding how much LBJ appreciated *South to a Very Old Place*, especially Murray's account of a conversation among elderly Alabamians about Johnson's civil rights policies. Receives Alumni Merit Award from Tuskegee. Speaks at Southern University, in Baton Rouge, Louisiana. Correspondents around this time include Michael Harper, James Alan McPherson, Ernest J. Gaines, Robert Bone, Martin Williams, and Leon Forrest. Spanish translation of *The Omni-Americans* is published by Editorial Letras in Mexico City. On October 7, 8, and 9, delivers Paul Anthony Brick Lectures at the University of Missouri.

1973 Serves as O'Connor Visiting Lecturer at Colgate University. Speaks at Yale University. Elected to executive committee of American branch of PEN. In spring Harvard undergraduate Lewis P. Jones III, editor of "Black Odyssey; A Search for Home," a special issue of the *Harvard Advocate*, invites Murray to contribute to the publication. Instead of an article, Murray suggests that the issue's chief theme, "the role and responsibilities of black artists operating in the larger American context," be the subject of a Harvard symposium and that the transcript be published in the *Advocate*. The symposium, moderated by Dean of Students Archie Epps and featuring Murray, Ellison, Harold Cruse, and Nathan I. Huggins, marks the beginning of Murray's decades-long friendship with Jones, who will later have a career in law, banking, and finance. Brick Lectures published as *The Hero and the Blues* by the University of Missouri Press. (An unsigned review in *The New Yorker* says that "[Murray] is succinct, funny, and marvelously original in defining what a hero is in fiction and drama—his reading of *Oedipus* is a knockout, and his comparison of Mann's Joseph to American black heroes is eye-opening.")

1974 Elected to membership in the Century Association, an exclusive club of writers, artists, musicians, and patrons of the arts in midtown Manhattan. Quickly becomes a regular for lunch and an active participant in club affairs. (The club will remain an important part of his life through 2005.) At St. Peter's Evangelical

Lutheran Church in Manhattan (famous for its ministry to the jazz world) serves on committee (along with Ruth Ellington, Phoebe Jacobs, Stanley Dance, and others) that organizes seventy-fifth-birthday concert for Duke Ellington on April 29. (Ellington will die on May 24.) In early May *Train Whistle Guitar*, a novel of childhood fashioned from approximately the first half of "The Briarpatch," is published by McGraw-Hill. The book, which will later that year win the Lillian Smith Award for Fiction from the Southern Regional Council, is well and widely reviewed. (John Edgar Wideman, writing in *The New York Times Book Review*, says that "the only way to appreciate the music of Murray's prose is to immerse yourself in long passages of dialogue and monologue, the lyric descriptions of countryside and fireside, which are nothing so much as the riffs and choruses of a blues artist translated into speech and action. . . . [They tell us] the truth about black experience just as resolutely as the runaway, star-climbing notes of a Charlie Parker solo.") At the invitation of Martin Williams, teaches at Smithsonian Institute in Music Criticism, where Gary Giddins is among his students. Is a regular at Upper East Side restaurant Elaine's. Speaks at public schools in Sacramento. Receives contract from McGraw-Hill for sequel to *Train Whistle Guitar*.

1975   Receives honorary doctorate from Colgate University. Social circle at this time includes Mary Hemingway, Robert Penn Warren, Sidney Offit, Herbert Mitgang, Drew Middleton, John Chancellor, Matt Clark, John Hammond, Romare Bearden, and Ralph Ellison. Michele, no longer with the Alvin Ailey company, teaches courses on dance and movement for actors at Howard University.

1976   In October *Stomping the Blues* is published by McGraw-Hill. A study of the history, aesthetics, rituals, and anthropology of jazz, focusing on its black derivation and affirmative disposition, the book is widely reviewed in both the mainstream and the music press. (Greil Marcus, writing in *Rolling Stone*, explains that for Murray blues music "is not involved with self-pity or resignation . . . but with affirmation and the act of creation. . . . *Stomping the Blues* is anything but the last word on the blues. It is, though, the best word anyone has offered in a long time.") For book party, McGraw-Hill throws a "Kansas City Jam Session" at its building on Sixth Avenue in midtown Manhattan, featuring jazz legends Budd Johnson, Eddie Durham, Buck Clayton, Oliver Jackson, Mary Lou Williams, Bill Pemberton, and Doc Cheatham. Murray's students and acolytes around this time include Gary Giddins, Henry Louis Gates, Jr., Charlayne Hunter-Gault, and Stanley

Crouch. Murray writes catalogue essay for Bearden's exhibition *Of the Blues* at Cordier & Ekstrom Gallery in New York.

1977   Jason Berry's essay "Musical Literature," the first long-form critical appraisal of Murray's oeuvre, appears in the January 15 issue of *The Nation*. Murray travels to West Germany in June for the United States Information Agency, speaking at the Free University of Berlin, the University of Bonn, and the University of Bremen. *Stomping the Blues* wins ASCAP/Deems Taylor Award for Music Criticism. Approached by Willard Alexander, longtime booking agent for Count Basie, to act as Basie's co-writer on an as-told-to autobiography. Agrees. Travels with Basie on and off through 1983. Repeatedly interviews old acquaintance Jo Jones, the drummer for the Basie band during its first decade, originally for background for the Basie book and then for a possible book on Jones's life. Exhaustively corroborates Basie's memories by interviewing bandmates, including Eddie Durham, Budd Johnson, Dan Minor, and Buck Clayton, and by checking Basie's memories against newspaper stories and publicity materials. Is "Special Guest Speaker" at conference of African and African American Folklorists at Indiana University–Bloomington. Speaks at the Studio Museum in Harlem.

1978   In spring is writer-in-residence at Emory University, where Mike Sager, who will become a prominent journalist, is among his students. Befriends literary scholar and biographer Richard Ellmann, also teaching at Emory. Conducts several long interviews with Jo Jones in the summer and fall. Writes wall labels for Bearden's *Profiles* series, on view at Cordier & Ekstrom. Presents lectures at Morehouse College and Howard University. Attends concert at the White House celebrating the twenty-fifth anniversary of the Newport Jazz Festival. Speaks at Long Island University's C. W. Post campus on several occasions throughout the 1978–79 school year under auspices of the political science department. Interviewed at his apartment by Henry Louis Gates, Jr., and Robert G. O'Meally (who sets up the interview). The interview is transcribed but is then set aside. O'Meally will find the transcription on the morning of what would have been Murray's hundredth birthday, May 12, 2016, and through the efforts of Gates, it will be published in the Winter 2016 issue of *The Paris Review* in December 2016 (after having been prepared for publication by Paul Devlin). In December, filmmaker Nelson E. Breen records joint conversation of Murray, Bearden, Alvin Ailey, and James Baldwin for the documentary *Bearden Plays Bearden* (1980).

1979   Writes recommendation on behalf of Eleanor Traylor to the Na-
            tional Endowment for the Humanities in support of Traylor's
            proposal for a fellowship to write a study of Richard Wright's
            creative process. Smithsonian interview with Hale Woodruff
            (1968) is published in the catalogue to Woodruff's exhibition at
            the Studio Museum in Harlem. Herbert Mitgang interviews
            Murray about his collaboration with Count Basie for his Book
            Ends column in *The New York Times* on November 18. Murray
            tells Mitgang: "My job is to help him get his voice right so readers
            will say 'I know that's Count Basie talking; what did Albert Mur-
            ray do to get his name on the book?'"

1980   Begins teaching creative writing at Barnard College as an adjunct
            associate professor. (He will continue on and off through 1983.)
            Declines Nathan I. Huggins's offer of a teaching position at Har-
            vard University. Stanley Crouch's laudatory essay "Albert Murray's
            Gourmet Chitlins" appears in the March 3 issue of the *Village
            Voice*. Works with Bearden and the photographer and movie
            producer Sam Shaw on *Paris Blues*, a book based on Shaw's 1961
            film of that title. (The book, commissioned by a French publisher
            but never realized, was to include photographs by Shaw, collages
            and other artworks by Bearden, and a text by Murray.) Writes
            catalogue essay for Bearden retrospective *Romare Bearden: 1970–
            1980* at the Mint Museum in Charlotte, North Carolina. Travels to
            Charlotte for the exhibition's opening. Appears in documentary
            Bearden Plays Bearden, several scenes of which are filmed on the
            balcony of Murray's apartment.

1981   Delivers lecture on Bearden at the Brooklyn Museum in October;
            a concert by Teddy Wilson follows Murray's presentation. Intro-
            duced by Stanley Crouch to nineteen-year-old Juilliard student
            Wynton Marsalis, a composer and trumpeter who will become
            Murray's most famous protégé in terms of thinking about culture.

1982   Serves as Colgate Professor of Humanities at Colgate in the fall,
            teaching junior-level course on regional writing and senior-level
            course "Implications of the Blues Idiom in Contemporary Amer-
            ican Literature." Attends an "All-Star Jazz Program" at the White
            House on December 4. Fires his literary agent, James Oliver
            Brown, whose firm, James Brown Associates, had merged with
            the New York office of prominent British firm Curtis Brown, Ltd.,
            in 1978. James Oliver Brown was serving as president of newly
            formed Curtis Brown Associates at the time, and Murray felt that
            his account was not receiving proper attention. *Stomping the
            Blues* reprinted by Vintage a few months after Nelson George's
            lament, in the *Village Voice*, that it had fallen out of print.

1983   Increases frequency of interviews with Count Basie. Makes several trips to Basie's home in Freeport, Bahamas. Speaks at Drew University. *The Omni-Americans* reprinted by Vintage. Speaks at the Jane Globus Seminar at Baruch College. Serves as judge of the Robert F. Kennedy Book Awards.

1984   Count Basie dies on April 26, just months after he and Murray had completed the first draft of his autobiography, *Good Morning Blues*. Speaks at Swarthmore College.

1985   Signs contract with Random House for *Good Morning Blues*. (Andrew Wylie, who represents him in the deal, will remain his agent for the rest of his life.) Book acquired by editor Erroll McDonald, who will publish all of Murray's future work, usually under Random House's Pantheon imprint. Collaborates with saxophonist David Murray (no relation) on musical stage adaptation of *Train Whistle Guitar*. (Producer Joseph Papp of the New York Shakespeare Festival shows serious interest in this work-in-progress, but the musical is never realized.) In July Murray conducts his last interview with Jo Jones, who dies, at age seventy-three, on September 3. Speaks at Harvard University in November.

1986   *Good Morning Blues: The Autobiography of Count Basie as told to Albert Murray* is published in early January. (By March twelve thousand copies are sold.) Black-tie book party for a thousand people at the Palladium in New York on January 17 is covered by national news media. Conducts long interview with Dizzy Gillespie, a truncated version of which appears in *Interview Magazine* for April. Murray is included in a fashion photo shoot in *New York* magazine. Receives award from literary journal *Callaloo*, which in December hosts a tribute to Murray at the convention of the Modern Language Association, featuring readings by Elizabeth Alexander, Thulani Davis, and Melvin Dixon. Joins board of directors of American Composers Orchestra, and will serve until 1989. Appears in "Black on White," episode five of Robert MacNeil's PBS documentary *The Story of English*.

1987   With Wynton Marsalis, Gordon Davis, and Stanley Crouch, Murray serves on committee that proposes the establishment of a classic jazz program at New York's Lincoln Center for the Performing Arts. (He will work closely with Crouch and Marsalis over the next several years on developing the project.) Delivers lecture to the Peter Rushton Seminars on Modern Literature at the University of Virginia. Speaks at Ohio University. German translation of *Good Morning Blues* published by Econ Verlag. Speaks at Dayton Art Institute, with concert by David Murray following presentation. Appears in documentary *Long Shadows: The Legacy of the American Civil War*. Interviewed twice at his apartment by V. S. Naipaul, in the spring and the fall. Helps make arrangements for Naipaul's visit to Tuskegee for his book *A Turn in the South* (1989). Mozelle retires from teaching in June.

1988   Romare Bearden dies on March 12, at age seventy-six. Murray becomes involved in creation of Romare Bearden Foundation. French translation of *Good Morning Blues* published by Éditions Filipacchi.

1989   On June 17, in honor of Murray's work with Central Pennsylvania Friends of Jazz, "Albert Murray Day" proclaimed in Harrisburg by Governor Bob Casey, Sr. Speaks at the New School for Social Research alongside Wynton Marsalis and jazz composer/arranger David Berger. Paperback edition of *Train Whistle Guitar* issued by Northeastern University Press with a new foreword by Robert G. O'Meally. Paperback rights to *The Omni-Americans* and *Stomping the Blues* licensed by Wylie to Da Capo Press.

1990   Appears in documentary *Lady Day: The Many Faces of Billie Holiday*. In spring spends two weeks at Dillard University in New Orleans, as United Negro College Fund Distinguished Scholar. In October takes long vacation with Mozelle and Michele to England and France, traveling from London to Paris to the Côte d'Azur, visiting friends along the way.

1991   Group of friends throws surprise party for the Murrays on their fiftieth wedding anniversary. Second novel, *The Spyglass Tree*, originally under contract with McGraw-Hill, is published by Pantheon in the fall. A sequel to *Train Whistle Guitar*, it continues the adventures of Scooter, now a student at a black college based on the Tuskegee of the 1930s. Novel is well received by critics, including Michiko Kakutani, who writes in *The New York Times* that "the book, as a whole, works beautifully. . . . Like all good *Bildungsromane*, it leaves the reader with a vivid portrait of a young man and his struggles to come to terms with his receding past and his beckoning future." In December receives Directors Emeriti Award from Lincoln Center for outstanding service to the institution in a volunteer capacity. Writes script for and appears in British television documentary *Count Basie: Swingin' the Blues. South to a Very Old Place* reprinted in paperback by Vintage.

1992   On his birthday has conversation with Wynton Marsalis onstage at Lincoln Center. Endures operation on back and neck, after which he will walk with a cane for several years, and later with a walker. Speaks at the Center for American Culture Studies at Columbia University. Writes captions for photographer Ming Smith's book *A Ming Breakfast: Grits and Scrambled Moments*.

1993   Serves as Du Pont Visiting Professor at Washington and Lee University in the fall. Appears as commentator, with blues scholar Robert Palmer, in documentary *Bluesland: A Portrait in American Music*.

1994   Attends eightieth birthday dinner for Ellison on March 1 at Le Périgord in New York. Ellison dies on April 16 after a brief illness. In April Murray is interviewed at his apartment by Wynton Marsalis, and in July is interviewed by Robert G. O'Meally for the Smithsonian's Jazz Oral History Project. (These wide-ranging discussions will appear, along with a much longer version of Murray's 1986 interview of Dizzy Gillespie, in *Murray Talks Music* [2016], edited by Paul Devlin.)

1995   *South to a Very Old Place* republished in hardcover by Modern Library. *The Hero and the Blues* reprinted in paperback by Vintage. Paperback edition of *Good Morning Blues* issued by Da Capo.

1996   In February Pantheon publishes two new books to an avalanche of attention: a third Scooter novel, *The Seven League Boots*, and an essay collection, *The Blue Devils of Nada*. (In the daily *New York Times*, Richard Bernstein calls the novel "a prose poem full of character and wisdom" in which Scooter, now a young man, "becomes part of a famous jazz band, travels the country, conquers Hollywood, goes to France, and is loved by several glamorous women, all the while reflecting on history and mythology, on Odysseus and Telemachus . . . and above all on the folks back in Alabama who sent him into the world to do great things." Charles Johnson, praising Murray's "wise and authoritative essays" in the Sunday *Book Review*, writes: "What deserves very close appraisal in *The Blue Devils of Nada* is Mr. Murray's acute awareness of how the 'on-going dialogue with tradition' across cultures, races, and countries forms the basis for the works —especially American ones—deservedly enshrined in the pantheon of world-class masterpieces.") Murray is profiled in February 22 issue of *Newsweek*. Receives National Book Critics Circle's Ivan Sandrof Award for outstanding contribution to American arts and letters. Profile by Henry Louis Gates, Jr., entitled "King of Cats," appears in April 8 issue of *The New Yorker*. Murray participates in "An International Celebration of Southern Literature" at

Agnes Scott College in June, a "Literary Olympiad" event affili-
ated with the Olympic Games in Atlanta. Receives honorary
doctorate from Spring Hill College in Mobile. Speaks at Cornell
University at invitation of Cornell's president. Interviewed by
Brian Lamb on C-SPAN's *Booknotes* program and by Charlie
Rose on his PBS talk show. Gives a reading, combined with a
performance by Wynton Marsalis, at PEN/Faulkner event at the
Folger Shakespeare Library in Washington, D.C., in November.
In December speaks at MLA convention in Washington as part of
panel celebrating release of *The Norton Anthology of African
American Literature*, which includes an excerpt from *Train Whis-
tle Guitar*. Jazz at Lincoln Center becomes full constituent of
Lincoln Center for the Performing Arts, and is now on par with
the New York Philharmonic, Metropolitan Opera, and New York
City Ballet. Murray will be an active board member through mid-
2005.

1997   In January elected to membership in the American Academy of
            Arts and Letters. Receives lifetime achievement award from the
            Anisfield-Wolf Book Awards "for important contributions to our
            understanding of racism and our appreciation of the rich diver-
            sity of human cultures." *Conversations with Albert Murray*, a col-
            lection of new and selected interviews edited by Roberta S.
            Maguire, published by the University Press of Mississippi. Deliv-
            ers lecture in "Eye of the Beholder" series at the Isabella Stewart
            Gardner Museum in Boston. Receives honorary doctorate from
            Hamilton College, alma mater of his Tuskegee mentor Morteza
            Drexel Sprague. Speaks at Vassar and at Yale. Reads from his fic-
            tion at the Unterberg Poetry Center of the 92nd Street Y with
            John Edgar Wideman. Reads at twenty-fourth annual Faulkner
            and Yoknapatawpha Conference at the University of Mississippi.
            Appears on cover of *The New York Times Magazine* for March 9
            alongside George Plimpton, Geoffrey Beene, Ed Koch, Allen
            Ginsberg, Cynthia Ozick, Eartha Kitt, Brooke Astor, Uta Hagen,
            and others under the headline "Funny, We Don't Feel Old."

1998   Participates in tribute to Ellison at the 92nd Street Y along with
            Saul Bellow, James Alan McPherson, John F. Callahan, and
            R.W.B. Lewis. Elected to membership in the American Academy
            of Arts and Sciences. Serves on literature awards committee of
            the American Academy of Arts and Letters with William Weaver,
            Charles Simic, Robert Stone, Reynolds Price, Anne Tyler, and
            Anthony Hecht. Receives inaugural Harper Lee Award from Ala-
            bama Writers' Forum. *Train Whistle Guitar* is reprinted by Vin-
            tage. Two lectures from the 1980s appear in Robert G. O'Meally's

compendious reader *The Jazz Cadence of American Culture* from Columbia University Press.

1999   Receives honorary doctorate from Tuskegee University (formerly Tuskegee Institute), with which he and Mozelle have maintained many connections over the past six decades. On June 18 participates in reading from Ellison's posthumously published novel *Juneteenth* with Toni Morrison and Peter Matthiessen at Barnes & Noble bookstore on Seventeenth Street in Manhattan. Speaks at Ellison symposium at CUNY Graduate Center at the invitation of Morris Dickstein. Jazz at Lincoln Center staff presents him with an enormous birthday card thanking him for being its "resident scholar and guru of the blues." Presents lectures at Iowa Writers' Workshop at the invitation of James Alan McPherson. Italian translation of *Stomping the Blues* published by Cooperativa Libraria Universitaria Editrice Bologna.

2000   *Trading Twelves: The Selected Letters of Ralph Ellison and Albert Murray* published by Modern Library. Receives honorary doctorate from Stony Brook University, through the efforts of philosophy professor Lorenzo Simpson. Good friends around this time include Paul Resika, Bernard Holland, Matt and Phyllis Clark, Sidney and Dr. Avodah Offit, and John Hollander and Natalie Charkow. Favorite restaurants include Daniel and Bistro du Nord. Delivers keynote address to Ralph Ellison–Albert Murray Symposium at Dallas Institute of Humanities and Culture.

2001   Appears in Ken Burns's documentary *Jazz* and in the University of Alabama/Alabama Public Television's *Coat of Many Colors: A Tapestry of Alabama Artists*. Speaks at University of North Carolina–Chapel Hill in February. In March receives Clarence Cason Award from the School of Journalism at the University of Alabama–Tuscaloosa. Paul Devlin, an undergraduate at St. John's University in Queens, New York, sends letter to Murray expressing interest in his work. Murray and Devlin meet on March 28, beginning what will become a close friendship. (Devlin will quickly become the latest of Murray's many intellectual apprentices, as well as his chauffeur and all-around assistant.) In May buys diamond and platinum ring for Mozelle from Tiffany & Co., a gift for their sixtieth wedding anniversary. On 9/11 Mozelle is in Rhode Island visiting friends as the attacks on New York and Washington unfold. (Murray is especially shocked by the attack on the Pentagon, calling it unthinkable from the perspective of a retired officer.) Appears in "Giants of Jazz" photo shoot in October issue of *Talk* magazine, alongside several musical legends and

up-and-coming performers. *Talk* feature also includes a philosophical statement by Murray in response to 9/11. Pantheon publishes two new books in November: a volume of new and
previously uncollected essays, *From the Briarpatch File*, and a
collection of poems, *Conjugations and Reiterations*. Real estate
developer Jack Rudin throws grand book party for Murray at the
Four Seasons restaurant in the Seagram Building in Manhattan
on December 5, with performance by Wynton Marsalis.

2002   Participates in Mobile's tricentennial celebration. Attends exhibition opening for painter Richard Mayhew in New York and renews old friendship with him. Maintains demanding schedule of
working on fourth and final Scooter novel and judging student
essays for Jazz at Lincoln Center's "Essentially Ellington" band
competition. *Good Morning Blues* is reprinted by Da Capo with a
new introduction by Dan Morgenstern.

2003   Receives award for literary achievement from the Alabama
Council on the Arts in Montgomery in May. Visits Tuskegee for
the last time. Loans one of several works he owns by Romare
Bearden, the 1985 monotype *Celebrations: Trumpet Spot, Wynton*,
to the National Gallery of Art's major retrospective traveling exhibition *The Art of Romare Bearden*, and attends the show's
opening in Washington in September. Speaks at St. John's University on September 30. It will be his last lecture at a college or university.

2004   Attends numerous events throughout the fall celebrating the
opening of the new home for Jazz at Lincoln Center in the Time
Warner Center at Columbus Circle. Attends black-tie gala at Co-
lumbia University for Basie's centennial. *The Art of Romare
Bearden* travels to the Whitney in New York and Murray appears
on a panel to mark the exhibition's opening on October 14. "Jazz:
Notes Toward a Definition" published in the *New Republic* in
October. It is the last piece of his nonfiction published during his
lifetime. Attends book party for Dan Morgenstern's *Living with
Jazz: A Reader* at Rutgers–Newark in November. With novel *The
Magic Keys* delivered to Pantheon, begins to imagine a work fo-
cusing on several minor characters in the Scooter sequence.

2005   Spends long afternoon in January in the Bearden retrospective,
now at the Whitney Museum. Excerpt from *Train Whistle Guitar*
centering on Jack Johnson is read in Ken Burns's documentary on
the boxer, *Unforgivable Blackness*. Interviewed on Bearden at the
Metropolitan Museum of Art in February. Falls from chair at
home on May 15 or 16 and injures his head, possibly sustaining a

concussion. Refuses to go to the hospital, citing several important events on his calendar. *The Magic Keys* published on May 17 to generally warm reviews. Extraordinarily heavy traffic the following evening delays his arrival for Q&A with John Edgar Wideman at New York's Housing Works Bookstore, but even after an hour's wait the capacity crowd does not thin out. Private publication party held in the rare book room at the Strand Bookstore on May 19, with performance by a combo featuring Wycliffe Gordon, Kengo Nakamura, and Aaron Diehl, followed by a public Q&A and book signing. Pleased by review of new novel in the May issue of *Harper's*, in which John Leonard calls it "less kiss-kiss bang-bang . . . than elegy, reverie, memory book, and musical score, as well as thank-you note to the entire sustaining community of black America." (Leonard describes the Manhattan sections, which include an *à clef* rendering of Ralph Ellison, as "the creation myth of the postwar black intelligentsia.") By mid-June it becomes almost impossible for Murray to stand up without assistance. For past few years he has been able to walk short distances but has used a wheelchair for excursions in public places such as airports, museums, and Lincoln Center. Severe back pain becomes worse. Begins to lose control of legs in late June. In July, at Mozelle's insistence, is admitted to Lenox Hill Hospital in Manhattan for battery of tests; remains in hospital through late August. Upon discharge is attended by nurses twenty-four hours a day and will be for the rest of his life. Makes rebound toward the end of the year, regaining energy and liveliness missing since his fall in May. Reads newspapers every morning at kitchen table. Assigns power of attorney and executorship of his estate to Lewis P. Jones III, his good friend since the *Harvard Advocate* symposium of 1973. (Jones will oversee the Murray family's personal affairs and finances as their attorney-in-fact and executor.)

2006   Enjoys cheerful, crowded ninetieth birthday party at his apartment on afternoon of May 12, and receives numerous visitors over the course of birthday weekend. Encourages Paul Devlin to listen to his 1977–85 interviews with Jo Jones to see if they might be turned into a book.

2007   Awarded W.E.B. Du Bois Medal from Du Bois Institute at Harvard University. Henry Louis Gates, Jr., bestows medal at a packed-house ceremony in Murray's apartment on afternoon of June 3. In hospital again from mid-December through January 2008.

2008   In January Auburn University hosts "Albert Murray and the Aesthetic Imagination of a Nation," the first symposium on his work alone. Italian translation of *Good Morning Blues* published by Minimum Fax.

2009   In final public appearance (and his first since 2005), receives Ed Bradley Award for Leadership from Jazz at Lincoln Center at concert portion of its fall gala in November. Receives standing ovation from sold-out concert audience. His hearing, which has been worsening for years, is now almost completely gone. Visitors must talk into a microphone attached to a headset, speak almost at a shout, or write questions and comments on paper to be understood.

2010   Photographed by Jake Chessum for photo-essay "Nine Over 90" in September 26 issue of *New York* magazine. Fellow nonagenarians profiled in the essay include Robert Morgenthau, Carmen Herrera, Elliott Carter, George Avakian, Ruth Gruber, Andy Rooney, Zelda Kaplan, and Hugh Carey. Enjoys the attention and commotion of the elaborate photo shoot in his apartment. Papers from the Auburn symposium, along with other articles and interviews, published as a book by the University of Alabama Press in June.

2011   Commemorates seventieth wedding anniversary with a small party at home. *Rifftide: The Life and Opinions of Papa Jo Jones*, as told to Albert Murray, is published by University of Minnesota Press in September. (The book, edited by Paul Devlin, is well received: in *The New York Times Book Review*, Colin Fleming writes that it is "the kind of book that delights jazz fans: the straight-talking, defiantly espousing firsthand record. Anyone interested in authenticity of voice is going to be on the verge of fist-pumping the air throughout, or else exclaiming, 'You tell it like it is, baby,' as if partaking in a call-and-response with the book.") In October becomes Director Emeritus of Jazz at Lincoln Center. The board's citation honors him as "Jazz at Lincoln Center's guiding spirit, shaping its values with the lessons of jazz and providing the pedagogical foundation for all its programs." Continues to receive visitors, but decline is noticeable. Talks of Mobile often. Mozelle, too, begins to need around-the-clock nursing care.

2012   Selection of five works from Murray's art collection (three by Bearden, two by Norman Lewis) exhibited at D.C. Moore Gallery in New York; the show, with wall text by Paul Devlin, runs from January 6 through February 4. In June receives lifetime achievement award from the Jazz Journalists Association.

2013   Strength and energy, declining for some time, fade rapidly in the late spring. Loses what had been a handshake with a viselike grip. Eats less and less, and then stops completely for a period in May. Makes modest rebound through June and July, but stops eating again in August. Dies in his sleep at home on the evening of August 18, at age of ninety-seven. Cremated. He is survived by Mozelle, his wife of seventy-two years, and by their daughter, Michele, now sixty-nine. (Mozelle will die in her sleep at home on July 3, 2015.) Wynton Marsalis and Jazz at Lincoln Center host memorial service on September 13. About five hundred people attend the midday event in the Appel Room, facing Columbus Circle, with an overflow crowd of approximately one hundred watching on screens in an adjacent room. In November Henry Louis Gates, Jr., delivers a tribute at the American Academy of Arts and Letters. "This was Albert Murray's century," he remarks; "we just lived in it. And as we keep on living, we will never forget what he meant to our American story or the music animating it with a soul force he taught us to hear."

NOTE ON THE TEXT

In June 1962 Captain Albert Murray, diagnosed by military doctors with arteriosclerosis, voluntarily retired from the U.S. Air Force with the grade of major. Upon completing his final assignment, at Hanscom Field in Bedford, Massachusetts, he moved with his family to Harlem to start a long-deferred career as a full-time writer. A sometime college instructor in literature, Murray had received an MA in English from New York University in 1948 and was, in 1962, the author of "The Briarpatch," a semi-autobiographical fiction manuscript that would eventually yield the novels *Train Whistle Guitar* (1974) and *The Spyglass Tree* (1991). He had also begun a long essay on "the blues tradition in modern fiction" that ten years later would provide the basis of *The Hero and the Blues* (1973). In Harlem Murray continued working on these projects, but also, through introductions arranged by his close friend Ralph Ellison, began soliciting book-review assignments from Ellison's editorial acquaintances at *Life*, *The New Leader*, and other publications.

By early 1967 he had published a dozen or so reviews, mostly of novels by contemporary black writers or of works of social science examining black life in America. That April he was invited by Nelson W. Aldrich Jr., editor of *The Urban Review*, to write a piece on Harlem for the journal. In this and subsequent assignments from *The Urban Review*'s parent organization, a New York–based education policy institute called the Center for Urban Education (CUE), Murray began to treat at length certain ideas about urban black culture and American life that placed his book reviews in a larger intellectual and aesthetic context. "When I got into these [CUE] pieces," Murray said in an interview with Louis Edwards in 1994, "I realized I was writing on a theme, the theme of identity. [America is] a mulatto culture. . . . You can't be American unless you're part *us*, and you can't be American unless you're part *them*. . . . I knew I was writing a book. . . . It *had* to be a book. . . . I wanted to deal with the richest possible context . . . all these other things which I was dealing with at the time—jazz, literature, style."

By 1968 Murray was pitching a proposal for a volume of articles and reviews, then called "The All-Americans," to various New York trade publishers. Later that year, two of CUE's top editors, David E. Outerbridge and Harris Dienstfrey, left CUE to start their own small book-publishing firm, and invited Murray to contribute to their list. Murray delivered the manuscript of *The Omni-Americans* to Outerbridge and Dienstfrey, New York, in the summer of 1969 and completed correcting the page proofs the following November.

Most of the pieces collected in *The Omni-Americans* had previously appeared in books and periodicals. The history of their composition and publication is given below.

Much of the essay "The Omni-Americans" was developed, at the request of Herbert Hill, labor director of the NAACP, for the unrealized volume "Revolt of the Powerless: The Negro in the North," a collection of original essays that Hill, under contract with Random House, commissioned from more than a dozen black writers from 1963 to 1969. An abridged version of the essay first appeared, as "The Omni-Americans," in *The Urban Review* 3.6 (June 1969), 38–45.

"Image and Unlikeness in Harlem" was commissioned by *The Urban Review* to accompany a suite of contemporary black-and-white photographs by Fred W. McDarrah. The text and photographs were published, as "Image and Likeness in Harlem," in *The Urban Review* 2.2 (June 1967), 12–17.

"Oneupmanship in Colorful America" first appeared, as "Another Name for Another Game," in *The Center Forum* (a newsletter of the Center for Urban Education) 2.4 (October 5, 1967), 8.

"The Illusive Black Middle Class" grew out of research done by Murray in early 1968 for "The Subculture of Suburbia in Crisis," a multimedia education initiative of the Center for Urban Education. It first appeared in *The Omni-Americans* (1970), 86–96.

"Claude Brown's Soul for White Folks" first appeared, as "Social Science Fiction in Harlem," in *The New Leader* 49.6 (January 17, 1966), 56–59.

"Gordon Parks Out of Focus" first appeared, as "Out of Focus," in *The New Leader* 49.10 (May 9, 1966), 18–20.

"Who That Say, What Dat, Every Time Us Do That?" grew out of research done by Murray in early 1968 for "The Role of the News Media in the Urban Crisis," a multimedia education initiative of the Center for Urban Education. It first appeared in *The Omni-Americans* (1970), 113–20.

"Star-Crossed Melodrama" first appeared, as "Star-Crossed Activists," in *Book Week* 4.19 (January 15, 1967), 6, 16.

"Warren Miller and His Blackface Vaudeville" first appeared, as "White Man's Harlem: The Novels of Warren Miller," in *The New Leader* 47.25 (December 7, 1964), 28–30.

"William Styron and His Troublesome Property" first appeared, as "A Troublesome Property," in *The New Leader* 50.24 (December 4, 1967), 18–21.

"James Baldwin, Protest Fiction, and the Blues Tradition" first appeared, as "Something Different, Something More," in Herbert Hill, editor, *Anger, and Beyond: The Negro Writer in the United States* (New York: Harper & Row, [February] 1966), 112–37.

"A Short History of Black Self-Consciousness" first appeared in *The Omni-Americans* (1970), 171–80.

"The Role of the Pre-American Past" first appeared, as "African Culture and Black Identity," in *Interplay: The Magazine of International Affairs* 3.6 (February 1970), 12–14.

"Black Pride in Mobile, Alabama" first appeared, as "Whose Dues for Good Black News? (Some Notes from a Journey to Mobile)," in *The Center Forum* 3.5 (March 1969), 22–24.

"Black Studies and the Aims of Education" first appeared in *The Omni-Americans* (1970), 203–17.

The epilogue, "Situation Normal: All Fouled Up," was written in October 1966 at the invitation of William Phillips, editor of *Partisan Review*, for the quarterly's symposium feature "What's Happening to America." The questions posed by the editors of *Partisan Review* to Murray and to other public intellectuals and social critics are enumerated in the note at 185.3–5. Murray's response ran long, and despite his efforts to shorten it in page proof, it was not among the sixteen that the editors published in their Winter 1967 number. It first appeared in *The Omni-Americans* (1970), 221–27.

The Omni-Americans was published, in hardcover, by Outerbridge and Dienstfrey, New York, in March 1970. The first edition bore the subtitle "New Perspectives on Black Experience and American Culture," but reprint editions, beginning with the Vintage Books paperback of 1983, bore Murray's preferred subtitle, "Some Alternatives to the Folklore of White Supremacy." Except for adoption of the revised subtitle, the text of the Outerbridge and Dienstfrey edition of *The Omni-Americans* is used here.

This volume presents the text of the original printing chosen for inclusion but does not attempt to reproduce nontextual features of their typographical design. The text is presented without change, except for the correction of typographical errors. Spelling, punctuation, and capitalization are often expressive features and are not altered, even when inconsistent or irregular. Errors in quoted material are not corrected, since they can reflect how Murray understood or read the quotations. The following is a list of typographical errors corrected, cited by page and line number: 7.10, mislead; 11.13, consciousness and; 15.2, *unim*; 26.13, *Change* is; 31.12, Steppin'; 41.19, sems; 41.21, desparately; 44.23–24, possibilities; 44.25, incidentaly; 45.7, clubs,; 48.7, exicted; 68.4, as Moynihan; 69.11, anti-sceptic; 78.30, wih the; 81.1, ante-bellem; 86.29, *Ramparts*'; 87.16, in not; 88.15, Mohammad; 88.16, Leroi; 89.24, guitar!'"; 97.2, that; 97.32, Paranasi.; 103.12, Parks', life; 103.26, Matthew; 104.1–2, Kaufman;

106.29, high fallutin'; 107.28, phoney; 108.16, mislead; 108.19–20, bibliographies and; 108.22, (and; 109.28, chauffers,; 109.24, cooks),; 113.19, ladies; 115.20, wtih; 117.4, ladies; 120.19 (and *passim*), *Seige*; 124.5, intanglements); 124.23, 1966),; 126.30, mislead; 129.29–30 (and *passim*), Hard Bought; 133.11, Greenwhich; 133.13, existentalists,; 134.7, *Gentlemen's*; 135.2, erectible; 135.4, traditions As; 136.26, essay,; 142.2, koolade.; 143.17, imaginary.); 145.26, ambitions.; 146.5, muscial; 150.21, *Charley*; 153.23–24, *Soldier's*; 161.27, "Koko"; 162.10, generation whose; 162.23, did) is; 166.11, forceably; 167.15, Tschombe,; 169.10, were; 170.9, soulfullness; 173.13, History which; 176.24, *Malcom*; 180.9, *Yearbook*;; 181.24, *the the*; 184.14 (and *passim*), Pritchard; 184.17, folk's; 185.20, development and; 195.25–26, *Goodbye Mr.*; 196.7, mislead; 199.3, *1967,*; 199.5, *in America?*"; 201.7, effects; 201.10, Morganthau,; 203.5, or.

NOTES

In the notes below, the reference numbers denote page and line of this volume (line counts include headings). No note is made for material included in standard desk-reference books. Biblical quotations are keyed to the King James Version. Quotations from Shakespeare are keyed to G. Blakemore Evans, editor, *The Riverside Shakespeare* (Boston: Houghton Mifflin, 1974). For further biographical detail than is contained in the chronology, see Roberta S. Maguire, editor, *Conversations with Albert Murray* (Jackson: University Press of Mississippi, 1997); Albert Murray and John F. Callahan, editors, *Trading Twelves: The Selected Letters of Ralph Ellison and Albert Murray* (New York: Modern Library, 2000); and Paul Devlin, editor, *Murray Talks Music: Albert Murray on Jazz and Blues* (Minneapolis: University of Minnesota Press, 2016). The tribute volume *Albert Murray and the Aesthetic Imagination of a Nation* (Tuscaloosa: A Pebble Hill Book/University of Alabama Press, 2010), edited by Barbara A. Baker, collects critical essays, biographical articles, interviews, and reminiscence, including "King of Cats" (1996), a *New Yorker* profile by Henry Louis Gates Jr., "An Interview with Michele Murray" (2010), by Paul Devlin and Lauren Walsh; "Albert Murray and Visual Art" (2010), by Paul Devlin; "Albert Murray and Tuskegee Institute: Art as the Measure of Place," by Caroline Gebhard (2010); "Wynton Marsalis on Albert Murray," by Roberta S. Maguire (2001); and "At the Bar and on the Avenue with My Pal Al Murray" (2010), by Sidney Offit. See also Robert G. O'Meally's Smithsonian Jazz Oral History Project interview with Murray (1994); Kurt Thometz's interview with Murray (circa 2001) for Thometz's "Private Library/The Well-Dressed Bibliophile" series at colophon. com; Brian Lamb's interview with Murray (1996) for C-SPAN's *Booknotes* program, available at booknotes.org; and David A. Taylor, "Albert Murray's Magical Youth," in *Southern Cultures* 16.2 (Summer 2010).

Grateful acknowledgment for answering queries pertaining to the notes and/or chronology is made to Dana Chandler, Harrietta Eaton, Gary Giddins, Diedra Harris-Kelley, Ida Hay, Joyce Johnson, Kristin Jones, Lewis P. Jones III, the late Harris Lewine, Michele Murray, Sidney Offit, Juanita Roberts, and Melissa Stevens.

3.1–7 The individual stands . . . intends to feed.] From Malraux's preface to his novel *Days of Wrath* (*Le Temps du mépris*, 1935), translated from the French by Haakon M. Chevalier (New York: Random House, 1936).

5.2 counter-statements] See *Counter-Statement* (1931), a work of rhetorical criticism by American literary theorist Kenneth Burke (1897–1993). In his introduction to the book, which is largely an essay on taste, style, and the effectiveness of persuasive prose, Burke writes: "We have chosen to call it *Counter-Statement* solely because . . . each principle it advocates is matched by an opposite principle flourishing and triumphant today. Heresies and orthodoxies will always be changing places, but whatever the minority view happens to be at any given time, one must consider it as 'counter.' Hence the title—which will not, we hope, suggest either an eagerness for the fray or a sense of defeat."

6.10–11 Gilbert Murray . . . *Greek Religion*] Murray (1866–1957) was Regius Professor of Greek at Oxford University from 1908 to 1936. *The Rise of the Greek Epic* (1907) is a study of Homer and his world, and *The Five Stages of Greek Religion* (1951) the third and final edition of a work first published in 1912.

7.6–7 *Report of the National Advisory Commission on Civil Disorders*] In July 1967, President Johnson appointed a commission (1) to examine the causes and consequences of race riots that since the summer of 1965 had erupted in several American cities, and (2) to recommend a national course of action to prevent further race riots. The commission, led by Illinois governor Otto Kerner, reported its findings in February 1968. They concluded that the nation was "moving toward two societies, one black, one white—separate and unequal," and warned that unless conditions were remedied, the country faced a "system of 'apartheid'" in most of its major cities.

8.31 dramatic sense of life] Murray alludes here to Dramatism, a poetic theory of "what people are doing and why they are doing it" developed by Kenneth Burke (see note 7.2–3) in his book *A Grammar of Motives* (1945).

10.11–12 folklore of white supremacy . . . fakelore of black pathology] Murray's terminology was influenced by that of American historian Marshall W. Fishwick (1923–2006), especially as used in the article "Folklore, Fakelore, and Poplore" (*Saturday Review*, August 26, 1967).

12.15 Professor "Clinkscales"] In his autobiography *Music Is My Mistress* (1973), Duke Ellington named one "Mrs. Clinkscales" as the best of his childhood piano teachers.

15.3 the prelude to *Joseph*] "The Descent into Hell" ("*Höllenfahrt*"), in *The Tales of Jacob* (*Die Geschichten Jakobs*, 1933), book one of the tetralogy *Joseph and His Brothers* (*Joseph und seine Brüder*, 1933–43), by Thomas Mann. Murray's quotations are from the English translation by H. T. Lowe Porter (New York: Knopf, 1934).

15.18 Lord Raglan . . . *The Hero*] Richard FitzRoy Somerset, Fourth Baron Raglan (1885–1964), a British soldier and writer, was the author of *The Hero* (1936), a study in comparative literature and anthropology that catalogued themes and motifs of hero tales across cultures and centuries.

17.3 Constance Rourke] Writer and educator Constance Rourke (1885–1941), a native of Ohio, was a pioneer in the fields of American studies, American folk art, and

American popular culture. Her books include *American Humor: A Study of the National Character* (1931) and the posthumous collection *The Roots of American Culture and Other Essays* (1942), edited by Van Wyck Brooks. These two works were touchstones for Murray and are alluded to throughout his nonfiction.

17.29–30   *homo Americanus . . . homo Europaeus*] Paul Valéry's essay "Homo Europaeus" was published, in France, in 1922. In a 2003 interview with Paul Devlin collected in *Murray Talks Music* (2016), Murray remarked that "*The Omni-Americans . . .* had two definitive sources. During the war I read a book called *The Heart of Europe* [Klaus Mann, ed., New York: L. B. Fischer, 1943]. And in that anthology there was an essay by Paul Valéry called 'Homo Europaeus.' He said *Homo Europaeus* was Greek logic, Roman administration and law, and Judeo-Christian morality. A few years later I came across a book by Constance Rourke, who is one of my patron saints. It was called *American Humor* but it could have been called *Homo Americanus . . .*"

19.6–7   the arrival of a Dutch ship . . . in 1619] According to John Rolfe, the secretary and recorder-general of Virginia (1614–19), the first Africans to be sold into slavery in America were traded at the end of August 1619, when "a Dutch man of Warr . . . arrived at Point-Comfort [Hampton, Virginia] [with] 20 and odd Negroes." See Susan Myra Kingsbury, ed., *Records of the Virginia Company, 1606–1626* (1909).

19.18–23   "The whites," . . . coastal trading centers."] See Benjamin Quarles (1904–1996), *The Negro in the Making of America* (New York: Collier, 1964).

20.30–31   "a nobler, higher spirit . . . human form."] William H. Seward (1801–1872), U.S. secretary of state (1861–69), in a testimonial to Tubman solicited by Sarah H. Bradford for her biography *Harriet, the Moses of Her People* (1868).

21.31–22.2   "that considering the condition . . . most meritorious man in the United States."] It was through John Eaton (1829–1906), U.S. commissioner of education during the Civil War, that Lincoln first met Frederick Douglass, in Washington, D.C., on August 10, 1863. Eaton, in a letter of condolence to Douglass's widow dated February 21, 1895, wrote that the president, upon learning of his and Douglass's friendship in July 1863, paid Douglass the compliment that Murray quotes here. Eaton's letter was printed in Helen Douglass's tribute volume *In Memoriam: Frederick Douglass* (1897).

24.12   Negro pilots of the 332nd Fighter Group] The so-called Tuskegee Airmen, all of whom were graduates of the Army Air Force pilot training programs at Alabama's Moton Field and Tuskegee Army Air Field from 1941 to 1945.

25.23   HARYOU-Act Program] Harlem Youth Opportunities Unlimited (HARYOU), founded in 1962 by black psychiatrist Kenneth B. Clark (1914–2005), merged with Associated Community Teams (ACT), founded in 1963 by U.S. congressman Adam Clayton Powell Jr. (see note 85.14), to form HARYOU-ACT in 1964. The organization, dedicated to increasing educational and employment opportunities for Harlem youth, dissolved in 1968.

26.11–12   *Youth in the Ghetto*] Kenneth B. Clark's 664-page report was distributed for free by HARYOU in 1964–68. Its publication was subsidized by grants from President Johnson's Committee on Juvenile Delinquency and the Office of the Mayor of New York City.

26.14–20   Brimmer . . . Davis . . . Stokes . . . Johnson] Andrew Brimmer (1926–2012), first black governor of the Federal Reserve Board (1966–74); Benjamin O. Davis Jr. (1912–2002), first black general officer in the U.S. Air Force; Carl Stokes (1927–1996), Democratic mayor of Cleveland, Ohio (1968–71); John H. Johnson (1918–2005), publisher of *The Negro Digest, Ebony,* and *Jet.*

26.22   antagonistic cooperation] Term coined by American sociologist William Graham Sumner (1840–1910) in his book *Folkways* (1906). Antagonistic cooperation, writes Sumner, "consists in the combination of two persons or groups to satisfy a great common interest while minor antagonisms of interest which exist between them are suppressed." Murray appropriated Sumner's term as a non-Marxist way of talking about a *thesis* and an *antithesis* that yield a desirable *synthesis.*

28.6–7   Moynihan Report] Report (*The Negro Family: The Case for National Action*) by then Assistant Secretary of Labor Daniel Patrick Moynihan (1927–2003), issued in January 1965 by the Labor Department's Office of Planning and Policy. Among Moynihan's more controversial statements was that life among America's lower-class urban black families is a "tangle of pathology" at the center of which is "the weakness of the Negro family": "The family structure of lower class Negroes [with its absent fathers, single mothers, and illegitimate births] is highly unstable, and in many urban areas is approaching complete breakdown. . . . The Negro community has been forced into a matriarchal structure which . . . seriously retards the progress of the group as a whole and imposes a crushing burden on the Negro male and, in consequence, on a great number of Negro women as well." Moynihan concluded: "The policy of the United States is to bring the Negro American to full and equal sharing in the responsibilities and rewards of citizenship. To this end, the programs of the Federal government bearing on this objective shall be designed to have the effect . . . of enhancing the stability and resources of the Negro American family."

34.26–27   Organization Man] *The Organization Man,* by sociologist William H. Whyte (New York: Simon & Schuster, 1956), was a best-selling analysis of postwar American business corporations, in which, the author argued, cooperation within a hierarchical organization was more prized than individual initiative and creativity.

34.31   Jack Lemmon and Tony Randall] Lemmon (1925–2001) and Randall (1920–2004) were American comic actors who, in the 1950s and '60s, were often typecast as henpecked husbands or neurotic, buttoned-down suburban "squares."

36.18   An American Dilemma] *An American Dilemma: The Negro Problem and Modern Democracy* (New York: Harper & Bros., 1944), best-selling two-volume study in World War II–era U.S. race relations by Gunnar Myrdal (1898–1987), Swedish sociologist and, later, Nobel Laureate in Economics.

39.1   Stanley M. Elkins] American historian (1925–2013) who, in his best-selling *Slavery* (Chicago: University of Chicago Press, 1959), posited the "Sambo" theory of black dependency upon the dominant white society, arguing that the institution of slavery had created a "totalitarian environment" that had infantilized blacks, robbing them of the ability to form positive relationships among themselves and with "mainstream" American culture. The book was controversial, and when, in 1969, a second, revised edition was released, it occasioned a collection of fourteen critical essays, *The Debate*

Over "Slavery": Stanley Elkins and His Critics, edited by Ann J. Lane (Urbana: University of Illinois Press, 1971).

39.3–4   *Dark Ghetto*] *Dark Ghetto: Dilemmas of Social Power*, by Kenneth B. Clark (New York: Harper & Row, 1965), grew out of Dr. Clark's experience as director of HARYOU (see note 25.23) and as an "involved observer" of ghetto life in Harlem. As the author writes in his introduction, the book's "emphasis on the pathologies of American ghettos"—that is, on "the delinquency, narcotics addiction, infant mortality, homicide, and suicide statistics"—"attempts to describe and interpret what happens to human beings who are confined to depressed areas and whose access to the normal channels of economic mobility and opportunity is blocked. . . . The truth about the dark ghetto is not merely a truth about Negroes; it reflects the deeper anguish and torment of the total human predicament."

39.7–8   Charles Evers . . . H. Rap Brown] Evers (b. 1922), brother of slain civil rights activist Medgar Evers (1925–1963), was the mayor of Fayette, Mississippi, from 1969 to 1981 and again from 1985 to 1989; Brown (b. 1943) was chairman of the Student Nonviolent Coordinating Committee (SNCC) in 1967–68 and, later, an outspoken member of the Black Panther Party.

39.33   *Black Rage*] Best-selling book (New York: Basic Books, 1968), by William H. Grier, M.D. (1926–2015), and Price M. Cobbs, M.D. (b. 1928), "two black psychiatrists," the jacket copy stated, "[who] reveal the full dimensions of the inner conflicts and the desperation of the black man's life in America."

41.8   Talcott Parsons] American sociologist (1902–1979) who created and headed Harvard's sociology department (1927–73). He and Kenneth B. Clark coedited *The Negro American* (1966), a volume of sociopsychological essays commissioned by the American Academy of Arts and Sciences.

49.19–20   patent-leather glossy coiffure to Brillo] James Brown switched from the conk to the so-called Afro hairstyle circa 1968.

50.27   shirt collar ad Anglo-Saxon and Gibson Girl images] Early-twentieth-century mass-culture images of American masculinity (as found in Arrow Collar advertisements created by J. C. Leyendecker [1874–1951]) and femininity (as found in magazine illustrations by Charles Dana Gibson [1867–1944]).

53.5   Kenneth Burke has equated stylization with strategy.] See *The Philosophy of Literary Form: Studies in Symbolic Action* (Baton Rouge: Louisiana State University Press, 1941).

54.33   *homo ludens*] *Homo Ludens* ("Man the Player," 1938), by Dutch cultural theorist Johan Huizinga (1872–1945), is a comparative study in the significance of games and athletic contests to human culture. *Homo Ludens: A Study of the Play Element in Culture*, translated from the German by R.F.C. Hull, was published in London in 1944.

56.3   *la condition humaine*] *La Condition humaine* ("The Human Condition," 1933), a novel by André Malraux concerning the failed 1927 communist revolution in Shanghai, was translated into English, by Haakon M. Chevalier, as *Man's Fate* (1934).

57.6–7 "emblems of a pioneer people . . . trait."] Constance Rourke, in *American Humor* (see note 17.3).

58.22 Guevara . . . Fanon] Che Guevara (1928–1967), Argentine-Cuban Marxist revolutionary and a theorist of guerilla warfare; Frantz Fanon (1925–1961), Afro-Caribbean psychiatrist, philosopher, and Marxist critic of colonialism whose books include *Black Skin, White Masks* (1952) and *The Wretched of the Earth* (1961).

60.23–25 *magnanimity of the black mammy . . .* worldly wit and wisdom of Uncle Remus] Throughout his writings Murray evokes "Aunt Hagar" and "Uncle Remus" as archetypal black elders who transmit life lessons, moral principles, and black folk culture to the children of the black and, especially, the white communities.

68.14 Bigger Thomas' response] Thomas is the twenty-year-old protagonist of *Native Son* (1940), a deterministic novel by Richard Wright (1908–1960) that suggests that Thomas's criminal nature is attributable mainly to his social environment, the slums of Chicago's South Side during the early 1930s.

69.5 As James Weldon Johnson noted] See "Harlem: The Culture Capital," by James Weldon Johnson (1871–1938), in Alain Locke, editor, *The New Negro* (1925).

70.33 Leontyne] Soprano Leontyne Price (b. 1927), who in 1961 became the first black American singer to join the Metropolitan Opera Company.

71.19 *An American Dilemma*] See note 36.18.

78.23 Reichianism] System of Austrian psychologist Wilhelm Reich (1897–1957), developed in such books as *The Mass Psychology of Fascism* (1933) and *The Sexual Revolution* (1936). Reich's mixture of far-left politics, sexual frankness, and mystical pseudoscience was embraced by the counterculture of the 1950s and '60s.

81.9 *From Slavery to Freedom*] The first edition of *From Slavery to Freedom: A History of American Negroes* was published in 1947, when John Hope Franklin (1915–2009) was a junior professor of history at Howard University. A standard work on its subject, the ninth edition was published posthumously in 2010.

81.32 *Life and Labor in the Old South*] Social and economic history of the antebellum South (1929) by Yale historian Ulrich Bonnell Phillips (1877–1934), a Georgia native educated at the University of Georgia and Columbia University.

83.32–33 Mays . . . Gibson, Big O . . . Simpson] In 1970, when Murray published *The Omni-Americans*, Willie Mays (b. 1931) was a power-hitting center fielder for the San Francisco Giants; Bob "Hoot" Gibson (b. 1935) a pitcher for the St. Louis Cardinals; Oscar "Big O" Robertson (b. 1938) a guard for basketball's Cincinnati Royals; and O. J. Simpson (b. 1947) the Heisman Trophy–winning running back for the Buffalo Bills.

84.2 Negro senator] In 1966 Edward W. Brooke III (1919–2015), then the Republican attorney general of Massachusetts (1963–67), became the first black person to be popularly elected to the U.S. Senate. He served from 1967 to 1979.

85.14 Adam Clayton Powell] New York Democrat Powell (1908–1972), a pastor of Harlem's Abyssinian Baptist Church (from 1937), served as a U.S. congressman from 1945 to 1971.

86.2–3 Farmer . . . Moses . . . McKissick . . . Carmichael] James Farmer Jr. (1920–1999), head of the Congress of Racial Equality (CORE) and an organizer of the Freedom Rides; Robert Parris Moses (b. 1935), leader of the Student Nonviolent Coordinating Committee (SNCC) and voting rights advocate; Floyd McKissick (1922–1991), civil rights lawyer and Farmer's successor at CORE; Stokely Carmichael (1941–1998), leader of both the American civil rights movement and the global Pan-African movement.

86.11–12 *Autobiography* . . . a magazine writer] *The Autobiography of Malcolm X* was written by Malcolm X (1925–1965) with American journalist Alex Haley (1921–1992). Their collaboration began when Haley, then a staff writer for *Playboy*, interviewed Malcolm X for the magazine in 1963. The *Autobiography*, published mere months after Malcolm X's assassination, was one of the best-selling books of the late twentieth century.

86.27 Whitney Young] American civil rights leader (1921–1971) who, in 1961, after serving the organization since 1947, became executive director of the National Urban League.

86.28 Eldridge Cleaver] American political activist (1935–1998) who was a member of the Black Panther Party (1966–71) and the author of *Soul on Ice* (New York: Ramparts Press, 1968), a collection of memoirs and polemical essays written from Folsom State Prison, where in 1965–66 he served time for rape and attempted murder.

86.29 *Ramparts* magazine] Glossy magazine (1962–75) that, by the late 1960s, had evolved from a monthly of liberal Catholic opinion into a leading news organ of the American counterculture.

87.30 Claude (Manchild) Brown] Brown (1937–2002) was a juvenile delinquent from Harlem who, with guidance from a reform-school psychiatrist, entered Howard University and later studied law at Rutgers and Stanford. Murray's review of his memoir, *Manchild in the Promised Land* (1965), appears on pages 90–96 of the present volume.

88.16–19 Jones . . . Hooks . . . Anderson . . . Kilson . . . Epps] LeRoi Jones (1934–2014), later known as Amiri Baraka, cultural critic, poet, and playwright; Robert Hooks (b. 1937), actor, producer, director for stage and screen; Jervis Anderson (1932–2000), versatile staff writer at *The New Yorker*; Martin Kilson (b. 1931), professor of government at Harvard University; Archie Epps (1939–2003), longtime dean of students at Harvard University.

88.19 *Freedomways*] Quarterly journal (1961–85), founded by Louis E. Burnham and Edward Strong (both of the Southern Negro Youth Congress), that chronicled what the editors called the Negro Freedom Movement—not just the American civil rights movement but also the Pan-African, Négritude, and Black Arts movements.

88.30 Julian Bond] American civil rights leader (1940–2015). The son of academics, he was educated at Morehouse College, and in 1970, when Murray published *The Omni-Americans*, was known as the Atlanta-area leader of the Student Nonviolent Coordinating Committee (SNCC).

90.9 CLAUDE BROWN'S SOUL] See note 87.30.

91.1   earth dark womb!] See John Milton's poem "On the Death of a Fair Infant, Dying of a Cough" (circa 1625).

91.18–19   Smith . . . Robinson . . . Powell . . . Motley]   Four prominent figures in twentieth-century Harlem: Willie "The Lion" Smith (1893–1973), stride pianist; Sugar Ray Robinson (1921–1989), prizefighter; Adam Clayton Powell Jr. (see note 85.14); Constance Baker Motley (1921–2005), the first black woman to serve as a federal judge (1966–86).

91.19–20   Lenox Terrace . . . Smalls Paradise . . . *Amsterdam News*]   Postwar Harlem apartment complex (and, after 1962, Murray's place of residence); Harlem nightclub (1925–mid-1980s); and Harlem-based weekly paper (founded 1909).

93.18–19   J. William Fulbright]   Arkansas Democrat (1905–1995) who served in the U.S. Senate (1945–74) and chaired its Foreign Relations Committee (1959–74). His book *The Arrogance of Power* (1966) was an indictment of America's Vietnam policy.

93.20   Mary McCarthy]   American writer (1912–1989) whose novel *The Group* (1963) chronicled the adult lives of eight Vassar graduates from the 1930s through the early 1960s.

93.25–27   Mailer . . . Hentoff . . . Podhoretz . . . Wolfe]   Novelist Norman Mailer (1923–2007) wrote a jacket blurb for Brown's book; jazz critic Nat Hentoff (b. 1925) reviewed it in *Book Week*; Norman Podhoretz (b. 1930), editor of *Commentary*, interviewed Brown on WNET Television's *Open Mind* program; and journalist Tom Wolfe (b. 1931) profiled Brown in *The New York Herald Tribune Magazine*.

94.24–31   Negroes like Duke Ellington, Louis Armstrong . . . how you get that way.]   Cf. the following passage, deleted from "Something Different, Something More" (in Herbert Hill's anthology *Anger, and Beyond*, 1966) when Murray revised it, as "James Baldwin, Protest Fiction, and the Blues Tradition," for *The Omni-Americans*: "This music, far from being simply Afro-American (whatever that is, the continent of Africa being as vast and as varied as it is), is, like the U.S. Negro himself, All-American. This is why so many other American musicians, like Paul Whiteman, George Gershwin, Benny Goodman, Woody Herman, Gerry Mulligan, and all the rest, identify with it so eagerly. The white American musician (excluding hillbillies, of course) sounds most American when he sounds like an American Negro. Otherwise he sounds like a European."

96.8   GORDON PARKS]   Parks was born in Fort Scott, Kansas, in 1912, and died at home in Manhattan in 2006. His memoir *A Choice of Weapons* (1966) was followed by three further volumes of autobiography: *To Smile in Autumn* (1979), *Voices in the Mirror* (1990), and *Half Past Autumn* (1998).

98.11–12   *The Learning Tree*]   Parks's autobiographical first novel, concerning the lives of black adolescents in a segregated Kansas town of the 1930s, was published by Harper & Row in 1963. A feature film based on the book—written, produced, directed, and with music by Parks—was released in 1969, and in 1989 was selected for inclusion in the National Film Registry of the Library of Congress.

104.1–2   Mydans . . . Kauffman] Carl Mydans (1907–2004) and Mark Kauffman (1923–1974) were, like Parks, contract photographers for *Life* magazine.

105.2   New York newspaper pundit] Baltimore native Murray Kempton (1917–1997), a columnist for several New York papers from the 1930s to the 1950s, wrote, in "To Be a Negro," a 1962 essay for the London *Spectator*, that "there is no Negro so alienated that he does not trust some white man somewhere for at least a limited distance down the road."

105.19–20   Amos and Andy and Lawyer Calhoun] Farcical characters created by blackface writers and actors for the radio series *Amos 'n' Andy* (1928–55).

109.2–3   Odetta . . . Joan Baez] Odetta (1930–2008), black folksinger, musician, and civil rights activist, and Joan Baez (b. 1941), white folksinger, musician, and social activist, shared record labels, festival dates, and campus and coffeehouse concert circuits throughout the 1960s.

111.1–2   Lemberg Center for the Study of Violence] Domestic policy institute, based at Brandeis University, that from 1965 to 1973 conducted research into the causes of social violence, particularly race riots.

113.7   "very essence of adventure and romance"] From *Freedom Bound*, a popular history of the Reconstruction era by the white independent scholar Henrietta Buckmaster (1909–1983), published by Macmillan in 1965.

113.22   *Five Smooth Stones*] First novel (1966) by American writer Dorothy Fairbairn Tait (1905–1972), using the pseudonym "Ann Fairbairn." Tait was the longtime manager of New Orleans clarinetist George Lewis (1900–1968) and, under the name "Jay Allison Stuart," the author of his biography, *Call Him George* (1961).

116.1   *Mojo Hand*] First novel (1966) by California poet Jane Phillips (b. 1944), who also publishes under the name J. J. Phillips. A revised version of the novel, *Mojo Hand: An Orphic Tale*, was published in 1985 by City Miner Press, San Francisco.

116.25   Hi-de Hi-de Hi-de-ho] "Hi-De-Ho" (1934) was a trademark tune of singer and bandleader Cab Calloway (1907–1994).

117.25   WARREN MILLER] American writer Miller (1921–1966) was educated at the University of Iowa and then taught in the writing program there until his death, from lung cancer, at age forty-four. His novel *The Cool World* was published by Little, Brown, in 1959. A stage version, adapted by Robert Rossen and starring Billy Dee Williams, played for two nights at the Eugene O'Neill Theater, New York, in February 1960. A film version, produced by Frederick Wiseman and starring Hampton Clanton, was released in 1963.

118.9   U.S. white negro] See Norman Mailer's essay "The White Negro: Superficial Reflections on the Hipster" (*Dissent*, Fall 1957), collected in *Advertisements for Myself* (1959). Mailer argues that white youth should embrace rebellion, hedonism, and hypersexuality, which he associated with blackness, in response to the existential threat of nuclear war.

120.23   Joel Chandler Harris] Atlanta-based journalist and folklorist (1848–1908) whose tales of Brer Rabbit, learned from slaves on Turnwold Plantation, near Eatonton, Georgia, were collected in *Uncle Remus: His Songs and His Sayings* (1880) and other volumes.

120.24   Cohen . . . Bradford] Octavus Roy Cohen (1891–1959), a white writer from South Carolina, contributed "downhome" tales in black dialect to *The Saturday Evening Post*. Roark Bradford (1896–1943), a professor of English at Tulane University, also wrote in blackface. His collection of tales *Ol' Man Adam an' His Chillun* (1928) was the inspiration for Marc Connelly's Pulitzer Prize–winning play *The Green Pastures* (1930).

121.3–4   Apollo Theatre . . . Markham] The Apollo (1934), on 125th Street, is Harlem's premier music hall. Black vaudevillian Dewey "Pigmeat" Markham (1904–1981) was the Apollo's unofficial house entertainer, appearing there more frequently than any other performer.

121.7   Father Divine] The Reverend M. J. Divine (circa 1876–1965) was founder and charismatic leader of the International Peace Mission Movement (1932–   ), a ministry whose tenets include racial equality, economic self-sufficiency, and the power of positive thinking.

122.32–33   *If you see dear Mrs. Equitone . . . careful these days.*] From "The Burial of the Dead," the first section of T. S. Eliot's poem *The Waste Land* (1922).

123.1   WILLIAM STYRON] Virginia-born writer (1925–2006) whose fourth novel, *The Confessions of Nat Turner* (1967), was awarded the Pulitzer Prize for Fiction. The controversy that the book occasioned culminated in *William Styron's Nat Turner: Ten Black Writers Respond* (Boston: Beacon Press, 1968), a collection of essays edited by John Henrik Clarke, and *The Nat Turner Rebellion: The Historical Event and the Modern Controversy* (New York: Harper & Row, 1971), edited by John B. Duff and Peter M. Mitchell.

124.20–21   Warren . . . Woodward . . . Clark] Three white intellectuals concerned with American race relations: poet, novelist, and critic Robert Penn Warren (1905–1989), whose nonfiction included *Segregation* (1956), *The Legacy of the Civil War* (1961), and *Who Speaks for the Negro?* (1965); historian and educator C. Vann Woodward (1908–1999), whose histories of Reconstruction and the New South culminated in *The Strange Career of Jim Crow* (1955); and civil rights lawyer Ramsey Clark (b. 1927), who as a justice official in the Johnson administration was architect of the Voting Rights Act of 1965 and the Civil Rights Act of 1968.

125.2–3   "room for many more."] Phrase from the chorus of the traditional American spiritual "The Gospel Train": "Get on board, children, / There's room for many a more."

125.17–20   Well you can be milk-white . . . gaining ground] See "traditional song (circa 1831)" published by the folklorist Lawrence Gellert in his article "Two Songs About Nat Turner," *The Worker* (June 12, 1949).

125.28   Stanley M. Elkins') Sambo] See note 39.1.

125.31   neo-Reichean] See note 78.23.

126.32   Aptheker] American Marxist historian Herbert Aptheker (1915–2003) wrote about Nat Turner's rebellion in his study *American Negro Slave Revolts* (New York: Columbia University Press, 1943).

127.10   U. B. Phillips] See note 81.32.

128.3–10   "an event . . . with them always."] From Kenneth Stampp, *The Peculiar Institution: Slavery in the Antebellum South* (New York: Knopf, 1956). Murray's later quotes from Stampp are from the same volume.

129.21   author of Uncle Remus] See note 120.38.

129.12–13   "Freedom's a Hard-Bought Thing"] Short story (1940) by American writer Stephen Vincent Benét (1898–1943) evoking the inner life of Cue, an American slave, as he escapes to Canada via the Underground Railroad.

130.2   Schillinger exercises] Musical composition exercises developed by Russian-born music theorist Joseph Schillinger (1895–1943).

131.1   JAMES BALDWIN] American man of letters (1924–1987) whose works include the novels *Go Tell It on the Mountain* (1953) and *Another Country* (1962), the play *Blues for Mister Charlie* (1964), and several volumes of essays.

131.7   "Everybody's Protest Novel,"] Baldwin collected this essay, together with its sequel "Many Thousands Gone," in his book *Notes of a Native Son* (1955). Murray's quotes are from the book versions of these essays.

132.24–25   hero of . . . *Native Son*] See note 68.14.

132.28   *Uncle Tom's Children*] Collection of short stories (1938; expanded 1940) by Richard Wright (see note 68.14).

134.7–9   *Gentleman's Agreement* . . . *Sound and the Fury*] Laura Z. Hobson's *Gentleman's Agreement* (1947), an exploration of institutional anti-Semitism; James M. Cain's *The Postman Always Rings Twice* (1934), a noir novella of infidelity and murder; Sinclair Lewis's *Kingsblood Royal* (1947), an allegory of a prosperous white man who discovers he has a black ancestor; Chester Himes's *If He Hollers Let Him Go* (1945), a tale of racial politics and union organizing in Los Angeles; William Faulkner's *The Sound and the Fury* (1929), four views of the fall of a distinguished Mississippi family.

141.6   *negritude*] Négritude was an international literary movement (fl. 1930s–60s) founded by Francophone African and Caribbean writers living in Paris in protest of French colonial rule. Its leaders—including Léopold Sédar Senghor, of Senegal, and Aimé Césaire, of Martinique—argued that black assimilation was a betrayal of black specialness, and that blacks everywhere should honor their connection to traditional African folkways as a balm against the soullessness of Western culture. The French intellectual Jean-Paul Sartre, in his 1948 essay "Orphée Noir" ("Black Orpheus"), called Négritude the necessary antithesis to colonialism that would one day result in the synthesis of racial equality.

141.17   "black arts"] The Black Arts movement of the 1960s and early '70s grew out of a populist American aesthetic in literature that reflected political ideas of the Black Power movement. It led directly to the creation of several black presses, periodicals, and theater companies, and indirectly to the establishment of black studies departments in colleges and universities.

142.20–25 Jean Genet . . . *The Blacks*] *The Blacks: A Clown Show* (*Les Nègres: Clownerie,* 1958), by the French writer Jean Genet (1910–1996), was, in its English translation by Bernard Frechtman, the longest-running off-Broadway drama of the 1960s. A farcical study in white racist attitudes, it featured an all-black cast, with some of the actors in "whiteface." It had its U.S. premiere at St. Mark's Playhouse on May 4, 1961, and closed in 1964 after 1,408 performances. Sartre's study of the playwright, *Saint Genet,* was published in 1951. Its English translation (1963), by Frechtman, was reviewed by Susan Sontag (see "Sartre's *Saint Genet,*" in *Against Interpretation and Other Essays,* 1966).

143.1–2 *The New Negro*] Anthology (1925) edited by Alain Locke (1885–1954) and published in New York by Albert and Charles Boni. Locke, a philosopher, writer, and professor at Howard University, commissioned and collected a group of stories, poems, and commentary that both articulated the aims and embodied the achievement of the Harlem Renaissance movement. Among the contributors were Countee Cullen, E. Francis Frazier, Langston Hughes, Zora Neale Hurston, James Weldon Johnson, Claude McKay, Kelly Miller, and Jean Toomer. Locke wrote five pieces for the volume, including the title essay.

143.19–20 ersatz tiger noises . . . boom boom and all.] See "Under the Bamboo Tree," song (1902) by J. Rosamond Johnson (1873–1954) with lyrics by his brother, James Weldon Johnson (see note 69.5), and Bob Cole (1868–1911). It was popularized by Judy Garland and Margaret O'Brien in the film *Meet Me in St. Louis* (1944).

145.7–9 Thus does the American . . . and Marxist environs.] Cf. the opening sentence of James Joyce's *Finnegans Wake* (1939): "riverrun, past Eve and Adam's, from swerve of shore to bend of bay, brings us by a commodius vicus of recirculation back to Howth Castle and Environs."

147.26 Ralph Ellison wrote an article] "Richard Wright's Blues," a review of *Black Boy* (1945), a memoir by Richard Wright, collected in Ellison's *Shadow and Act* (1964).

148.33 Nexø] Martin Andersen Nexø (1869–1954), Danish writer on underclass themes.

150.14–15 address at the New School] According to Nat Hentoff, in his article "Uninventing the Negro" (*Evergreen Review,* November 1965), Baldwin, as the keynote speaker at the New School/Harlem Writers' Guild symposium "The Negro Writer's Vision of America," said, in April 1965, that "my models—my private models—are not Hemingway, not Faulkner, not Dos Passos, indeed not any American writer. I model myself on jazz musicians, dancers, a couple of whores and a few junkies."

150.21 *Blues for Mister Charlie*] Baldwin's three-act play, based on events surrounding the 1955 lynching of Mississippi teenager Emmett Till, opened in New York on April 23, 1964, and was published later the same year by Dial Press.

150.27 *An American Dilemma*] See note 36.18.

150.27–28 *Mark of Oppression*] Abram Kardiner and Lionel Ovesey, *The Mark of Oppression: A Psychological Study of the American Negro* (New York: Norton, 1951).

150.30   sounds more like the reds than the blues.] In an earlier version of this essay, published in Herbert Hill's anthology *Anger, and Beyond* (1966), this paragraph ended with a parenthetical statement: "(Incidentally, when down-home people used to speak of having the reds, the mean old reds, they meant they were in a fighting mood, that they could see red. But being down-home blues people, and Joe Louis people to boot, they did what they were going to do and talked about it later, if at all.)"

159.17   they knighted Benny Goodman] The Benny Goodman Quartet (white clarinetist Goodman, white drummer Gene Krupa, black vibraphonist Lionel Hampton, and black pianist Teddy Wilson), which formed in 1937, was the first high-profile integrated jazz group. A year earlier, Teddy Wilson had joined Goodman's previously all-white big band.

160.7   *Black Power*] *Black Power: A Record of Reactions in a Land of Pathos* (1954) is Richard Wright's nonfiction account of his visit to Ghana on the eve of independence from Britain.

160.16   "Blue Print for Negro Writing."] Uncollected essay by Richard Wright, published in *New Challenge* 1 (Fall 1937).

161.4–5   "How 'Bigger' Was Born,"] Essay by Richard Wright, dated March 3, 1940, published in *Saturday Review* (June 1, 1940). It appears as an appendix in most reprint editions of *Native Son* (1940).

163.28   first concert at Carnegie Hall] On January 23, 1943.

163.9   Eldridge Cleaver] See note 86.28. After 1966 Cleaver was a staff writer for *Ramparts* magazine (see note 86.29).

163.13–14   Rinehart and Ras the Exhorter] Characters, one a black hustler of fluid identity, the other a West Indian black separatist, in Ellison's *Invisible Man* (1952).

163.17–18   Norman Mailer] See note 118.9, on Mailer's essay "The White Negro."

163.27–28   Mickey Spillane] Prolific writer of "American noir" crime novels (1918–2006), some twenty of which feature the detective/antihero Mike Hammer.

164.22   "puerile controversy and petty braggadocio."] See "The Negro Digs Up His Past," by Arthur A. Schomburg (1874–1938), in Alain Locke, ed., *The New Negro* (1925). Schomburg was a pioneering collector of books and manuscripts of the African diaspora. Harlem's Schomburg Center for Research in Black Culture, a research library in the New York Public Library system, had its basis in his collection.

165.6–8   Woodson . . . Brawley . . . Wesley . . . Du Bois . . . Johnson . . . Quarles . . . Franklin] Carter G. Woodson (1875–1950), pioneering black historian, author of *The Negro in Our History* (1922), and founder, in 1915, of the Association of American Negro Life and History and, in 1926, of Negro History Week (later Black History Month); Benjamin Brawley (1882–1939), first dean of Morehouse College and author of *A Short History of the American Negro* (1921) and *Negro Builders and Heroes* (1937); Charles H. Wesley (1891–1987), author of some twenty works in black history; W.E.B. Du Bois (1868–1963), sociologist, historian, cofounder of the NAACP, editor of its journal *The Crisis*, and author of *The Souls of Black Folk* (1903); James Weldon Johnson (see note 69.5), whose historical works include *Black Manhattan* (1930); Benjamin Quarles (see note 19.18–23); and John Hope Franklin (see note 81.9).

167.15–16 Lumumba, Tshombe, or Nkrumah] Patrice Lumumba (1925–1961), short-lived prime minister of independent Congo (June–September 1960); Moïse Tshombe (1919–1969), one of his embattled successors (1964–65); and Kwame Nkrumah (1909–1972), first president of the Republic of Ghana (1960–66).

168.18 John A. Kouwenhoven] Professor of American studies and American literature (1910–1990), long associated with Barnard College, whose books on American culture—high, folk, and pop—include *Made in America: The Arts in Modern Civilization* (Garden City, N.Y.: Doubleday, 1948) and *The Beer Can by the Highway: Essays on What's American about America* (Doubleday, 1961). Kouwenhoven's work was a touchstone for Murray and is alluded to throughout his nonfiction.

173.11–12 Woodson and . . . Brawley] See note 165.6–8.

173.20–21 Logan . . . Franklin . . . Quarles] Rayford Logan (1897–1992), professor of history at Howard University and author of more than a dozen books; John Hope Franklin (see note 81.9); Benjamin Quarles (see note 19.18–23).

174.1–2 Du Bois . . . Frazier] W.E.B. Du Bois (see note 165.6–8); E. Franklin Frazier (1894–1962), American sociologist whose chief field of study was the urban black American family.

176.1 *Bull Connor and Al Lingo*] T. Eugene "Bull" Connor (1897–1973) was commissioner of public safety in Birmingham, Alabama, from 1937 to 1963. During the 1963 civil rights protests in his city, he approved the use of cattle prods, fire hoses, and attack dogs on the demonstrators. Connor's superior at this time was Albert J. Lingo (1910–1969), director of the Alabama Department of Public Safety (1963–65).

176.16–17 *high yallers . . . peola*] A "high yellow" is, in antebellum parlance, a mulatto with very light skin. A "peola," in 1930s Harlem slang, is a mulatto woman with skin so light as to be able to "pass" for white, after Peola Johnson, the heroine of Fannie Hurst's novel *Imitation of Life* (1933).

176.28 NOW] Neighborhood Organized Workers of Mobile, Alabama, was a civil rights and economic improvement organization (1966–75) founded by local activist Dorothy Parker Williams and educator David Jacobs.

180.7 Miller . . . Locke . . . Brown] Polymath Kelly Miller (1863–1939) was a mathematician, sociologist, writer, and teacher at Howard University; Alain Locke (see note 143.1–2); Sterling Brown (1901–1989) was a poet, folklorist, and literary critic.

180.8 Monroe N. Work] American sociologist (1866–1945) who edited several pioneering reference works, including the *Negro Year Book: An Annual Encyclopedia* (1912–45) and *A Bibliography of the Negro in Africa and America* (1928).

180.10 Ira De A. Reid] American sociologist and anthropologist (1901–1968) who published nine book-length academic studies, most of them documenting the lives of urban black workers.

180.11 Charles S. Johnson] American sociologist (1893–1956) and the first black president of Fisk University (1946–56).

180.27 Denmark Vesey and Nat Turner] American slaves Vesey (1767–1822) and Turner (1800–1831) each led a slave revolt that ended in his execution.

181.28 *Rockefeller*] Businessman Nelson Rockefeller (1908–1979) was governor of New York (1959–73) and, in 1960, '64, and '68, a Republican candidate for U.S. president. He was later vice president under Gerald Ford (1974–77).

181.31 *Wallace*] George Wallace (1919–1998), three-time governor of Alabama and, in 1968, an independent candidate for U.S. president.

184.5 rather be a lamp post in Harlem than the mayor of Mobile] Catchphrase in the Harlem of the 1920s, sometimes attributed to the poet Langston Hughes.

184.13 Benjamin F. Baker] Dr. Baker (d. 1953?) was the principal of Mobile County Training School (MCTS), Murray's junior high and high school, from 1926 to 1947. In 1950 he became the first principal of Mobile's Central High.

184.14 Ella Grant] Ella Grant (d. 1937) was a master teacher at Meachem Elementary School, in the Mobile County Public School district. In 1944 the Prichard School, a Mobile district grade school, was rechristened the Ella Grant School in her honor.

191.6–14 "[Some black Americans . . . other resources."] Tom Mboya, "The American Negro Cannot Look to Africa for an Escape," in *The New York Times Magazine* (July 13, 1969). Mboya (1930–1969) was assassinated a week before his essay appeared.

193.24–25 Charles Houston] Prominent black lawyer (1895–1950) who was dean of Howard University Law School (1929–35) and special council to the NAACP (1935–50).

193.31 David Susskind's vaudeville hour] After a career as a theatrical producer, David Susskind (1920–1987) was the host of an hour-long New York–based talk show on NET/PBS television from 1958 to 1986.

195.25–26 *Goodbye, Mr. Chips*] Novel (1934) by English writer James Hilton (1900–1954) that sentimentally dramatizes the twilight years of a teacher of classics at a second-tier boys' school.

199.3–5 *In the fall of 1966 . . . "What's Happening in America."*] The symposium feature "What's Happening to America" was published in *Partisan Review* for Spring 1967. The editors sent to writers whom they invited to participate the following questionnaire, which was also published as a preface to the symposium:

> *There is a good deal of anxiety about the direction of American life. In fact, there is reason to fear that America may be entering a moral and political crisis. If so, the crisis isn't to be explained by any single policy, however wrong or disastrous. There seems instead to be some more general failure or weakness in our national life. The deterioration in the quality of American life during the last few years has been made evident in several ways. The rhetoric through which issues are created and argued and which seemed during the Kennedy years to have some relation to the seriousness of the problems facing the country has become jingoistic and question-begging. The economy seems to be out of control. The civil rights movement has become more desperate as the government has become more cautious and the white population less sympathetic. U.S. foreign policy is becoming more and more indistinguishable from John Foster Dulles', if in fact it isn't even more an adjunct of our military power. Throughout the country, there is a sense of drift and frustration and confusion—and a growing sense of urgency.*

Of course there are many people who don't think conditions are so bad, who regard the idea that we are in some kind of crisis as extremist, and who in any case feel sure that our problems can be solved within the terms of our current methods and policies.

To give the discussion some focus, we suggest the following questions. But you are free, of course, to approach the problem of what is happening to America in any way you choose.

1. *Does it matter who is in the White House? Or is there something in our system which would force any President to act as Johnson is acting?*
2. *How serious is the problem of inflation? The problem of poverty?*
3. *What is the meaning of the split between the Administration and the American intellectuals?*
4. *Is white America committed to granting equality to the American Negro?*
5. *Where do you think our foreign policies are likely to lead us?*
6. *What, in general, do you think is likely to happen in America?*
7. *Do you think any promise is to be found in the activities of young people today?*

Partisan Review published responses from Martin Duberman, Michael Harrington, Tom Hayden, Nat Hentoff, Robert Lowell, Harold Rosenberg, Susan Sontag, Diana Trilling, and eight other public intellectuals and social critics.

199.16–17 "not nostrums . . . but serenity."] Republican presidential candidate Warren G. Harding (1865–1923), in a campaign speech of May 14, 1920, promised American citizens a "return to normalcy" after World War I.

200.10–11 Elijah Muhammad . . . Mailer . . . Wallace . . . Buckley] Elijah Muhammad (1897–1975), leader of the Nation of Islam from 1934 until his death; Norman Mailer (see note 93.25–27); George Wallace (see note 181.31) and his wife, Lurleen Wallace (1926–1968), governor of Alabama from 1967 until her death; William F. Buckley Jr. (1925–2008), conservative talk-show host and founding editor of the weekly *National Review*.

201.4 *The Walnut Trees of Altenburg*] André Malraux's fragmentary final novel (*Les Noyers de l'Altenburg*, 1943), translated from the French by A. W. Fielding (London: John Lehmann, 1952).

201.9–11 Bundy . . . Katzenbach . . . Taylor . . . Jessup . . . Kennan . . . Morgenthau . . . Howe] McGeorge Bundy (1919–1996), American national security expert; Nicholas Katzenbach (1922–2012), U.S. attorney general (1964–66); General Maxwell Taylor (1901–1987), diplomat and chairman of the Joint Chiefs of Staff (1962–64); John K. Jessup (1907–1979), editorial-page writer for *Time* magazine (1944–66); George Kennan (1904–2005), Princeton professor and Cold War strategist; Hans Morgenthau (1904–1980), German-born American writer on international politics; Irving Howe (1920–1993), socialist critic of American life and literature.

201.30 Moynihan Report] See note 28.6–7.

202.16 Norman Podhoretz] See note 93.25–27.

203.1–2 Senator William Fulbright] See note 93.18–19.

INDEX

This book is set in 10 point Minion Pro, a digital typeface designed
by Robert Slimbach in 1990 for Adobe Systems and inspired by
Renaissance-era fonts. The name comes from the traditional nomenclature
for type sizes, the smallest of which was diamond, followed by pearl,
agate, nonpareil, minion, brevier, bourgeois, long primer, small pica, pica, etc.

Two sans-serif fonts are used for display and running heads:
Trade Gothic LT, designed by Jackson Burke during the 1950s for Linotype,
and the condensed typeface Steelfish, created by the independent designer Ray
Larabie in 2001 and inspired by twentieth-century newspaper headlines.

The paper is acid-free and exceeds the requirements for permanence
established by the American National Standards Institute.

Text design by Donna G. Brown.
Composition by Dianna Logan, Clearmont, MO.